Cascais, No[...]

For Tony Baker

You may be amused
by some of the memories
within,

With all good wishes

Charles Wallace

———————

The Valedictory

THE VALEDICTORY

Charles Wallace

Foreword by
The Rt. Hon. The Lord Pym, M.C.

The Book Guild Ltd.
Sussex, England

For GW,
who made it all possible

The Book Guild Ltd.
25 High Street,
Lewes, Sussex

First published 1992
© Charles Wallace 1992
Set in Baskerville
Typesetting by Raven Typesetters
Ellesmere Port, South Wirral
Printed in Great Britain by
Antony Rowe Ltd.
Chippenham, Wiltshire.

A catalogue record for this book
is available from the British Library

ISBN 0 86332 765 6

Contents

List of illustrations between pages 146 and 147   6
Foreword   7
Introduction   9

Part One
1   Baghdad, 1960   19
2   The Shooting Party   28
3   Northern Iraq   34
4   The Siege of the Embassy, 1963   49

Part Two
5   The Road from Damascus   65
6   Bahrain, 1953–1956   73
7   The African Department, 1957–1960   109

Part Three
8   Mexico, 1973–1975   135
9   Guadalajara, October 1973   146
10   Paraguay, 1947–1949   166

Part Four
11   Peru and the Falklands: Lima   197
12   Peru and the Falklands: London   217

Part Five
13   The Birth of a Legend   267
14   A Great Naval Occasion   279
15   Uruguay, 1983–1986   292

Select Bibliography   301
Index   302

List of illustrations between pages 146 and 147

Baghdad. The Chancery, British Embassy, 1962.

The gap left by Residence burned down in 1958.

The Political Resident, Lt. Col. Sir Rupert Hay and his Head of Chancery, Martin Le Quesne. Bahrain.

Bahrain. The Political Agent (Mr John Wall) and the Shaikh of Bahrain. The Adviser (Sir Charles Belgrave) in the bow tie behind the Ruler.

The Sultan of Muscat and Oman, Said bin Taimur, arrives in Bahrain from London. In addition to the Ruler of Bahrain, he is greeted by the acting Political Resident, the acting Political Agent, the acting Adviser and the acting Commandant of Police.

The British Political Agent and his staff, 1953.

The Ruler of Bahrain receives a visiting US Admiral.

The Everest conquerors at Manamah Airport, Bahrain, 1953.

New Year's Day at the Political Residency in Jufair.

Mexico, 1975. Sanitised 'Charreada' for Royal visitors from Britain.

President Belaunde's inauguration, 1980.

The Lord Mayor of London and the Swordbearer in Lima, 1981.

Sir Ronald Gardner-Thorpe on his way to Machu Picchu.

Mr Cecil Parkinson inaugurates a viaduct at the Majes Project, Arequipa, 1981.

Montevideo, 1984. Defaced walls of British Embassy, calling for release of Raul Sendic, imprisoned leader of Tupamaro terrorists who kidnapped Sir Geoffrey Jackson in 1971.

FOREWORD

'Despite being an institution which as an instrument of policy is admired, envied, or imitated by almost every country in the world, the Foreign Office and its servants abroad are conditioned to a bad press in the UK.'

These words of Charles Wallace are profoundly true. Our Foreign Office is not surpassed by any in the world, and very few are its equal. Its history goes back over more than two centuries and spans an almost infinite range of differing circumstances. In this sense, its wealth of experience is unrivalled. Inevitably its performance has varied but overall the consistency and quality of its advice stand favourable comparison with any counterpart.

This is no accident. Young men and women going into the service are selected with great care, and so are those who apply for late entry. They receive excellent training and as their career progresses much time and trouble are given to match the requirements of each post to the talents of each diplomat.

This delightful book recounts some of the experiences of just one diplomat and reveals what that life involved for one individual. The reader will be surprised by the range of challenges he faced, the unexpected happenings to which he had to respond, the personalities he had dealings with, and the responsibility he carried for his country. It is a very human story. It traces Charles Wallace's ascent up the Diplomatic ladder and gives a lively account of many incidents on the way. The first part relates to Iraq in the early 1960's and is of particular interest today after the Gulf War. There is a vivid description of Bahrain in the 1950's and of life in the African Department in London. For the latter part of his career, Charles Wallace was Ambassador to Paraguay and then Peru where his time included the Falklands War. His telegrams at that time were obviously extremely important and his full account of these events and the controversies surrounding them will be of special interest to many.

By comparison with the life described here, most people lead very dull lives. This is a fascinating story and through it all comes Charles Wallace's integrity, his charm and his sound sense.

In the UK we are fortunate to have a diplomatic service staffed by men and women of this calibre and character. So why, it may be asked, does it sometimes receive a bad press? The reason is not far to seek. The Foreign Office exists to identify and promote British interests everywhere in the world. When the perception of those interests coincides with the perception of the man on the Clapham omnibus, everyone is happy. But when those perceptions do not coincide, which is often the case, the political problem arises as to how to reconcile the two; or, if they cannot be reconciled, how best to deal with the issue. On occasions this can lead to great difficulties. If the Foreign Secretary and his Cabinet colleagues decide on a course that strains the loyalty and support of the man on the omnibus rather far, the press will naturally give full expression to the omnibus view, and for good measure have a bash at the Foreign Office for being so daft as to suggest an alternative. In fact, the Foreign Office may be right in its assessment of where British interests lie: its whole purpose is to gauge these interests accurately and not to adjust them for convenience. If the result is a political problem, that is for the Foreign Secretary and his colleagues to deal with and they must take full responsibility. The Foreign Office cannot answer back, and some of the less courageous newsmen enjoy the impunity they think this gives them. Chapter 12 in this book describes a most unusual occurrence when Charles Wallace was invited to give evidence before the House of Commons Select Committee on Foreign Affairs about the wild allegations that had been made in the press and elsewhere about the peace initiative emanating from the President of Peru and the US Secretary of State and its connection – or lack of it – with the sinking of the Belgrano.

This is a book of recent history, of unexpected incidents and personal impressions. It is a sparkling read.

November 1991   Francis Pym

INTRODUCTION

Lives of great men all remind us
We can make our lives sublime,
And, departing, leave behind us
Footprints on the sands of time.

Henry Wadsworth Longfellow, *The Song of Hiawatha* (1855)

There is a tradition that British ambassadors, when about to retire, address a valedictory despatch to the Secretary of State for Foreign Affairs in which they may cover much ground. Understandably, they tend to concentrate on those professional and geographical areas they know best. Their assessment of those events in which they were involved is valuable; their opinions and perspectives are significant; their recommendations for those that might follow in their footsteps, both in Whitehall and abroad, are relevant.

Some of the authors analyse the geographical distribution and balance of political and economic power, and consider the prospects before the government of the day. Their views and opinions have been formed as a result of long experience in the privileged observation posts they have occupied for many years, and the weight of the author's professional trajectory tends to create a receptive frame of mind in some of the readers in Whitehall. Few can avoid reflecting on the changes in the diplomatic service during their time. Some argue that recent reforms have tended to dehumanize the service and made it less personal; it has, in other words, become more mechanical and thus less effective. Others praise the manner in which the service has retained its identity in spite of successive reviews, while yet others believe the reforms have not gone far enough.

The writer may be forgiven if he includes a paragraph on some personal experience during his years of service to Crown and government: breaches of diplomatic relations, threats against his person or premises, revolutions and undeclared wars. This sort of violence has been an occupational hazard of envoys and their missions in some parts of the world since ambassadors were invented. Sadly, it has today acquired and even wider currency and ever new dimensions.

I never failed to read with particular interest all the valedictory despatches that came my way, most of which were widely circulated in Whitehall and posts abroad. Many of my senior contemporaries acquired an early reputation for evocative narrative and literary brilliance, even during a period when the increasing use of telegrams imposed severe limitations on content and elegance of style. Some exceptional despatches created benchmarks which may no longer be matched in today's prevailing preoccupation with speed and brevity. Originally the ambassadorial valedictory was one despatch he was obliged to draft himself, although this rule became less significant in later years when successive cuts in staff and the consequent debasement of the professional currency left some ambassadors with no alternative but to do most of their own drafting. The ultimate accolade bestowed by the Foreign Office on a formal despatch was to have it printed for a wide distribution at home and abroad. Valedictories were almost always included in this category. This tacitly recognized the despatch as being of more than parochial interest, and it was therefore circulated to those concerned in Buckingham Palace, 10 Downing Street, the Cabinet Office, and other Whitehall departments, as well as all British embassies and high commissions.

As the years went by and the volume of official paper relentlessly increased, I tended to concentrate on those valedictories written either by colleagues I knew or about countries in which I had served. Other despatches by exceptionally gifted authors were sometimes given a wide distribution. One such author was Sir John Russell, whose reports from such disparate capitals as Addis Ababa and Rio de Janeiro made compulsive reading. His account of the carnival in Rio de Janeiro in 1967 was a masterpiece of the art, and by no means lacking in perceptive political and social content, even if, at first blush, the carnival in Rio might not be deemed the best peg on which to hang a comprehensive think-piece on the state of the nation. Inevitably, in recent years the demands of instant communications have sacrificed the despatch, in its traditional form, to the cause of economy of words and immediate decisions.

When the time arrived for me to write my own valedictory, I became uncomfortably aware that my retirement, due inexorably on the day before my sixtieth birthday in January, coincided with my obligation to submit the Annual Review for the previous year. These were routine reports sent to the Foreign Office by all embassies abroad. Covering the principal events of the year they provided hard-pressed desk officers in Whitehall with a useful summary of visits, negotiations, agreements and other developments which might already have been the subject of more detailed reporting at the appropriate time but which, if worthy of a mention in the Annual Review, were thus put into their proper perspective. When this was accompanied by a brief assessment of current prospects and past errors or achievements, the value of the despatch was enhanced. As Annual Reviews were also given a wide distribution some authors were tempted to include their recommendations for future action, hoping that their suggestions might catch a sympathetic eye in high places. Others, with more temerity, gazed into the crystal ball and tried to foretell the future.

The Annual Review had to be submitted before the end of January, but the prospect of two formal despatches within the same month raised doubts in my mind. I was naturally reluctant to give up my last opportunity to offer the Secretary of State my opinions on a wide variety of subjects. I could offer him solutions to many of the problems I had encountered during my service. Some of the experience I had acquired was too valuable to lose in the sands of time, and my suggestions and recommendations were worth recording for the benefit of my successor, if not posterity. But *two* despatches from me within a few days of each other? It would be thought that I had lost my sense of proportion. Was there anything I had to say that had not been better said previously? My consideration was much influenced by the constant injunctions on brevity, circulated at regular intervals to posts abroad and departments at home. Annual Reviews had been limited to a maximum of 2500 words, and anyone who exceeded his quota had his despatch either rejected or arbitrarily excised and edited by the Foreign Office. Those who compressed the volume of their views and opinions to a single side of foolscap were hailed as examples to be emulated. Valedictory despatches were regarded with greater tolerance, however, even if the author had little to add to what he had been saying for the previous decade.

In the event, the ceaseless official appeals for restraint and the genuine despair made manifest by those colleagues serving in Whitehall departments won the day. I drafted the Annual Review (the more enduring document, I thought) in commendably economic terms, and added a short valedictory paragraph in which I drew attention to my impending departure and briefly recalled, in much the same way as a drowning man is said to visualize images from his past, some of the salient experiences in my career. I think I mentioned my youthful tribulations as an assistant judge of Her Majesty's Court in Bahrain, the siege of the embassy in Baghdad, the Queen's visit to Mexico, and the Falklands crisis in Peru, concluding that the service had enriched me with a rewarding career, even though some of the events listed above I could cheerfully have done without. But, given the nature of the vehicle I had chosen for my final words, I felt bound to refrain from including references to many other occasions which, though unrecorded in history, contributed in large measure to my professional education and to the acquisition of much personal ballast.

My own service began in posts regarded as geographical and political backwaters. Some subsequently became theatres of political importance, though usually after my own departure, and few events of international significance had involved me professionally. Having spent most of my service abroad in posts once officially described as outside our 'area of concentration', it was clear that my experiences could not compare with those usually featured in the memoirs published by those diplomatic heavyweights who had served principally in those capitals previously known as 'the inner circle', whose own contributions to the making of contemporary history were accurately reflected in their biographies.

Yet I also found that, with very few exceptions, even those books written by former ambassadors to Third World countries dwelt principally on the history and origins of their peoples and their economic and political development. The easy flow of obscure historical background and the educated reflections on cultural and religious trends all revealed the practised hand of the erudite and percipient observer. The analysis was comprehensive; the wealth of detail commanded respect. Their diary entries dwelt on conversations and meetings which merited more than an ephemeral record. Their critical appraisals withstood the test of time and never failed to impress. Sometimes there might be included a short chapter headed 'My day in the office', unfolding a well-ordered sequence of programmed events which seldom matched my own recollection of a typical day, even making allowances for the manifest differences between then and now.

We are not all privileged to encounter greatness, either in people or events, though once or twice I found myself on the fringes of situations which were to make their way into the history books. There were, however, many other occasions which remained vivid in my mind, not always for the best of reasons. There were also personalities and individuals who made an impression on me, some in strange places and circumstances. I had served with the great and the good, and with some of the others as well. There are places abroad where a distinguished predecessor is still recalled with admiration and affection many years after his departure; the fact that nobody remembers his successor or mentions the name of the most recently departed incumbent helps to retain a sense of proportion in nearly all aspiring ambassadors, at least in our service. But there were many senior colleagues who contributed much to my professional formation. Their influence, friendship or example remained a source of inspiration for many years after the initial contacts, which sometimes even compensated for a not always appetizing diet of occupational monotony, extremes of climate, primitive facilities, irregular leave and inadequate pay.

Few of my diaries have survived the ruthless destruction always generated by an imminent move, but those that have show that my most consistent diary entry for many years was the mandatory monthly appointment with the administration

13

officer to check the accounts. Most of us deal with trivia some of the time, even if this is not always recognized in the memoirs of the eminences of the profession. I thought it might be a measure of their intellectual stature that they recalled but little of the dross and drudgery which in my experience made up a large proportion of the daily fare. Perhaps the olympian pinnacles attained by the giants of an earlier generation prevented them from seeing the lower reaches of the mountains they had successfully scaled. Perhaps not. One such giant under whom I served published after his final retirement several books of political memoirs which were widely acclaimed as 'throwing new light on some of the vagaries of western policies' and 'a personal record of the utmost importance'. His style was praised as 'terse, intelligent and sympathetic', his narrative as 'valuable to the historian of the period'. The books were based on his tours of duty as head of mission in Peking, Cairo, Baghdad and Moscow; a record few outside 'the inner circle' could equal in modern times. But shortly after, Lord Trevelyan (as he had then become) surprised and delighted those of us who had sat mutely during his Friday-morning meetings in Baghdad by publishing a light-hearted book* of his reflections on life in the service, incorporating personal reminiscences and observations, the whole sparkling with humour, wit and mischievous fun. The contrast could not have been more marked. One swallow does not make a summer, however, and Humphrey Trevelyan was an unusual man.

In the pages that follow I have set out my account of some of the events which I refrained from including in my valedictory paragraph giving my brief, drowning-man's review of the life I was leaving. I was tempted to mention my feelings of total inadequacy when, the day after my arrival in Bahrain, I was invited to sign a manumission certificate conferring a life of freedom upon the man who was even then kissing the shoes I was wearing. How I was bitten by an alligator in the offices of the British legation in Asunción was also difficult to resist, albeit for very different reasons. The kidnapping of the honorary British Consul in Guadalajara in 1974 proved to be a memorably dramatic experience, even though much of my

* Humphrey Trevelyan, *Diplomatic Channels*, Macmillan, 1973.

recollection of the episode is one of a recurring nightmare, which began every morning when I woke up and went on for much of the night as well. Fortunately, this lasted only for ten or twelve days, but the same applies to the Falklands crisis in Peru which went on for much longer. I also refer to some unusual personalities, both in my service and outside it. In most cases these were men whose guidance and advice I valued; whose friendship I recall with gratitude; or whose memory I respect. That having been said, this narrative lays no claim either to eminence or revealment, it being no more than a superficial account of glimpses from the sidelines and marginal comments. If some of these appear to illustrate the transient nature of individual achievement and the impermanence of personal success, so be it.

There are two additional comments I should make. Some of the episodes described take place in the Middle East. We have all read books in which Arabic places names and the names of individuals are spelt in English in different ways. For many years the prevalence of the English transliteration of Arabic names made their use customary in other languages, and articles in Spanish or Italian journals for years transcribed the traditional English spelling, frequently with curious phonetic results. This is seldom the case now, but in writing Arabic words I have followed the advice given to me when I arrived in Bahrain by the then Political Agent, a gifted orientalist and Arabic scholar: 'You can spell it any way you like,' he said, 'so long as it sounds like the original in Arabic.' Since then, of course, many place names have acquired a conventional spelling from which it would have been pretentious to depart, though other, less well-known names may differ in some ways from the transliteration now used by more expert authors. If so, I regret any confusion this may cause.

Some of the individuals I mention I first met many years ago, before they attained any eminence they were later to achieve. In the case of members of my own service I have refrained from bracketing, even in a footnote, their final rank or later honours and titles, other than where it flows from the narrative. It would have been invidious as well as inelegant to single out some of my colleagues by referring to them as Joe Bloggs (later Sir Joseph, now Lord Bloggs), so I have simply recalled them as they were at the time of the episode described. I know they will forgive me.

15

Finally, the title. I first thought I would call this collection of reminiscences 'Footprints on the sands', despite Longfellow's suggestion that permanent footprints on the sands of time may indeed be left by some men. In my experience, footprints on any sands tend to get blown away very quickly, much as the memory of the average diplomat's transit through different countries which, if successful, he usually leaves with little trace of his passing. But my wife thought this was a bit complicated and decided on the present, more relevant and, indeed, apposite title.

I must, of course, add that the opinions expressed are my own, and do not necessarily represent those of the Foreign and Commonwealth Office. It is also appropriate to mention here that the extracts from the Foreign Affairs Committee Report (session 1984–85), *Events surrounding the weekend of 1–2 May 1982*, are reproduced by kind permission of the Controller of Her Majesty's Stationery Office.

PART

1

You throw the sand against the wind,
And the wind blows it back again.

William Blake, MS notebooks 1800–03

1

Baghdad, 1960

When I arrived in Baghdad in May 1960, Sir Humphrey Trevelyan was the ambassador. He was then only 52, but his aura of authority and experience made him appear older. He was widely respected by Iraqis and foreigners alike. Even then his career was impressive, and was to become even more so. A distinguished member of a distinguished family, he had joined the Indian Civil Service at an early age in 1929. A varied and rewarding career in India, during which he achieved a high position in the External Affairs Department of the Government of India came to a premature end in 1947 when partition and independence came about. India's loss, however, was our gain, and he was smoothly translated to the foreign service in which his first post was, appropriately, Baghdad, were he served as counsellor until he was promoted and seconded to the Control Commission for Germany. He then went as head of mission to Peking and Cairo, being appointed Ambassador in Baghdad in 1958, a bare five months after his predecessor had been shot at point-blank range (and miraculously missed) by one of the mob which ransacked the embassy after General Qasim's revolution on 14 July 1958.

For months after my arrival I stood in awe of the Ambassador, despite the many kindnesses shown to me by both Sir Humph (as he was known to the staff behind his back) and his wife, Peggy, a woman of great charm, dignity and beauty. She was the daughter of an eminent military family which had served India for generations. In difficult circumstances, her contribution to the generally high morale of the staff in Baghdad was considerable. She had an easy and unassuming manner and endeared herself to all by the way in which she sought them out in turn, on suitable occasions, when she

19

contrived to leave her interlocutors with the impression that she was more interested in what they had to say than in anything or anyone else. She had the engaging habit of retailing, with seeming indiscretion, ambassadorial comments or remarks which always flattered: thus, 'Humphrey told me what a good speech you had drafted for him for tomorrow's inauguration,' or, 'Humphrey mentioned how well your husband has done during the Oriental Counsellor's leave; he found the press summaries invaluable.' These snippets of gossip ensured that husbands and wives were made aware of some of the opinions of the usually enigmatic Ambassador, whose most eloquent praise was normally limited to the silent return of those drafts submitted by their author for ambassadorial approval. If these had been initialled off without additions or deletions this was high praise indeed.

On our Friday-morning staff meetings, the Ambassador normally sat at his desk writing copious notes while the assembled staff, sitting in a semicircle round the room, spoke up in their turn (though only if they had a contribution of substance to make; Sir Humphrey had a reputation for not suffering fools gladly, and his lifted eyebrows and curt nod towards the next speaker seldom failed to stem the flow from all but the hardest skinned). With the exception of one or two irrepressible characters, the presence of senior heads of sections normally resulted in the more junior members of the staff rarely getting a word in; even if the ambassadorial eyebrow courteously cocked itself in their direction on its brisk way round the room. After weeks of silence one youthful third secretary, sitting in his customary place at the tail-end of the assembled semicircle, decided to break with tradition. Having listened to a thorough analysis of the latest political and economic developments and a review of the week's vernacular press, and taken note of forthcoming visits and events, the Ambassador looked at his watch and turned to this most junior member of the assembly, while he placed his hands on the arms of his chair obviously anticipating the customary, mute shake of the head. But Adrian Sindall, recently arrived with his wife from the Middle East Centre for Arab Studies in Shemlan, set his jaw and leaned back in his seat. 'I had a daughter yesterday,' he drawled unexpectedly, to his eternal credit.

Humphrey Trevelyan was then a man of medium height

with sparse, greyish hair, penetrating eyes, and rather prominent ears. These he had the habit of moving, fast and furiously, while he wrote his notes. Any new arrival whose turn it was to speak, unsure of the degree of attention being accorded to his analysis of the import figures for the previous quarter, sometimes found his concentration undermined and his own attention increasingly drawn to those remarkable ears. His delivery tended to falter, until perhaps brought to a halt by the brief 'Yes?' when this coincided with the end of a paragraph in the ambassadorial notes. When it did not and the hesitating flow eventually dried up, a kindly Counsellor or Head of Chancery intervened with improvised comments of their own. The Military Attaché was always good at staging a diversion. But if none of this happened there followed an awkward pause, unbroken until the scribbling figure at the desk put down his pen and asked a highly relevant question which made it clear he had not missed a single word. Even more awkward was the possibility that an ambassadorial question prompted by the speaker's remarks might be addressed to a third party who knew the answer but whose attention had also wandered, having likewise allowed himself to become fascinated by those unusual ears. The floundering which ensued revealed more of the mental agility of the victim than any of the tests devised by the Civil Service Commission in many years. Those who knew the Ambassador best claimed that there was always a twinkle in his eye on these occasions.

Some of the new arrivals at first found the weekly meeting a bit of an ordeal. The deputy head of mission and senior counsellor, at the time Peter Hayman, sat in a chair next to the Ambassador's desk and spoke first. The others sat round the room more or less in order of seniority, with the Head of Chancery and the Military and Air Attachés in the middle of the semicircle which coincided with the three-seater sofa and armchairs directly facing the ambassadorial desk. I recall my first meeting at which, having previously taken advice and been told to sit somewhere in the middle, I made a beeline for the sofa where I ensconced myself comfortably next to the Military Attaché, who affably bade me good morning. Throughout the meeting, in which I was first presented to the assembly by the Counsellor, I was a silent participant. Not so the Arabic experts, most of whom retailed comments from the local press, as well as gossip and speculation from their own sources. The consul was also a contributor of some importance, being closely in touch with the long-established British community, some of whose members had lived for many years in Iraq and had excellent sources of information of their own. The commercial staff also had the opportunity of picking up useful bazaar gossip and rumour. It was therefore a normally well-informed group of people who offered their contributions at the weekly meetings. These were made sometimes even more interesting by the accounts of those members of the staff who had travelled to some area outside Baghdad, from which foreigners at the time (and particularly members of the British embassy) were normally barred. It was essential to have previously obtained a travel permit from the Military Governor of Baghdad, which was never actually refused, but seldom granted in time for the trip to take place as planned. Yet perhaps the best informed of all, though seldom a major contributor to the meeting, was the Ambassador himself, whose seemingly inexhaustible energy was reflected in his daily list of appointments and engagements. He had the additional advantage of having previously served in Baghdad just ten years before, even though most of the friends and contacts he had made in his earlier sojourn were either dead, in exile, or keeping out of public sight – in the political conditions prevailing at the time, for good and valid reasons of their own.

In May 1960 there were still several members of the staff in Baghdad who had been through Qasim's rebellion and the looting of the embassy on 14 July 1958. The advice I had been given before leaving London was not to take to Baghdad 'anything I did not wish to lose'. Some of the staff still slept with a packed suitcase by the bed in case the unpredictable Qasim decided to expel the British without notice. Infrequent visitors to the embassy had their names taken down by plain-clothes policemen at the gates. The more suspicious members of the staff were under constant surveillance. Telephones were tapped and conversations taped. A curfew existed from 20.00 hours until dawn. Members of the British embassy were restricted in their movements to a radius of twenty miles from the centre of Baghdad. There were also other constraints which made life interesting if at times a little difficult. Lord Trevelyan included an account of this time in a book he published in

1970,* which illustrated comprehensively the uncertainties of the Iraqi political situation during this period of Qasim's regime and how closely we were affected by his internal and foreign policy preoccupations. Having already suffered one or more attempts on his life, his principal objective was to survive in power; to this end he unhesitatingly played both ends against the middle, both domestically and in his relations with other countries.

Nevertheless, as time passed, conditions improved slowly in a number of practical ways. The all-night parties (sometimes forced upon reluctant hosts by the evening curfew) gave way to a concerted rush through Baghdad streets at midnight. Customs clearances came through with less delay, and essential supplies began to trickle through with some regularity. Iraqi guests reappeared at some of our houses. Restaurants and night clubs resumed business. Best of all, permits for travel outside the capital began to filter through the government bureaucracy. This last was a concession all of us had been eagerly awaiting, the number of places of interest to be seen within a radius of twenty miles from the centre of Baghdad not being very extensive. Among other things, this meant that I could plan to visit development projects on which British firms of consulting engineers (as distinct from contracting firms) were still employed. Some of these were names which had been associated with Iraq for generations and were highly regarded and respected by all technical departments of the Iraq government. Many of the British and other contractors engaged in various development schemes around the country had not had their contracts renewed, however, and others had not been paid on completion. One of my tasks at that time, therefore, was to pay regular calls on the directors general of several government departments in order to persuade them to settle the outstanding bills. Sometimes they did, though not very frequently, but the consultants, by and large, continued to be paid regularly, although sometimes there were delays. Being on the spot and providing the essential supervision on works actually under construction at the time put them in a much stronger position when it came to the end of the month.

The Iraqi Director General of Irrigation at this time was a

* Lord Trevelyan, *The Middle East in Revolution* Macmillan, 1970

career civil servant who had retained his post through the revolution and the subsequent convolutions of the Qasim regime. He was a highly qualified engineer who spoke English and had an attractive presence and personality. My regular calls at his office gave me the opportunity to talk of many things, once the ritual enquiries on the progress of payments had been completed. In the process I also acquired an addiction to *haamud* (a delicious orange tea always generously available) which even in the ferocious heat of the Baghdad summer was fragrant and refreshing and made a welcome change from the more frequently offered *bebsi*. Gradually I learned something of the complexities of the irrigation systems in Iraq and of their impressive network of dams, canals, barrages, watergates, irrigation channels and drainage ditches which distributed the waters of the Tigris and Euphrates and some of their affluents and tributaries. Many of the original canals and watergates had originally been built from about 1750 BC by the Babylonians, who had of necessity to rely on gravity to get the flood waters across hundred of miles of waterless lands. The systems were further developed and improved by the Assyrians from about 1400 BC, and it was said that modern survey teams found that they could not improve on the work carried out by their Babylonian and Assyrian predecessors, many of whose ancient canals and ditches, long since disused and abandoned, were uncovered and recommissioned as a result.

Mesopotamia, the land between the rivers, was said to have once been the granary of the Middle East. I learned that the problem in modern Iraq was not so much the lack of water, but rather that there was too much of it, all at once, and not at the best time of the year. The solution was therefore to be found in conservation and distribution. In modern times several dams and barrages had been built to complement the ancient irrigation networks. The idea was to store some of the flood waters generated by the winter rains in the northern mountains and brought down by the Tigris and Euphrates which in the region around Baghdad flow at their closest to each other, before parting again on their separate ways to Al-Qurna, the Shatt-al-Arab and the Gulf.

A firm of British consulting engineers, Binnie, Deacon and Gourlay, was employed by the Iraq government in the design and supervision of one of the new dams and some irrigation canals. Ken Snelson was one of Binnie's engineers directly concerned, and also a friend. A colleague called Christopher Herdon and I decided to apply for the essential permits to visit the north of Iraq, where the dams were located. Under Ken's tutelage we proposed to travel by train to Kirkuk and then continue by road to the recently completed dam at Dokhan, then going on to another one, then under construction, at Derbendi Khan. We also hoped to see something of Kurdish Iraq and visit Suleimaniyah, close to the Persian border, returning via Erbil and Mosul, the capital of northern Iraq and an important commercial centre which also had an interesting museum and a notable mosque with a leaning tower.

Would we get the permits? Ken Snelson had no problems, being a member of the engineering team with acknowledged responsibilities in the area. One of his jobs was to redesign the irrigation networks which would carry the waters to the fertile plains between Samarra and Khanaqin. The Dokhan dam had been built on an affluent of the Tigris called the Lesser Zab close to the Persian border to the south of Rowanduz. The Lesser Zab meandered across the valleys north of Kirkuk and joined the Tigris well to the north of Samarra, where the Tharthar barrage had already been built. The other dam, at Derbendi Khan, was on another river called the Diyala which also flowed into the Tigris just south of Baghdad. Altogether the prospect was an exciting one and I felt particularly happy with my choice of travelling companions.

Christopher Herdon, one of the oriental secretaries at the embassy, was a proficient Arabist. He was also one of the few remaining members of the embassy who had been through the 1958 attack by the hostile mob, in which he had particularly distinguished himself by his personal courage in circumstances which could have been even more disastrous than they were. His conduct had been the subject of an unusual commendation by the Secretary of State. He was then about thirty and, together with his attractive wife, Virginia, was much in demand on all social occasions, when he tended to be one of the first to arrive and the last to leave. Cheerful, humorous, and gregarious, he showed no signs of the trauma one could still sense in some of the other embassy veterans of 1958, whose attitudes to conditions in Baghdad and life in general had been understandably affected by the event. He had a large circle of friends and was generally popular and well informed. In spite of his late nights he was always up at dawn to go riding, a form of exercise in those days still easily available. I had joined him on his early morning rides two or three times (we were also neighbours, living in houses on the same street at Karradat Mariam) and we had become friends. The third member of the party, Ken Snelson, was a rather lanky figure with fair hair and a ready smile who was a mine of information on Iraq and its history, not to speak of barrages, water-wheels and irrigation since biblical times. He and his vivacious wife, Moyna, were another very popular couple, always to be found at parties in the centre of an animated group of people to whom Moyna was retailing the latest news and gossip while Ken sucked at his empty pipe with an appreciative grin. Her rapid-fire comments and amusing descriptions never failed to provoke shouts of laughter from her audience. When we met again years later in Rome, where Ken was then working for the FAO, we spent several evenings together, our conversation constantly interrupted by 'Do you remember . . . ?' Needless to say, we went on to remind each other just the same.

Now the important question was the essential permits. Christopher was due to leave Baghdad shortly on transfer to another post, and Ken also had commitments which could not be postponed indefinitely. If the permits did not turn up in the next week or so, we would have to call off the trip, for the time being at any rate. But my fears proved groundless. A couple of days later Christopher put his head round my door one morning and waved a piece of paper. 'Look what I've got,' he said cheerfully. 'Now that we have it, I think we'd better leave as soon as possible. I've already telephoned Ken and he's ready to go. Shall we leave this evening?' But I was already reaching for my phone to ask my wife to pack a bag for me. Our superiors had given their consent to our proposed trip, and there was nothing to do except to clear my desk and get someone to take my place on the duty roster. Alec Stirling, then the chancery first secretary, was, as always, ready to help. He sighed and said, 'Congratulations! I wish I could to go too,' eyeing the heaps of files on the table in front of him. Cutting off my thanks with a grin and a wave he added, 'Have fun, and don't get into trouble!'

We were indeed to be congratulated on getting our permit. I think we were probably the first civilian members of the embassy to be allowed to roam about the north of Iraq without a permanent escort since the revolution in 1958. For some months previously the Military and Air Attachés had been allowed to go off on day trips to shoot over the cotton fields to the south of Baghdad near Suwaira. They had been authorized to leave the capital long before the civilian members of the embassy. This was due not only to their close working relations with their Iraqi military contacts but also to the absence of any official with authority in the lower reaches of the foreign ministry, where the civilian personnel were neither empowered nor inclined to take a decision without prior reference to the military. Those of us who perforce had to submit our requests for travel permits to the Ministry of Foreign Affairs were conditioned to the sight of the applications mouldering in the same in-tray for weeks on end without any sign of onward movement. After five or six fruitless calls one tended to give up. But not our services colleagues. They were dealt with under a different set of rules. They submitted their applications direct to the military governor's office in Baghdad and usually got it approved straight away. The corollary was the Jeep-load of plain-clothes and uniformed policeman who followed them wherever they went, sometimes giving rise to amusing situations. Once or twice the following Jeep ran out of fuel and had to ask their quarries for a loan of petrol. On another occasion one of the security men had a wedding to attend at a village close to their destination. All were put on their honour to return to the village at the appointed hour in order to return in close company to Baghdad, having spent the day shooting over the neighbouring cotton fields without supervision. The shooting party took with them a supply of canned beer and other provisions which were always shared with the invigilators, the more readily when they actively and usefully participated in the shoot, as I learned one day when I managed to break into this particular closed shop.

2

The Shooting Party

The fact that these expeditions took place at all was at first not generally known, for reasons that will become evident. Attendance was further restricted by the need to possess a shotgun and ammunition (very difficult to come by at the time), not to speak of transport and the essential official permit. No suitable dogs were available. But the glowing accounts brought back by the participants as well as the large quantities of partridges generously but unattributably distributed on return made me determined to join the shooting party on the next suitable occasion. After one or two fruitless attempts to get my official permit to leave Baghdad by fair means, it was the Air Attaché, Wing Commander Bob Horsley, a pilot with a particularly distinguished war record, who thought up the simple solution with the carefree approach to the established procedures which was such a characteristic feature of his jovial personality. Overnight I became Major Wallace and as such was included with the half-dozen names typed on the group permit which was approved and stamped, without a second glance, by the real major to whom it was submitted in the military governor's office the day before the shoot.

It was therefore an augmented and exhilarated military party which set out in two cars at dawn next morning, closely followed by the Jeep-load of security men. During our drive to the cotton plantations which were our destination I learned that these were on some of the estates expropriated by the government after the revolution. While cotton was still cultivated in most of the irrigated fields, these had not been shot over since 1958. I was told that the whole area was literally teeming with birds; that the hen bird was similar in colouring to the European partridge but twice the size; and that the cock had a black head and chest and usually took off from under one's feet with a startling rattle of wings. But, above all, I was enjoined not to shoot any of the security men who, anxious as always to join in the fun, would scour the fields ahead of the line of guns for wounded or dead birds, always difficult to find in the ditches between the serried rows of overblown cotton bushes. A hazardous and dangerous task this, but no more, I was to find, than that facing the guns themselves.

By the time we arrived at the cotton plantation the sun was up and it was beginning to get warm. We parked the cars under some trees and had a coffee from our Thermos flasks while we were given our order of battle by the Military Attaché, Colonel Guy Bowden, who was now in command. The guns were given their appointed places, told to maintain a distance of fifteen or twenty yards between each position, and not to fall behind the line. We would be shooting across the field with the rising sun behind us. The two men at the ends of the line were to stick close to the boundary fences and to keep slightly ahead of the centre of the line. In his quick-fire mixture of Arabic, Urdu, Hindi and Pushtu, Guy Bowden briefed the security party on our plan of attack, and with a cheerful, 'Come on, chaps!' strode across to the gates and led the way into the chosen field. He proposed to do three fields before lunch and two more, including the first one shot over in the morning, in the afternoon. It was clear he assumed that all members of the party were as fit as he was. This was made evident to me when I took my place on Guy's left of centre and viewed the prospect before me, while our invigilators took up their positions half-way up the field and we waited impatiently for the rest of the guns to get to their places at the ends of the line.

The cotton fields were irrigated by a simple system of sluice gates, ditches and gravity. To take full advantage of this the cotton bushes were planted on piled-up ridges of earth running parallel to each other straight across the breadth of the field. Each ridge was about eighteen inches high and separated from the next ridge by a ditch about two feet deep. At that time of the year the bottom of each trough contained about six inches of muddy water. The distance between ridge and trough made it impossible for anybody of my size to take two consecutive steps from ridge to ridge or, for that matter, from trough to trough. It had to be, at best, a scramble to the top of a ridge followed by a landing half way up the next one. At worst you landed at the bottom of the trough or sitting astride the ridge. Shotgun and cartridge belts further diminished the agility of the participants, and I was by this time uncomfortably aware of the perspiration already running down my back. My musings were interrupted by Guy bellowing, 'Ready?' up and down the line. The waves by the two boundary men were followed by a stentorian, 'We're OFF!' and the eager colonel set off at a cracking pace, his long legs enabling him to step from the top of one uneven ridge to the other unless, as was frequently the case, the space between the ridges had not been laid out with military precision. In my case my shorter stride made it clear that I could not take two consecutive paces without coming to grief in the third ditch, from which I had to emerge by clambering to the top of the following ridge, whence I launched myself hopefully across to the next row unless, of course, my path was barred by a particularly robust cotton bush. I had not travelled more than a few yards in this manner when my painful progress was made even more complex.

A shot, followed closely by another, signalled the opening of hostilities by Guy. I was just in time to see two dead birds falling to earth a few feet in front of him when, with an exciting explosion of beating wings, three birds flew up from the ditch into which I was even then plunging. I could have hit them with my gun barrel as they flew up past my face. This was my first encounter with the Iraqi partridge and I could hardly fail to be impressed by the size of the birds. I had put up two cock birds and a hen and they made a gorgeous picture against the clear blue sky from the bottom of the ditch where I was by now lying. The cock birds' black and shiny head and chest plumage had a greenish sheen in the strong sunlight, and all had a tinge of red in the eye, mottled greyish-brown bellies, and grey legs and feet. Having gained a little height they banked to fly off low to my left front. As I struggled to regain my feet while holding my shotgun aloft out of the mud and water, my scattered thoughts were rudely concentrated. 'Shoot 'em, you fathead!' roared Guy. But I had time only to take a snap shot at one of the cock birds as I leant my heaving chest against a cotton bush while kneeling in six inches of slimy water.

By this time regular volleys were coming from both ends of the line, and a few yards further on I counted five dead birds in the air between me and the boundary gun on my left. Some of the birds we put up flew across the line of guns, which gave rise to a veritable fusillade across the field unless brought down by a lucky first shot. The need to reload and pick up dead birds played havoc with our line abreast, not to speak of our bursting lungs and aching muscles. But Guy was having none of this. 'No laggards!' he bellowed. 'Come along, keep in line!' and charged on at such a pace that we began to overrun some of the more lethargic partridges, with the result that some broke cover behind us, frequently taking off just a few feet away to our rear. This gave rise to potentially lethal situations, with guns aiming to the front, the sides and the rear more or less at the same time. When I walked back two or three steps to pick up a bird I had shot just behind me, I disturbed two more partridges which erupted into the air from under my feet just as I was bending to pick up my bird. As I fumbled to reload my empty chambers I found myself looking at the business end of three sets of gun barrels all aiming at a point approximately three feet above my head. 'Fore!' shouted the ever vigilant Guy. But I was already face down in the ditch, thinking of the report on cotton production in Iraq I had to produce before the end of the quarter. This was all useful experience.

We thus made our strenuous progress to the end of the field, where we caught up with our beaming leader unburdening himself of a large number of dead birds and breaking open fresh boxes of cartridges. We were all drenched in perspiration and covered in mud. Our breathing was laboured and harsh. Some had run out of ammunition. One had been lucky to escape injury when one of the barrels of his shotgun had burst when he fired after unwittingly thrusting them into the mud when falling into a ditch. But the combined bag was satisfactory by any standards and the morning was yet young. Barely giving us time to regain our breath, 'Come on, chaps! To your places!' from Guy was greeted with groans. Heedless of our appeals for another few minutes' grace, he left the birds in the care of one of our invigilators and strode off to his place in the middle. Now that we were one gun short he changed the order of battle and put our disarmed colleagues at the end of the row. 'And don't fall behind, you can always hit them over the head with a stick!' he shouted, rather heartlessly, I thought. But by the middle of the morning all were back in business, Guy having produced from the boot of his car a second shotgun which he generously made available when we retraced our steps to the field near the parked cars. As the day wore on some of us tried different techniques for dealing with the ridges and troughs. One or two developed a left leading, sideways, crab-like step and lunge, the more effectively to fire (if right-handed) without being knocked off balance by the recoil as was wont to happen if standing facing front with both feet on top of a ridge. Others adopted a sort of hop, skip, and jump which was effective in dealing with the terrain but less so in bagging the birds, the degree of concentration required by the two objectives being almost mutually exclusive. I found it best to take aim from the bottom of a ditch even if this meant giving up birds put up while scrambling over to the other side. It was also less dangerous for all concerned, and there was clearly no shortage of game.

It was a cheerfully dishevelled and exhausted group which gathered for lunch by the cars under the trees, where our indefatigable escorts joined us. Cold beers, hard-boiled eggs, and sandwiches were shared and exchanged with chapatties and boiled rice, followed by large quantities of coffee and tea. There was no time for conversation. A few minutes later, regardless of the blazing sun high in the heavens, the implacable Guy was sharing out the remaining ammunition among those who had run short. 'I told you you'd need more;' he said, 'Isn't it wonderful?' A laugh and further exchanges with our friendly custodians in his incomprehensible vernacular were followed by the relentless: 'Come on, chaps!' Mercifully for some of us, the shortage of ammunition made it pointless to plan on doing more than a final sweep over our first shoot, which still produced an inordinate quantity of birds.

When we finally gathered under the trees for the last time, we counted the birds, disposed of the remaining food and drink, and made plans for a further shoot a fortnight later, the while recalling enthusiastically the individual highlights and exciting moments of the day. I was delighted when I was invited to resume my military rank in two weeks' time. Our enthusiasm was only slightly dampened when Guy reminded us that as the season wore on the cotton harvest would reduce the cover for the partridges, which meant that our pace across the fields would have to be even faster. The suggestion that we should march in line with and along the ridges and troughs was scoffed out of court, it being clear that the birds would simply scamper on ahead of the marchers, at least along those ditches which had little water. In fact I found that, as the season progressed, the nature of the shoot changed considerably, the bare cotton bushes, waterless ditches, and hard earth bringing about several changes in the rules of engagement. The birds took flight further away, the going for the guns was less exhausting, and, while the day's bags were always prodigious by any standards of rough shooting, they never matched the quantities achieved on the first few days of the season. Nevertheless, we always returned to Baghdad tired, aching and filthy, but happy to have several brace of birds to distribute to friends and neighbours. For days after a shoot our kitchens would be filled with flying feathers, and invitations to dinner parties which were known to serve partridges were always eagerly sought-after. One bird provided an ample meal for two normal people, especially as the Mesopotamian partridge, like the East African francolin to which the experts claimed it was closely related, had virtually no dark meat and was remarkably fat and juicy.

3

Northern Iraq

During my first few months in Iraq the shooting expeditions, in which I participated two or three times with my honorary military rank, were the only opportunities I had to travel outside the capital until the day Christopher Herdon came to my office waving the piece of paper on which my name appeared for the first time, so to speak, in my own right.

We agreed to meet that same evening at the West Baghdad railway station packed and ready for our great adventure. Ken Snelson had already booked our sleepers in an air-conditioned coach and his firm had kindly undertaken to provide the transport in the north. For this purpose they had hired a Baghdad taxi driver, inevitably called Ali, and his 1957 Chevrolet. Both were to meet us the following morning on arrival at Kirkuk railway station. As we settled into our comfortable compartment it was Ken who had to field all our questions about the new dams, the Kurds, Mosul, Derbendi Khan, the Rowanduz gorge, the mountains, and the irrigation networks. Ken had an engaging habit of producing a paper and pencil and drawing plans and diagrams in order best to illustrate his explanations. The train left Baghdad punctually, and while we pored over Ken's sketches the hours slipped happily and swiftly away as the meter-gauge train trundled on its northward journey at a sedate thirty miles an hour.

When we arrived at Kirkuk the following morning I had a headache. It was a gloriously clear and sunny morning and we had all been up and about long before we were due to arrive in order to see something of the scenery. The previous evening, however, had been very convivial: I had brought along a couple of cold partridges, and somebody produced a bottle of whisky. As a result the excitement and conversation had gone on until the small hours and I was clearly short of sleep. Ken had arranged for us to repair first to the oil company's guest-house in Kirkuk where we would breakfast and freshen up. During the day we planned to see something of the oil capital of Iraq and spend the night there, leaving the following morning at the crack of dawn with our friend Ali and his taxi who had met us at the station as arranged. A hearty and very English breakfast was served to us at a long mess table with a cheerful checked tablecloth and bottles of HP sauce and other condiments spaced along the centre. My headache disappeared and we prepared eagerly to see what Kirkuk had to offer.

Even though the town dated back to the time of the Assyrians I had been warned that there was now little to see of any interest. Undaunted, we set out to visit the souk first; we also wanted to visit the tomb of the prophet Daniel who was said to have been buried in Kirkuk. But the bazaar was, unusually, not very interesting. Ali the driver dismissed the souk with a shrug: 'Nothing here but fruit and vegetables,' he sniffed, 'These people make nothing!' although Ken had by this time found a merchant with a goodly stock of Persian carpets. But the prices were higher than in Baghdad and the merchants did not seem to be disposed to bargain. The oil industry seemed to have given a different character to the city. When we visited the oil company's offices we were given an interesting account of the origins, nature and extent of the oil company's operations, which provided such a large share of the Iraq government's revenues. The Kirkuk oilfields were among the oldest in the Middle East, but the uncertainties of the situation since 1958 had inhibited the oil companies from assuming new undertakings while their protracted negotiations continued with Qasim's government. There were other complicating factors. The relations of the local authorities with the central government in Baghdad were not as cordial as they might have been. About a year earlier Kirkuk had been the setting for a pitched battle between communists, nationalists and Ba'athists. Inevitably, the foreign oil companies were a natural target for all political parties and opposition groups.

We returned to the guest-house for an early lunch, followed by a long siesta which we justified by the lack of sleep the previous night on the train. The guest-house, although comfortable and clean, had the impersonal atmosphere usually found in most such establishments, as provided by hospitable oil companies for the benefit of their own staff in transit and benighted travellers in general in many parts of the world where hotel accommodation is unavailable. This one was manned by a cook, a major-domo and a couple of cleaners who all did their jobs efficiently and with a minimum of fuss, seldom intruding other than to replenish the ice bucket on the sideboard or put a fresh bottle of HP sauce on the table. The sitting-room had a radio and a gramophone, and we were able to listen to the BBC news. By the time we gathered for an evening drink in the comfortable sitting-room I was again full of questions and looking forward to our departure the following morning. As the evening shadows closed in, our view through the windows became quite spectacular, the skyline of the town with its oil installations silhouetted against the suffused orange-red glow which seemed to surround us on all sides.

Even what I had been told about the effect of the oil flares by night had not prepared me for the real thing. Although some of the oil installations surrounding the city were clearly visible during the day, time (and dust) seemed to have given them a degree of protective colouring which enabled them to merge with the undistinguished houses and featureless buildings in the suburbs where we were staying. But at night the oil industry took over. The tongues of flame and muted roar of the oil flares burning off surplus gases provided a spectacular backdrop to the view from the window. The effect was most notable at twilight when the natural process of day turning into night seemed to be retarded by the increasingly intrusive radiance. After dark, the sky above acquired an unnatural luminosity. Christopher and I were gazing out of one of the windows in fascination when our attention was distracted by a laugh from Ken standing by the gramophone. He had noticed that there was only one record available, although dozens of paperback novels were stacked on one of the shelves by the radio. 'Just listen to this,' said Ken with a grin, as he put the record on the turntable. As we gathered round we heard the clear, musical tones of a song which had been an instant success. I think the opening line was a melodious and beguiling description of the plain, simple tastes professed by the singer. These included diamonds, large estates and, to the best of my recollection, luxury motor cars. But the last verse conveyed the topical message of the single record with its amusing reference to the musical sound of oil wells slurping into barrels. An early night followed by a call at 04.00 found us packed and ready to go when the punctual Ali drove up in his taxi just as dawn was breaking.

Our trip was an unqualified success. The only problem was that our planning had been more than a trifle ambitious and we had to cover a great deal of ground in the time available. For six days we were on the go from dawn till well after dusk and, one memorable night, much later. But there was so much to see and learn in the few days available to us. Our visits to the two dams were the highlights of the trip. The Dokhan dam was then virtually finished. There had been some problems with the so-called 'apron' of cement grouting in the porous rock formation on both sides of the dam. As a result the water intakes were partially open, in order to reduce the level of the backed-up reservoir of water, while additional grouting was carried out to stop the small leaks. Ken described this process as similar to the squeezing of toothpaste into the appropriate nooks and crannies, the toothpaste being a special kind of quick-drying, non-porous cement. The dam had what was called a bell-mouth spillway, rather like a gigantic, horizontal funnel which would prevent any flood waters raising the level of the reservoir over the approved limits. There was provision for hydroelectric generation in the chambers which regulated the normal downstream flow, although none of the machinery had so far been installed. This enabled Ken to take us into the bowels of the dam, where we stood thoughtfully on one of the large concrete pipes through which flowed a then modest but still impressive outflow into the river below; for my part keenly aware of the vast volume of water confined above our heads by the retaining cement.

The contrast between the man-made structure and the surrounding countryside could not have been more stark, the more so because of the few other signs of human enterprise at that time visible in the area. The building contractors had withdrawn and the machinery installation had not commenced, so the site was virtually deserted. In order to reach the dam we had travelled along dusty desert roads which in due course brought our taxi to equally dusty hills. These provided the first exciting change from the monotonous plains around Baghdad to which I had grown accustomed since my arrival. The hills had then given way to arid mountain formations which looked for all the world as though a superior hand had carelessly dropped a gigantic piece of crumpled brown sacking which had lain undisturbed for generations. The site was chosen and the dam built in the upper reaches of the Lesser Zab where it threaded its course through the folds in the sacking. On our way there we had been taken aback by our driver's perplexity at his car's reluctance to climb hills in third gear, Ali never having previously encountered the need for any gear other than top after starting up when cruising the flat streets of Baghdad in search of fares.

I was interested to find, however, that our desert roads were by no means deserted. On our way north we met a number of large American cars with as many as seven or eight occupants, all with headcloths and scarves wound round their necks and mouths against the heat and dust. This was the normal means of transport between towns and villages in the north, each passenger paying an agreed fare to the owner-driver, who would also make room available in his boot and roof-rack for luggage and assorted bundles. Thus piled high with bags of flour, baskets of vegetables, and chickens in crates, the overloaded cars would race across the desert followed by a plume of evil-tasting dust. Each car bore two or more canvas water bags secured over the front bumpers, condensation, evaporation, and the speed of the vehicle combining to keep the water in the bags cool and satisfying. We met three or four such cars every hour coming in the opposite direction along those parts were the road had been surfaced. We also covered long distances off the road, however, over vast and empty tracts of level ground where numerous vehicles had chosen their own route across the desert, as the countless tyre marks snaking their way over the desolate landscape bore witness. On these sectors, unconfined by a narrow metalled surface, we were frequently overtaken by a heavily laden car racing ahead on a parallel course sometimes a hundred yards away, half-open boot lid tied down with bits of rope revealing intriguing glimpses of Gordon's Gin cartons, firewood, and other merchandise. Once we were caught up by a dilapidated station-wagon laden well above the Plimsoll line. Its springs visibly touched bottom whenever the surface was less than perfectly even. It was travelling at sixty or seventy miles an hour with a full complement of passengers and the customary pile of bundles and baskets on the roof-rack, the whole edifice crowned by an upright, pedal-driven sewing machine. The driver's efforts to avoid stones or other irregularities on his chosen track made the vehicle with its high cargo keel over like a schooner in a gale. Before it disappeared in a cloud of dust we watched it swaying from side to side. 'If they have a break-down, they'll sink without trace,' said Ken, and it was clear that we had all been thinking on the same lines. But we never came across any vehicles broken down by the wayside, although we sometimes encountered stationary cars, particu-larly in the evenings, with passengers and crew devoutly kneeling at prayer.

We were hoping to visit Mosul, Erbil, Rowanduz and Suleimaniyah before retracing our steps to Derbendi Khan where the dam on the Diyala river was being built. Although the distances involved were not great we were hard put to it to keep to our timetable because of the rich variety of historical antiquities on offer. We had little time for visits to the Winged Bull at Nineveh, or the ancient site of the battlefield outside Erbil. But we were now in the heart of Kurdish Iraq and the differences all around us were notable and interesting. The endless plains and arid deserts surrounding Baghdad had given way to horizons with imposing mountain ranges and green foothills and fields close by. Kurdish men seemed to be taller and heavier than the Iraqi Arabs of the plains. They were frequently fair and blue-eyed, and even when they were dark they might have green eyes and a reddish stubble. Their dress was colourful and exotic; they wore tasselled and fringed turbans, sashes, and baggy trousers, and some wore long-sleeved waistcoats with cartridge loops on their chests. Others habitually wore bandoliers which, together with their orna-mental daggers and rakish headgear, made them look for all the world like a cross between a Georgian cossack and an Italian *bersagliere*.

The women also wore colourful shawls and headcloths. Their faces were uncovered and most had gold necklaces or ear-rings made of gold coins and other ornaments. They usually wore their hair in thick plaits, and many were also fair-complexioned and blue-eyed, with cheerful, open countenances. The villages through which we passed were full of people bustling about, the men with sacks and bundles, the women herding children and animals before them. Their language was incomprehensible, and some did not appear to speak Arabic. They were neither hostile nor particularly friendly, but we were clearly foreigners and strangers to boot; once or twice we were asked if we were Russian.

Once when we stopped for petrol at a ramshackle service station outside one of the towns, we went into an adjacent teashop to get something of the atmosphere of the place. There were a number of raffish looking characters squatting with both feet on the wooden benches outside, drinking tea or companionably smoking hubble-bubbles. Christopher struck up a conversation with one of the tea-drinkers who spoke Arabic. He told us that he lived on one of the hill slopes about a day's journey away and had come into town to buy supplies in the market. He had never been to Baghdad. When he had established our nationality he made little attempt to disguise his sentiments towards Qasim and the central government in Baghdad. After some final exchanges about the weather and the shortage of wheat he got to his feet, belched politely, picked up his sack of flour or whatever, swung it lightly onto one broad shoulder and, with a contemptuous glance towards the hapless Ali, set off up the valley road towards his hillside home.

Kurdish dissatisfaction had not yet broken out into the open rebellion which put an end to any further visits to the north for the remainder of my time in Iraq. The Kurdish leader Mullah Mustapha Barzani was then thought to be in Moscow where he had already spent some years before Qasim's revolution, and was known as 'the Red Mullah' as a result. Shortly after his return to Iraq in 1961 he broke off negotiations with the central government and took to the mountains, raiding army posts and inciting other tribes to join him in what eventually became a full-scale revolt throughout Kurdish Iraq until it was crushed by Qasim's army and airforce. But while we sat in the shady *chaikhana* drinking tea and Coca-Cola all this was in the future. Some of our interlocutors seemed to think that the British were in a position to influence Qasim to grant autonomy to the Kurds. Many of the Kurdish leaders had been thorns in the sides of British administrations in Iraq ever since the end of the

First World War. Those responsible for drawing the dotted lines on the maps of the Middle East after the defeat of the Ottoman Empire could hardly make provision for all the ethnic minorities which gave such a rich diversity of peoples and cultures to several of the new nations in the area. The Kurds were perhaps the largest of these minorities, as well as the most fragmented by the international dotted lines: there are significant Kurdish populations in several of the countries whose boundaries are straddled by what used to be known as the 'Fertile Crescent' stretching from Iraqi Suleimaniyah and the areas across the Iranian border in the south, to Syria, Turkey and the Soviet Union in the north. The Kurdish highlanders had never found it easy to accept the authority of the central government in any of the countries in which they lived, their mountain fastnesses having provided home and refuge to generations of rebellious, raiding tribesmen. One old man with blue eyes and an impressive white moustache told us that in his youth he had fought many battles against the British and had indeed once been taken prisoner and subsequently released. He explained that he and his men never took any prisoners.

My head was filled with thoughts of raids and ambushes as we continued our journey north. I wanted to visit the Rowanduz gorge, which had so often featured in the chronicles of the early travellers in the area. We also hoped to get as far as Hajji Umran on the Iranian border, a mountain village at an altitude of some six thousand feet with pine-covered slopes and the snowy peaks of the Zagros mountains in the background. The Rowanduz gorge was a natural pass on the route through the mountains where the headwaters of the Greater Zab flowed on their way to the Erbil plains and the Tigris. It had been one of the main caravan routes between Turkey and Persia since biblical times. The Venetian traveller Marco Polo was said to have passed through the gorge on his journeys to the Far East. Its geographical significance was such that the British Government had maintained a vice-consulate at Rowanduz in the mid-1930s. In preparation for our trip I had searched through the rather barren library of the embassy in Baghdad for suitable background reading. Like everything else, the library had suffered from the looting and burning in 1958, but I was interested to find that one of the books which had survived was an elderly official tome by a Captain Rupert Hay of the Indian

Political Service who, in the company of a brother officer, carried out a topographical survey of the area for the Government of India in the middle twenties. This was without doubt the same official who, as Colonel Sir Rupert Hay, was the Political Resident in the Persian Gulf when I first arrived in Bahrain in 1953, the Persian Gulf Residency having established itself there on leaving its original headquarters in Bushire shortly after Indian independence in 1947, Britain's responsibilities in the Gulf having previously been administered by the British Government of India.

On hearing or our proposed trip, the Indian Ambassador in Baghdad, himself a former member of the Indian Political Service, had told me that in the bad old days the Government of India frequently had problems throughout the area then known as 'Kurdistan'. Mr Inder Sen Chopra was a charming gentleman of distinguished appearance, with iron-grey hair, a military moustache and a martial bearing, usually dressed in pinstripe suits of impeccable cut, regimental ties and highly burnished shoes. He was interested to hear that I had served in Bahrain under Sir Rupert Hay, Mr Chopra having also served with him in the Indian Political Service many years previously, when both were young officers. He confided that he 'found Rupert rather demanding', and had indeed once found it necessary to apply to rejoin his own regiment, after which there had been an improvement in the situation. I assured him that by the time I met him in Bahrain, Sir Rupert had obviously mellowed, then being just a few months short of retirement. Mr Chopra gave me much advice and useful information, and I was happy to meet him again, years later, when he was ambassador to Argentina and Uruguay; I was then able to return his courtesy in what was to him an unfamiliar country in an unfamiliar continent.

As one would expect, the official account of Captain Hay's survey concentrated on the nature of the terrain and vegetation, with detailed descriptions of the hills and mountains climbed, their formation, different levels and altitudes, and the places and number of times they had halted for observations (or a comforting brew of tea). Various meetings and conversations with friendly *agas* were also faithfully recorded. While we travelled in the comfort of our Baghdad taxi I tried to visualize a youthful Sir Rupert and his companion arduously

42

climbing mountain after mountain and covering vast distances with their mule trains and bearers. But communications in the north had greatly improved in recent years, and a number of villages in the mountains now boasted hotels and guest-houses. The magnificent mountain views, wooded slopes, clear streams and spectacular scenery made a welcome change from the dust and heat of the arid central plains; had it not been for the continuing communal and political instability, several areas of Kurdish Iraq might have become attractive holiday resorts. When I commented as much, Ken reminded me that only twelve or fourteen years before, a British consular officer in Mosul had been killed by a hostile mob, the sort of thing which he thought gave holiday resorts a bad name. The existence of much contraband (or traditional commerce) across the frontiers was a further complication. Police posts were few and far between, and well-armed local entrepreneurs conducted a thriving trade in smuggled goods and commodities not available even in the souks of Baghdad, including the very latest in Japanese electronic wizardry.

We were beginning to realize that we had bitten off more than we could chew in the time available to us. Even though we were on our way at dawn every morning and fell unconscious into bed at night, we could allow ourselves only cursory visits to some of the places we had originally aimed for. I found myself nodding off in the back of the car many times as we drove on to our next port of call, in spite of my determination to see everything in the areas through which we travelled. I was fast asleep the following evening when Ken dug his elbow into my ribs. It was quickly getting dark and he wanted me to see the mountain scenery as we approached Derbendi Khan. We were moving comfortably over a wide earth road, clearly of recent construction. In the failing light we saw two or three graders and rollers parked by the roadside. Otherwise there was little traffic although the road surface showed numerous tyre marks. Ken had warned us that the approaches to Derbendi Khan were almost as spectacular as the dam site itself. This had finally been chosen in a gap in the mountains where the Diyala flowed evenly on its way south just below the place where a lesser affluent joined it. The new road we were driving on twisted and turned through hilly country without any sign of human habitation. We were impatient to get to our destination and disappointed that we would get there in the dark. Our car headlights lit up the rock face on the right side of the road and the beams disappeared into empty space whenever we came to a right-hand bend, while I gazed apprehensively at the invisible depths a few feet to our left.

It was now completely dark and even Ken was straining forward in his seat and looking at his watch. 'We should be getting there fairly soon,' he murmured, not very confidently. Ali, normally an uncomplaining man of few words, brought another problem to our attention. 'We need petrol soon,' he said, adding, 'the tin is empty.' This last was a reference to the jerrycan we carried in the boot as an emergency reserve, which had been used as such earlier that evening. All we could get out of Ken was a far from reassuring, 'We should have been there already,' while I thought of the bandits said to infest the area. Each bend in the road brought us to the edge of our seat as we peered forward in the hope of seeing some sign of life. In the desolate darkness we were anxious, hungry, thirsty, and very tired. We had set off at dawn that morning and it was now well past our normal bedtime. Ali had been telling me how all these savages in the north were said to mutilate the bodies of their victims, and the flickering petrol gauge had been registering empty for the last half-hour. But the next bend in the road brought forth a fervent 'Al hamd-al-illah!' from Ali while we strained forward to gaze at the totally unexpected blaze of light in the valley below us.

We had passed the highest point in the road some while back, and I had noted with approval that Ali's newly acquired expertise in hill driving including slipping the gear into neutral and coasting down as far as the gradient would permit. But the site of the dam was surrounded by mountains which had prevented us from catching any glimpses of it until we reached the bend half-way down to the river on the valley floor. We were therefore quite close when we came to see it so dramatically, but far enough away to encompass the whole complex undertaking as well as the working areas surrounding the dam. It was as though we were viewing a large-scale table model of the project.

Powerful arc lights brilliantly lit up the whole area, and the vast site was teeming with activity. High-pressure jets of water aimed from all angles at the man-made rock barrier across the

44

ravine. Giant rollers were treading down the thirty-ton dumper-loads of rock and shale being delivered in ceaseless convoys up the approach road to the wide top of the great wall, which seemed to increase in height with every load. The noise was deafening, none of the huge dumper trucks or generators apparently bothering overmuch with silencers on their exhausts. Overhead cranes, transmission towers, elevated platforms and conveyor belts all added to the apparent confusion. On the valley floor there were countless Jeeps and vans, lorries and cars, mechanical shovels and graders and cement mixers. All this impressive display of machinery was attended by several hundred men wearing bright-yellow safety helmets. Here and there we could see helmets of other colours, as well as white overalls among the more numerous khaki and light green. Ali had stopped the car and we were all standing by the edge of the road staring at the extraordinary spectacle below. 'Well, what d'you think of that, eh?' said Ken, grinning, and obviously enjoying the effect upon us of the remarkable activity on all sides, the more impressive because it was so unexpected. After a quick technical briefing from Ken who was anxious to exploit the comprehensive, floodlit view from our vantage point, we climbed stiffly into the car again and coasted down to the seeming bedlam on the valley floor, where we were greeted hospitably in the comfortable staff quarters by the Yugoslav resident engineer, who had long ago given us up for lost.

The earthworks were approximately half-built at the time. Ken told us that, unlike Dokhan, the dam then under construction at Derbendi Khan was known technically as a rock-fill dam, which he described graphically as taking the top half of a mountain from the side of the valley, inverting it and dumping it across the river bed, having previously built a coffer dam to divert the waters during construction. At one end of the rock barrier you built the powerhouse and the spillway, to deal respectively with electricity generation and the overflow from the reservoir to be formed upstream behind the rock barrier. The river would then be funnelled through the entrails of the dam, which would thereafter regulate its flow and provide water for agriculture from the reservoir during the dry season. The spillway was already built. It looked like an oversized concrete ski-jump, the upward curve and lip at the bottom serving to break the force of the flood waters which would eventually pour through the overflow. With his customary drawings, Ken made it all look very simple, only the ceaseless activity which surrounded us conveying something of the magnitude of the undertaking. Among other reasons, the site had been chosen because of the impermeable nature of the rock formations on both sides of the rock-fill, thus reducing to a minimum the need for an additional expensive grouted apron. The Yugoslav engineer told us that the work never stopped. There were three shifts working round the clock. Everyone on the site worked in relays. This meant that as soon as one crew relinquished their place on the cranes, dumpers or rollers, another lot took their place. Workers were either eating or resting at all sorts of times, hence the unexpected luxury of our excellent meal in a comfortable mess hall, promptly produced and served in spite of the lateness of the hour. Everything worked twenty-four hours a day. Neither the gigantic dumpers with their ten-foot tyres, nor the rollers and graders, ever stopped their engines other than to refuel and for their standard maintenance and oil change. The wear and tear on the contractor's plant and appliances was tremendous, and the self-contained engineering and maintenance workshop never closed. A prefabricated village complete with dormitories, sick bays, mess halls and leisure amenities had been built to accommodate the workers.

All this was explained by the friendly Yugoslav engineer while we ate our belated dinner (and lunch). Although I believe that the original choice of the dam site had been made many years before by a British firm of consulting engineers, new contracts for the supervision and construction had been let after Qasim's revolution. As a result, several Eastern European state organizations were responsible for various bits of the project, working in harmony with the American consultants (Harza Engineering) and, of course, the Iraqi technical staff representing the Government's planning and irrigation departments. The workers were mainly Iraqi Arabs and Kurds, with a smattering of Iranians from over the nearby border. The Yugoslav resident engineer presided over this remarkable polyglot workforce with equanimity. When we asked him how he managed to communicate with all those concerned in such a highly technical undertaking, he said that he had picked up a smattering of Arabic in the past six months, but added that most of his meetings with his international staff were conducted in English. With a twinkle in his eye he also reminded us that in Iraq there was already a precedent, albeit not a very recent one. In any case, he added with a broad smile, the Tower of Babel had probably not been supervised by a Yugoslav resident engineer otherwise it might still be standing today, a sentiment to which we raised our glasses with one accord.

I cannot remember going to bed that night. I think I must have been asleep on my feet for some time before we were taken to the guest bungalow where we spent what was left of the night. In spite of the ceaseless noise, audible even in the sealed, air-conditioned comfort of our bedrooms, the warmth of the hospitality, the food and drink, the long day's journey, and the sense of achievement all contrived to ensure that I lost consciousness even before I went to bed. When the ruthless Ali shook me awake at dawn next morning he found me lying with my head at the foot of the bed and my feet on the pillow, fully dressed and with the electric lights on. On my stomach was Captain Rupert Hay's topographical report of the area, published so many years before by the Government of India, which I had thoughtfully borrowed from the remains of the looted library of the Baghdad embassy.

Our return to Baghdad was uneventful. Sadly, Christopher left us shortly after on transfer to another post, and to my eternal regret the deteriorating political situation in Kurdish Iraq prevented me during the rest of my time in Baghdad from making another trip to the north to see some of the things and places we had been obliged to miss out. However, my first-hand knowledge and understanding of dams and irrigation had increased prodigiously, as had my awareness of the problems and difficulties confronting British contractors and consultants trying to do business in Iraq at that time. Our efforts to obtain payment of overdue bills continued unabated, and British firms' representatives sent out by their companies to get the embassy to 'bring pressure to bear' on the Iraq Government were sometimes mollified to hear about our regular dunning visits to the corresponding government departments. For months after my northern trip my conversations with visiting British businessmen and my correspondence with their principals were both peppered with references to bellmouth spillways, sheep-foot rollers and grouted aprons; the fact that I had actually visited the site of some of these prestigious undertakings in the remote Kurdish mountains of northern Iraq seldom failed to bring about a marked change in the attitude of my interlocutors when the conversation reached a point where, at the appropriate moment, I was obliged to make this admission with becoming modesty.

4

The Siege of the Embassy, 1963

One Friday morning in February 1963, just after our customary staff meeting had begun, there was a tremendous explosion overhead which sounded like an aircraft's supersonic boom. It so happened that the meeting was being conducted in the Ambassador's room by John Robey, the deputy head of mission, who had succeeded Peter Hayman some months earlier. Sir Humph had himself been replaced by Sir Roger Allen at the end of 1961. The Ambassador had gone off earlier that morning to a newly uncovered archaeological site which the experts in the Iraqi Department of Antiquities were to show him.

The first man out of the room scanned the cloudless blue sky above the inner courtyard and concluded that some of the new Iraqi Soviet-built MiG fighter-bombers based at Habbaniyah must be out on exercises. These aircraft were capable of breaking the sound barrier, and more distant sonic booms had been heard over Baghdad on a number of previous occasions. But a second explosion shortly after, followed closely by a third and fourth, caused the assembled company to become increasingly restless, and there followed a concerted rush out of the Ambassador's office. Some went to their own rooms to make phone calls while others went up to the higher level of the rambling chancery offices in order to get a view of the city across the Tigris, which lapped the walls at the back of the chancery and meandered through most of Baghdad rather as the Thames does through London. It was Rab Munro, the Oriental Counsellor, who first brought concrete news to several of us apprehensively loitering in the central courtyard. 'The Iraqi air force is attacking the Ministry of Defence with rockets and somebody told me that there are reports of army tank

49

columns coming into town from Ba'quba,' he said. 'This is serious,' he added. 'It rather looks as though this time the plot has got off the ground.' This was a reference to the fact that it was generally known that in the last six months there had been many abortive coups against Qasim's increasingly psychopathic rule. But tanks from the army's armoured division base at Ba'quba east of the capital and air force MiGs from the air base at Habbaniyah to the west suggested a greater degree of co-ordination than previously achieved. Other members of the staff were by this time listening to the local radio and yet others were trying to reach the Ambassador in order to get him safely back into the fold. Miraculously, the chancery switchboard was working normally and our Iraqi telephone operator was doing a magnificent job getting through to anxious wives and to leading members of the British community who had a predetermined role to play in an emergency.

The embassy in Baghdad was once the palace of the Turkish governor, but little remained at this time of any splendour it might have had under Ottoman rule, or even during the years between the two world wars, when the spacious grounds included stabling for the troop of Indian cavalry which provided the formal escort for the High Commissioner (and, later, Ambassador). The ambassadorial residence had been burned down and looted by a hostile crowd on 14 July 1958, when elsewhere in Baghdad King Feisal and his family were killed by Qasim's troops. Of the original buildings, only the ballroom remained standing to one side, with a ceremonial pre-1914 war cannon and corresponding pyramid of ball shot at the top of the short flight of steps which now led to an empty space adjoining the ballroom, through which one could view the skyline of new buildings across the river. The continuing uncertainties of the situation in Iraq inhibited both the Treasury and the Ministry of Works from undertaking any rebuilding, only to see it (they argued with some justification) burned down and looted again. But the chancery offices (originally the servant's quarters of the Ottoman governor) had remained almost unscathed and had been repaired and improved; new furniture had arrived in my own time there. My office adjoined that of the head of chancery on the ground floor surrounding the inner courtyard. My single window to the rear overlooked the muddy banks of the Tigris where we normally berthed the embassy launch, the *Mary Rich* (imaginatively named after the tragic child bride of Charles Rich, one of the early East India Company Residents in Baghdad); it also framed a view of two of Baghdad's bridges as well as the skyscrapers of Bank Street and the commercial centre across the river. The Commercial Counsellor was on leave in the United Kingdom and I was acting in his place, which gave me unusual obligations and responsibilities in the emergency which now confronted us. I was trying hard to establish precisely what these were when the assistant Military Attaché joined the group in the courtyard. He was overflowing with news.

He reported that the air force was leading a major rebellion against Qasim. The attitude of some of the key army units was not yet clear; the armoured brigade at Ba'quba had joined the rebels; other units were still biding their time. The main radio station had been taken over by the rebels and was broadcasting martial music and appeals for calm. A twenty-four-hour curfew had been imposed; anybody on the streets would be shot. Qasim and his immediate staff and guards were in the Ministry of Defence (it was known that he habitually spent his nights there) and the policeman normally at our front gates had been replaced by a group of soldiers. This was reassuring; an assault on the British Embassy in those days was regarded by some as a useful diversion in any conditions of political uncertainty. We were also relieved to learn that army tanks had taken up positions on the 'bund' (a sort of dyke originally built on the outskirts to prevent the flooding of low-lying parts of the city). This now served mainly as a barrier between some of the new residential suburbs and the teeming sea of indigent humanity living in the mud and reed hovels known as *sarifas* which, viewed from the top of the bund, stretched in parts as far as one could see on the dusty horizon. These shanty towns gave shelter to some of the frightening crowds which had, on more than one occasion, filled the streets of Baghdad, looting, pillaging and generally laying waste whenever the normal order of things was disturbed.

The residence of the Ottoman governor had originally been in a commanding position on the banks of the Tigris in the centre of the city, but much new housing had been built in the suburbs and nearly all the embassies had by this time moved out of the less salubrious area where the British Embassy, traditionally a natural target for hostile demonstrations, still remained in its splendid riverside site surrounded by squalor. The main gates fronted on what we still called General Maude Square, although the statue of the defender of Kut al Amarah no longer graced the dusty plants and shrubs in the centre of the roundabout. On entering the gates there was a long driveway bordered by spacious lawns on the one hand and the swimming-pool complex on the other, shielded from the road by a hedge of laurel bushes. The drive ended in an open esplanade (with another dusty garden roundabout) in front of the chancery offices, with the burned-out residential quarters behind a low hedge on the left and garages and stores to the right, the whole backing on to the river bank. Six or eight feathery date palms surrounded the esplanade where we usually parked our cars, competing for the few spots where the tall palm trees cast a few square feet of blissful shade when the sun was high in the sky.

Tardy arrivals in the morning had no recourse but to leave their cars in the full glare of the unfailing sun which, by noon, produced unbearable temperatures within the vehicles. It was said that one wag had fried an egg on the bonnet of his car, before starting the engine. Air-conditioning in motor cars not being generally available, the unbearable midday heat resulted in a sort of ritual mating dance between a car and its owner when the time came to join forces and go home to lunch. Having been round the car once or twice gingerly opening all doors and windows, the driver would then take his ventilated 'cool seat' from the steering-wheel which it had been protecting from the sun and replace it on the seat, the while taking off his tie and jacket. This was followed by one or two tentative dabs at the steering-wheel to see if it was bearable to the touch. He would then stick his head and shoulders into the driver's door and either recoil violently or, having decided to venture forth, go round the car again closing the doors before driving off with ventilator quarter-lights turned in and fans going full blast.

Cars also parked along the shadier bits of the wall adjoining the chancery officers, where later in the morning they were joined by one or two official Land Rovers and the Bedford van which served as the school bus for those few children of school age who were in Baghdad with their embassy parents. This being a Friday morning the school bus and the official Land Rovers had not been out of the compound and were hogging the only shady corner of the esplanade. One of my tasks was to check that all official transport was accounted for and that the garages, storerooms and outhoused offices were locked and shuttered. The large, steel-backed doors leading into the chancery offices had been closed and barred, only the small gate within one of the two leaves remaining open. A member of the chancery staff was permanently stationed by this door. A notable disadvantage was that he could not see down as far as the outer ornamental iron gates at the end of the drive which curved gently between the car-parking area and General Maude Square. As the outer gates were always open, there was nothing to prevent a crowd storming up the driveway (yet again), a possibility uppermost in our minds during that first anxious morning. Any intruders would not be seen from the chancery doors and windows until they had virtually reached the top of the driveway and the parking area. The absence of firm news, the well-documented precedents, and the un-certainties of the situation at that stage left us with little alternative but to contemplate the prospect of yet another attack against the embassy. Some of us thought it was only a question of time, perhaps minutes, before the crowds concent-rated at our gates and forced their way up the drive in order to burn down whatever had been left unburned the last time.

While these reflections were going through my head, my ears were deafened by another aircraft searing past our radio aerials virtually at roof level. I was then detailed to go down to the main gates with another member of the staff to make sure they were properly secured. By this time one or two stragglers had driven in and others had been told to stay at home. Rab Munro had courageously gone out in search of news and, as I prepared to go down to the front gates, I was greatly relieved to see the trim figure of the Ambassador, dressed for a day's archaeology in the desert in a smart sports jacket and cavalry twill trousers, step out of his Rolls and walk briskly into his offices. He told us that, having set out an hour earlier from his home (a house rented from one of the oil companies), he was still in the suburbs when he became aware of the unusual air activity, the absence of other traffic on the roads, and the monotonous martial music on the local radio. I think his car was the last to enter the compound before we battened down all hatches.

Having completed our task at the gates, I retraced my steps up the drive with many a nervous backward glance. When I rounded the bend which brought the chancery offices into view, I was horrified to see clouds of smoke billowing from the roof. I was only partially reassured when my companion told me that orders had been issued to burn our files and sensitive papers, a task to which some of the more junior members of the staff were even then devoting much energy with rather unseemly enthusiasm. I panted up to the chancery doors, and the welcoming wicket gate clanged reassuringly shut behind us. But for months afterwards, whenever I was worried about something and slept badly, I had a recurring nightmare in which I ran up the drive with a howling mob at my heels only to have the small gate bang shut in my face just as I reached it.

I wanted to find a vantage point to see if I could make out what was happening across the river. Climbing up to the first floor, at the end of the verandah which gave access to the service attachés' office, I found the Air Attaché and his Flight Sergeant complete with camera and binoculars. They were leaning over a small platform adjacent to the suspended false roof, made of mud and wattle, which protected the ceiling of the Ambassador's office below from the blistering Baghdad sun. My erstwhile shooting companion had been transferred and his replacement had been in Baghdad a relatively short time. Wing Commander Hamilton greeted me amiably and drew my attention to a spot in the sky, well across the city on the other side of the river. 'Another one,' he said, adding, 'They seem to be coming in from Habbaniyah. They complete their turn well to the north, then come along the river flying very low in order to avoid anti-aircraft fire and then loose off their rockets at the Ministry of Defence. Then they go off to reload and back again.' Before I could make any comment, he said, 'Watch this one coming now!' With that he picked up his camera and began to photograph the rapidly approaching aircraft, the while calling out technical data which the Flight Sergeant jotted down on his clipboard. 'MiG 17 at eleven o'clock; height 3000 feet . . . turning south bearing 90 degrees . . . levelling out at one thousand feet . . . my word, he seemed to skim the top of that bridge . . . rocket one fired . . . rocket two gone!' This was followed by two explosions in quick succession as the aircraft flashed across our line of vision, flying so low that we could clearly distinguish the pilot in his transparent canopy. Only then came the high-pitched roar of the jet engine, which seemed to linger with us after the aircraft had disappeared from sight. None of this disturbed the imperturbable Flight Sergeant, who continued to take down the details with only a fleeting glance at the Ministry of Defence across the river in order to register a hit or a miss. 'No misses so far,' he volunteered in an aside to me, 'but then you can hardly expect them to miss at this range!'

Looking back from where I stood I could see the confidential file burning party on one of the flat roofs of the offices on the other side of the inner courtyard. Long-handled drums made of wire mesh were roasting our files on a spit while relays of sweating members of the staff brought up the bundles of paper from the registry below. The air was full of burning ashes and people took turns at the handles. 'At least we shan't have to deal with that lot!' from an irrepressible member of the registry produced a general titter and a worried frown from the Head of Chancery as another bundle of letters and files went up in flames. But he was right. For months afterwards we had a cast-iron excuse for unanswered correspondence. 'Destroyed in the recent emergency' in reply to demands for an answer was calculated to elicit sympathy and tolerance from all but the flintiest Whitehall departments. Meanwhile, the Flight Sergeant was checking his notes as dictated by his chief who was busily changing the lens of his camera while I aimed his binoculars at the Ministry of Defence across the river, which was very low. In the dry season the level of the Tigris in Baghdad can go down by as much as thirty feet. The steep banks and the additional height of our vantage point on the chancery roof gave me the impression that the aircraft had gone past us almost at eye level. By this time the Wing Commander had fitted a formidable looking telephoto lens to his camera. In those days some telephoto lenses were nearly three feet long and to counterbalance the weight on the 35 mm camera case one could purchase a sort of wooden rifle stock, to which the lens and the body of the camera could be attached, instead of using a more cumbersome tripod. Another aircraft had flashed past us while this was going on and the Air Attaché had resumed his dictation. 'MiG 17 at 10 o'clock . . . 6000 feet

. . . bearing 40 . . . levelling out at 1500 feet . . . rocket one gone . . . rocket two!' By the time the next aircraft appeared Bill Hamilton was aiming his telephoto lens at it, wooden stock at his shoulder looking for all the world like a bazooka. I swear I saw the pilot turn his head to glance at us while the Wing Commander chanted his litany for the Flight Sergeant's log.

Several other people had joined us at our vantage point which was, in fact, the only place from where one could see anything happening. There was now a lot of dust and smoke over the Ministry of Defence across the river, but there was little sign of activity in any other part of the city. We spotted one or two tanks guarding the approaches to those bridges we could see, and the river, which usually had some small boats plying across, was deserted. One of the latest arrivals to the verandah brought the news that three army tanks had taken up their position outside our main gates in General Maude Square. This was greeted with renewed speculation about the attitude of the army to the rebellion. Were the tanks there to protect us? Or were they there to prevent our escape? The assistant Military Attaché and Rab Munro (both fluent Arabic speakers) soon came back from the front gate with the news that the tank crews had confirmed that most of the army units in the neighbourhood of the capital had joined the rebels. The tank crews said that they were there to protect us; but they also said that we should not leave the embassy, as the situation in various parts of the city was far from clear and, in spite of the curfew, there were known to be bands of Qasim supporters ready to make trouble, particularly for foreigners. This came as no surprise. At that time, our own position in Iraq was held by some to be ambiguous, even though it was known that Qasim had overthrown a king and government which had been particularly friendly with the British. As a result of the sometimes convoluted logic which prevails in many parts of the world, many of our Iraqi friends actually accused the British of supporting Qasim, simply because it was well known in the bazaar that we were not actively plotting to bring about his downfall. It followed that we were on his side. The Iraqi military were therefore taking no chances, and were doubtless anxious to prevent a recurrence of the burning and looting of 1958. While I was pondering over the significance of these developments, yet another aircraft rocket attack on the

56

Ministry of Defence was heralded by the Air Attaché's renewed litany, 'MiG 17 at 12 o'clock . . . altitude 5000 feet . . . turning south . . . bearing 45 degrees – that's funny, he's not taking the same line . . . he must turn now – no, he's not! He's coming *straight for us!!!*' Unlike its predecessors, this aircraft was not flying on a parallel course to the river; it was unquestionably heading for us in a shallow dive at right angles to the river and clearly aiming at the threatening telephoto bazooka in the shadow of the Union Jack fluttering on the roof a few feet above our heads.

My recollection of the next few seconds is like an old photograph of a confused situation in a state of suspended animation. The small group on the verandah disintegrated rapidly as everyone sought cover. I stared in open-mouthed paralysis at the round black hole of the jet engine's air intake framed by the stabbing flashes of orange flame from the four cannon mounted on its rim. Providentially, someone then collided with me and knocked me over. Two or three of the slimmer and more agile members of our group had dived for cover in the space between the false sun-roof and the real ceiling of the Ambassador's office below. As this was no more than 18 inches high I had just time to catch a glimpse of three posteriors struggling to disappear into the murky cobwebs and bat droppings before I was trampled underfoot by those making for the protecting corner of the Military Attaché's office. There I joined them, scurrying on my hands and knees, a distance of a mere six or eight interminable feet, with those orange flashes of cannon-fire indelibly imprinted on my mind. Miraculously, none of the group on the verandah was injured; but an Iraqi driver, faithfully standing guard by his Bedford school van parked against the wall of the esplanade below, was wounded in the arm by a splinter from one of the cannon shells which hit the bus. This subsequently enabled the experts, by a careful calculation of angles and elevations, to conclude that the pilot was not really trying to hit the group on the verandah, but simply to give us a fright. If so it was just as well, as the mud roof on the Ambassador's ceiling would have given scant protection to those under it; not to speak of others, like myself, whose tardy reaction left them in exposed positions until well after the aircraft had screamed away overhead. But the experts also concluded that the position of the wounded bus driver, the estimated speed of the aircraft, and the range and trajectory of the cannon shells all suggested that only a fraction of a degree had separated the proposed fright from a real disaster.

After the first day the group in the embassy settled down to some sort of routine. I have the impression that conditions were not unlike those so graphically described by Dame Freya Stark in her account of the siege of the Baghdad Embassy in 1941* except, of course, that her siege lasted nearly a month, and we did not have the prospect of British troops arriving to relieve the beleaguered embassy. Fortunately, our telephones continued to function which enabled us to keep in touch with families and friends, not to speak of the informal and official contacts with individual military commanders as soon as we had established whose side they were on. Camp beds and emergency rations appeared in every office as though we did this every weekend. Portable generators supplied electricity during the frequent power cuts. A twenty-four-hour duty roster kept us all on three-hour watches on the lookout from several vantage points in the heights of the chancery building. Providentially, a forthcoming duty visit by the non-resident Naval Attaché had caused the prior acquisition of several cases of whisky for his use in the one or two cocktail parties he normally offered his Iraqi guests during his visits. This unaccustomed hoard was in one of our storerooms, where it was eyed speculatively by those responsible for our morale and defence. After some deliberation we concluded that our need was greater than his, and our garrison's morale, excellent from the beginning, rose even higher. Once or twice, when feeling the chill before dawn on duty at my lookout post above the administration block, one of the admirable ladies who had been cooped up with us from the beginning would clamber up the rickety wooden steps with a blanket and a cup of tea, all the more welcome for its strong smell of whisky.

At first tension was high and nerves were close to the surface. Ian Danson, one of the irreplaceable communications officers who worked twenty-four hours a day, always hastened to

* Freya Stark *Dust in the Lion's paw*, John Murray, 1961. Her chilling dedication 'to friends in Iraq who were imprisoned or murdered' can hardly fail to strike an evocative chord in those who have dwelt in the 'land between the rivers' since it was called into existence in 1920 to redress the balance in the Middle East (with apologies to George Canning).

deliver messages and telegrams hotfoot from the communications room. His natural exhuberance and youthful energy
frequently caused him to gallop across the courtyard or up to
the wooden verandah leading to the attachés' offices. The
sound of running feet was, at times, more than some of us could
bear; and the speed of our communications was permanently
affected when, during one particularly fast delivery in the
middle of the night, five separate voices from the dark offices
round the courtyard shouted in unison: 'Ian, DON'T RUN!'
But as the threat of a mob attack on the embassy appeared to
recede life became more relaxed. Dick Thomas, the press
officer, even managed to organize a highly successful film show
on the second or third evening we spent in the embassy. This
was preceded by a calm and comprehensive ambassadorial pep
talk in which Sir Roger also relayed messages of appreciation
and encouragement from the powers that be in London. But
there were also other diversions.

The first night, the sound of automatic and desultory rifle-
fire could be heard all around us. Afterwards we were told that
the army pickets deliberately kept up sporadic firing in order to
keep the streets clear and discourage would-be troublemakers.
Firm news was difficult to come by, and the wildest rumours
were retailed at our regular meetings with the Ambassador. He
had, by this time, formed a sort of 'war cabinet' consisting of his
most senior collaborators. This was made up of only four or five
people, a select group which included me only because of my
unaccustomed eminence as a result of my boss's absence.
Because of the risk of snipers (and snoopers) we had put
blankets on the windows of the Ambassador's office and always
kept the lights low; at night our meetings took place by the
solitary light of the table lamp on the large desk. The telegrams
which kept coming in (and going out) in large numbers
throughout the day kept me trotting in and out of the
Ambassador's room most of the night. Sir Roger Allen dealt
coolly and effectively with a formidable range of complex and
far-reaching problems which were relayed to us by the
ceaseless flow of telegrams from London. These reflected
international preoccupations with the local situation of which
our own predicament was but a minor aspect. Once or twice,
having previously discussed with us the various aspects of a
telegraphed requirement, he invited us to meet again in half

an hour with our respective individual draft replies, which he examined attentively and approvingly before producing from under his blotter, with a smile of apology, a draft that he had prepared. This never failed to cover all the points made in our drafts as well as some we had omitted to consider. When there was time for it, he (and we) regarded this as a useful and stimulating exercise.

After half the night employed in this manner, I collected my binoculars, police whistle, tear-gas canisters, alarm signals, and other assorted ironmongery, and climbed up to my lookout post. At the end of my guard duty in the early morning, I telephoned my wife to warn her that she was going to be asked to gather in the new house we had moved to in Saadun Park a girl secretary and a couple of young wives (including Ian Danson's) who were alone in their homes in our part of Baghdad; they would be delivered by the (British) district warden or someone from the local police station in due course. For my part I was signing off and going to sleep in my office until further notice.

Two or three hours later, at about 10.30 hours, I was wakened from a profound sleep by a terrifying explosion. My first befuddled thought was that we had been hit by a bomb. When I rushed to my door I recoiled from the strong, pungent smell of cordite. My dash across the courtyard to Rab Munro's office coincided with a second, equally loud and frightening explosion which seemed to have taken place almost within the courtyard; and more cordite. I found him smoking one of his habitual cheroots and calmly talking in Arabic on the phone. Keith Haskell, then newly arrived from the Middle East Centre for Arab Studies, was with him. When Rab finally put the phone down they told me that the tanks guarding our gates in General Maude Square had been ordered to open fire against the Ministry of Defence across the river in order to pin down any occupants who might be tempted, so to speak, to leave by the back door. The salvoes were taking place at minimum elevation and the only problem for the stationary tanks was that our offices were literally in their line of fire. Rab went back to his 'phone while Keith and the assistant Military Attaché raced down the drive to the front gates in order to parley with the tank crews. Feeling rather helpless, I went back to my office where I knelt under my new, two-pedestal steel

60

desk (first secretaries, for the use of) while the bombardment continued. The walls and ceiling shook with each explosion, the air was full of dust and smoke. Eventually, reason prevailed and the tanks were ordered to stop firing. But it was not until late in the morning of the fourth day, when the triumph of the rebellion was announced on the radio and the population of Baghdad had been shown Qasim's severed head on television, that the tank crews at the gates started up their engines and we were told we could go home.

There is little more to tell. Our siege had ended. I reflected that it would never compare with the siege of the legation in Peking in 1900 which lasted for fifty-five days or with that of the embassy in Athens during five weeks in 1944–45. But our beleaguered garrison did not get off scot free. Apart from the wounded driver and the wear and tear to which all were subjected, we suffered two casualties from gunshot wounds, both sustained in the line of duty. The administration officer, Ron Braithwaite, was shot in the leg while trying to deter, from the exposed upper verandah, somebody who was interfering with the embassy launch, abandoned on the mud bank below. He and a visiting journalist who had taken sanctuary in the embassy when the revolt began were both surprised by a burst of firing from some neighbouring houses. The journalist was lightly wounded when going to his aid. Happily, they both fully recovered in due course. It was not until I collected my car and drove out of the parking area that I noticed that most of the wireless aerials on the chancery roof had been shot away and, even more importantly, that the few feathery date palms which had provided the only shade for our cars had all been neatly decapitated.

We had been right to take every precaution. A tape, pre-recorded by Qasim, was subsequently found at his desk in the Ministry of Defence. In it he exhorted the populace to kill all foreigners and the British in particular. Only the rebel commanders' prompt action in seizing the radio station had prevented its broadcast. My own personal piece of anguish came the previous day when, ringing through to my wife to see if the isolated embassy girls had joined her, I was told by a hysterical houseboy that the *memsa'ahb* had been arrested and taken away by a Jeep-load of soldiers. In the fullness of time it turned out that, few streets in Saadoun Park having any names, or houses any numbers, the helpful police officer who was detailed with his men to collect the girls decided to begin at the end and enlist the help of my wife in his errand of mercy. He assumed correctly that she knew the persons to be rescued and could direct him to the houses where they lived; this would clearly save a lot of time. But for two hours I waited anxiously and impotently for news in ignorance of my wife's whereabouts, at a time when anybody on the streets was liable to be shot on sight.

A couple of months later we left Baghdad after almost exactly three years. Our thousand and one nights in the city of the caliphs had given us a lot of pleasure and, certainly, much excitement. Above all, we were sad to leave the many friends, Iraqi and others, we had made. Some we managed to see again in London or elsewhere. Every time we moved to another post we looked forward to the prospect of meeting friends and former colleagues, in different and unlikely places. Before the Trevelyans left Baghdad I attended the wedding of one of their daughters, Susan, to a West German diplomat then also serving in Baghdad. We were delighted when, many years later, we arrived in Lima to find Susan with her husband at the West German embassy there. When I was introduced to the children I was struck by the resemblance of the eldest boy, then aged about fifteen, to his grandfather. When I remarked upon it Susan smiled broadly and said, 'Yes, he does have the same ears, doesn't he?'

PART

2

He is crazed with the spell of far Arabia,
They have stolen his wits away.

Walter de la Mare, *Arabia.*

5

The Road from Damascus

I was transferred to Bahrain in April 1953. This came as a bit of a surprise to me, and I had to look up Bahrain in the atlas in order to establish precisely where it was. I thought the move was being made as part of the process of broadening my experience, and I was excited by the prospect of going to a part of the world about which I knew next to nothing. At the time the Foreign Office administration was encouraging youthful members of the service to volunteer for 'hard language' studies. One of the inducements was the payment of proficiency allowances which, compared with those paid for normal languages like French or Italian, were generous to a degree. One of my more ambitious contemporaries later worked out that if he passed the higher standard examination in Arabic, Serbo-Croat, and Russian he could double his salary as a second secretary, even though he would be paid the full allowance only for the language spoken in the country where he was serving. But even the reduced continuation allowances for 'hard' languages made the amount we received for proficiency in Italian look derisory. All these considerations were uppermost in the minds of impecunious would-be diplomats on the thresholds of their careers, and there is no doubt that the prospects ahead were affected in many cases by the youthful decision to specialize in one or more of the difficult languages, for which the Foreign Office arranged full-time study for a year of two, or even longer.

These thoughts were uppermost also in my mind while I looked up encyclopedias and reference books in order to improve my inadequate knowledge of the place which was to be my home for the next few years. Was this a turning point in my career? Was I destined to become a specialist on the Middle

East? I tried to read between the lines and search out hidden implications behind every word in the short formal communication. Alas, years later I found out that the main reason for my appointment to Bahrain was that I was then a bachelor and that there was a shortage of accommodation on the island. The letter added that the 'approved route' was by sea to Beirut and then overland to Damascus, Baghdad and Basra, where there was a British India steamer which sailed down the Gulf on its way to Bombay. As I was going on direct transfer without home leave, I found myself a ship that sailed from Brindisi for Alexandria and Beirut, where I was to board a Nairn Transport bus to Damascus and across the desert to Baghdad, then by rail to Basra to embark on the last lap of this exciting journey. Aeroplanes were still regarded as expensive alternatives to normal travel.

On arrival in Baghdad, however, I was told that my plans had been changed. My late arrival from Beirut (not, as I shall explain, through any fault of my own) and the prospect of further delays in Basra if I missed the boat there, had enabled the Political Agent in Bahrain, on whose staff I was to serve, to persuade the Foreign Office to authorize my flying direct to Bahrain where, it seemed, I was urgently needed. In the meantime, I was told I would spend two nights in Baghdad before catching the flight to Bahrain. This would still get me there much sooner than travelling by rail and boat. I was then invited to sign the visitors' book at the embassy residence, which I remember as an imposing house standing in its own park on the banks of the River Tigris, with ornamental cannon and a pyramid of ball shot guarding the main entrance at the top of a short flight of steps. Having collected my airline tickets and a modest advance of travelling expenses I was taken with my luggage to the Semiramis Hotel in Rashid Street, where I made the first of my unsuccessful attempt to get in touch with Leila.

The sea journey to Beirut was pleasant but unexciting. The trip on the bus, on the other hand, was unusual in that, after leaving Damascus and before reaching the Iraqi border, we were stranded in the flooded desert for about eighteen hours while we waited for the waters to subside, so that the bus driver could see the track. The first part of the road to Damascus was paved and well engineered; leaving Beirut the bus climbed up into the hills with wooded slopes and snow capped peaks, travelling smoothly until we reached Damascus where, with virtually no delay, we changed into larger, air-conditioned buses for our journey across the desert. It was customary for this part of the trip to be made by two buses in convoy, just in case. Besides air-conditioning they had comfortable reclining seats, and the passengers were fed at regular intervals with the sort of pre-packed cardboard luncheon box containing a piece of cold chicken, biscuits, cheese and fruit then also provided on aeroplanes. My bus was full, and as luck would have it I found myself sitting next to a Lebanese girl of about my own age who spoke perfect French and was learning English. She told me she was going to Baghdad to take up a position as a teacher in a girls' school. She had been there previously for a brief visit when she had stayed with a cousin of her mother's. Her application and interview had been successful and, although she confided that she had not been overly impressed by what she had seen ('Baghdad is not like Beirut' she said), she had decided to accept the position for a trial period. I was a little surprised to find her travelling by herself, but she was obviously thoroughly Westernized and well educated. She was also quite beautiful. She had long, dark hair and a pale complexion, regular if slightly Semitic features, showed even white teeth when she smiled, and her large almond-shaped eyes had the longest lashes I had ever seen. When I told her where I was going she volunteered to teach me Arabic if I would let her practice her English with me.

Thus studiously occupied, we bounced companionably across Syria until we were brought to an unexpected standstill by the flooded desert which, under sullen skies, rendered the waterlogged plains almost totally featureless as far as the eye could see. The bus drivers habitually chose the shortest distance between two points, and there were many stretches where the buses left the road (and the telegraph poles beside it) if only to choose more comfortable level ground. But the heavy rains had blotted out all the tracks and made the so-called 'Irish bridges' even more than usually hazardous. These were sudden dips in the road where subsidence or a natural gully dropped the level of the track several feet. If travelling at any speed in dry weather a vehicle usually took to the air before regaining contact with the ground where it rose again, but the watery landscape made it quite impossible to gauge the depth of the pool in the intervening hollow. There was therefore little alternative but to stop and wait for the waters to subside. The drivers told us that we were only a day's journey away from Baghdad and plied the passengers with more cardboard boxes containing chicken in plastic, fruit, and cheese. It was all quite new and exciting to me. Some of the more adventurous passengers disembarked and splashed around, swapping horror stories about Nairn buses which had gone missing in earlier years. I was told that in the late 40s, shortly after the war, one such bus with thirty-six passengers had disappeared on the route to Baghdad and that no trace of it or the passengers had ever been found.

In the meantime, my language studies were proceeding apace. I learnt how to spell Leila in Arabic without too much difficulty, the Arabic letter 'alif' being sufficiently like our 'L' to make my task simple. My tuition continued with each box of cold chicken handed round; these were inscribed with the words 'Nairn Transport' in blue letters in Arabic and English on opposite sides of the box. I munched my cheese and biscuits on a boulder by the roadside, the two travel-stained buses reflected in the watery waste under the darkening skies with no sign of human habitation in sight, while I concentrated on the Arabic letter 'noon' which was illustrated at both ends of the word 'Nairn' on my cardboard box. In spite of Leila's patient instruction I do not think we got as far as the word 'Transport' before the buses resumed their journey across a visibly drying landscape at dawn the following morning. I was told that we had already crossed the Jordanian border and had, in fact, spent the night on Iraqi territory, but that the buses were to stop at a place called Rutba in order to comply with the Iraqi customs and immigration formalities.

When we rolled to a halt at the customs post I was fascinated by all the new faces and sights which surrounded me. The fort with the Iraqi flag above it looked to me for all the world like the Fort Zinderneuf I had visualized many years before when devouring P.C. Wren's chronicles of Beau Geste and his brothers, their ladies, the Blue Water diamond, and, of course, Major de Beaujolais. I half expected to see him galloping out of the fort in his spahi uniform with his red cavalry cloak flying behind him. The fact that we were in the wrong country mattered not one bit. To my overheated imagination the contrast with what little I had seen of Beirut and Damascus could not have been more marked, and the assorted officials and hangers-on added excitement and local colour to the scene with their hawkish faces, fierce-looking eyes, and moustaches. A few (I was told that these were Jordanians) wore red and white checked *keffiyas*, with the black knotted *aghal* tilted rakishly over one eye, but most wore white headcloths which some wound round their necks to protect the lower part of their faces from the wind and sand. Two or three policemen, their smart khaki uniforms and Sam Browne belts contrasting markedly with their Arab headgear, provided an even more exotic touch. Having had my passport stamped I returned with a couple of Coca-Colas to the queue waiting to board the bus, to find that Leila was now wearing a shawl over her head, chastely masking most of her face below her enchanting eyes. I think it was this, more than the chattering crowd or the theatrical fort in the background, which made me realize how far we had travelled, in more senses than one, from the luxury hotels of Beirut overlooking the blue Mediterranean.

Some hours later we trundled into the suburbs of Baghdad, having left behind us a strangely colourful desert with an irregular patchwork of brief wild flowers already showing signs of urgent life, the result of the heavy rains which the parched land was to denied until the following year. At the bus depot I was met by someone from the embassy who told me about the changes in my onward travel arrangements and took me, after my brief call at the imposing office and residential compound by the Tigris, to the Semiramis Hotel where I slept well that night and most of the following day. When I finally got up, I saw that my room was at the back of the hotel and had a ceiling fan and a window which overlooked a lawn which sloped down to the river bank. On the lawn there were tables and chairs and, the sun being already close to the horizon, a goodly number of ladies and gentlemen gathered in convivial groups. It being the cool season most ladies wore dresses and cardigans. The men had rather florid complexions and wore mostly jackets and ties. Some had bristling white moustaches and looked like retired Indian Army colonels. The loud, cut-glass accents mingled with the tinkling of ice in glasses and the occasional shout of 'Boy!', answered almost immediately by an Arab or Indian bearer in a sort of white nightgown with a cummerbund. Having had a bath and a change I was tempted to join the chattering throng on the lawn, and I was certainly looking forward to a drink, but they all obviously knew each other well and I was reluctant to engage any of them in conversation. Having made a last fruitless attempt to get through to the number Leila had given me I went down to the indoor bar, which was virtually deserted. Unexpectedly, I found there a colleague I knew slightly, having met him briefly some time before in London. He had but recently arrived in Baghdad and was still staying at the hotel. We took our drinks to one of the tables and talked shop and exchanged gossip until the sun went down spectacularly across the river at the bottom of the hotel lawn. When he invited me to have a bite of dinner with him I readily agreed; I knew no one in Baghdad and I was anxious to see something of the romantic city of the caliphs, the thousand-and-one nights, Ali Baba, forty thieves and all. In the event, we had dinner in a nearby restaurant which turned out to be very occidental in both décor and cuisine. Not wishing to part company without returning my colleagues's hospitality, I pressed him to have a nightcap and was happy to fall in with his suggestion that we might have a final drink at a nightclub (I think it was called the Scheherazade) where he said there was a new floor show with a Spanish dancing troupe.

We took a taxi and arrived at the nightclub just as the floor show was beginning. Although the place was almost full we were given a table only a couple of rows back from the semicircular space in the centre where the performance was taking place. At the back of the room there was a raised dais stage facing the horseshoe-shaped arrangement of tables and chairs. Sitting on the dais were three or four musicians wearing red fezzes, playing their complicated instruments with expressions of profound melancholia. On the main floor in front of them were three robust ladies with prominent stomachs, attired mainly in bangles and beads. Their faces were bare, and with bold, dark eyes and cheerful countenances they responded to the rhythmic applause and coarse shouts of encouragement from the predominantly male audience with ever more enthusiastic gyrations of their abdominal muscles as they went round the tables in the front row, pausing now and then to undulate their plump hips in slow motion only inches away from the fascinated eyes of some spectator, while their hands wove complex patterns above their lustrous black hair. As they danced their separate ways round the floor, spreading a strong fragrance of patchouli, spotlights picked out individual feats of muscular control, each greeted with good-humoured shouts and whistles until a crescendo in the repetitive rhythm of music and drums coincided with their collapse on the floor, while their foreheads touched the ground in obeisance to the audience. When the house lights went up they got up together, acknowledged the applause and, with broad smiles and heaving chests, danced their way out through the curtains at the back of the room. Later I learnt that it was customary for nightclubs in Baghdad to open their shows with one of more belly-dancers as a sort of local curtain-raiser for the imported foreign numbers to come. Understandably, it was a popular act; some of the performers were well known and the audience was put into a good mood. That evening they were followed by a black American female singer who sang in French, by a German juggler and magician whose blonde female assistant seemed to get more attention from the audience than her principal, and by a troupe of Spanish flamenco dancers and singers who put on some excellent numbers and were deservedly much applauded. I called the waiter for the bill which he brought a few minutes later, during which time I noticed idly that nobody seemed to be making a move to leave. When I got up the waiter said, 'Why do you go now? Please wait for our star attraction, the great Mademoiselle Maisoun. She is something!' With that he kissed his fingertips and went off, leaving my bill on a plate. I raised my eyebrows at my companion who said, 'Ah, yes, somebody told me that a new belly-dancer was appearing tonight. She is supposed to be sensational!'

I looked at my watch. My long sleep had enabled me to recover from the uncomfortable bus journey across the desert, but my plane was leaving early the next morning and it was already well after midnight. Besides, I had already seen my first belly-dancers and thought that the number of variations on the theme must be a bit limited. While these thoughts were going through my mind the house lights went out, putting an end to any prospect of leaving. A dim spotlight then outlined the figure of a woman in the centre of the floor. Her hands were motionless above her head. She began to move gracefully as the lights went up slowly. Although she also was wearing mostly bangles and beads her face was veiled, which made a tantalizing contrast with the expanse of bare skin beneath her brief bodice. Unlike the curtain-raisers at the beginning of the show, she was slim and had long, well-formed legs, at first only glimpsed through the partings in her gauzy skirt. Baubles and anklets above her bare feet and tinkling cymbals at her fingertips sounded in counterpoint to the low background music and drums. Throughout her performance she never once raised her eyes to the audience, keeping them demurely cast down over the veil which covered the lower part of her face. In spite of the explicit nature of her dance, she conveyed an air of sensual innocence and fragile purity. Together with her modest bearing and downcast eyes, this combined to render her supple movements infinitely more erotic than any of the remarkable feats of muscular control achieved by the brazen curtain-raisers, good though they were. It spoke volumes for the different quality of her act that the previously rowdy audience sat throughout in enthralled silence. When she finished with a final clash of cymbals and drums she bowed until her glossy dark hair swept the floor and, as the lights went up, slowly took her veil off and smiled shyly at the thunderous ovation from the spectators, many of whom were standing on their chairs. My companion turned to me and said, 'Well, that really was – why, what's the matter?' I could not answer. I was dumbfounded. There, bowing in the centre of the floor was Leila.

6

Bahrain, 1953–1956

My flight next morning to Bahrain was uneventful. After a brief stop in Kuwait we landed at Muharraq airport where the acting Political Agent met me and kindly took me to his home for lunch, after which we went to the Political Agent's house, which was to be my home for the next few weeks at least until the rightful tenant came back from leave. At the time there was only one hotel in Bahrain in addition to the BOAC resthouse, where they normally put transit passengers, as in the days of the Imperial Airways flying boats. Other travellers could stay there only for a limited period. The number of European-style houses on the island was limited, although there were one or two expatriate romantics who lived in local-style houses with wind towers and Turkish lavatories.

The housing shortage had been aggravated by the earlier decision to move the seat of the Political Residency in the Persian Gulf to Bahrain. This was based in Bushire until Indian independence and partition obliged the Foreign Office to assume responsibility for the British Government treaty obligations with those states in the Gulf previously administered by the (British) Government of India. For his part, the Political Agent was the British Government's representative in and to Bahrain. He also acted as the Ruler's foreign minister in so far as Her Majesty's Government was responsible for the conduct of Bahrain's foreign affairs. The Political Agency had additional internal responsibilities resulting from the Crown's jurisdiction over those foreign nationals not subject to the Ruler (now known as the Emir) of Bahrain. Broadly, this situation then applied to all the British protected states in the Gulf, except Muscat which was in a different category. As a result, Bahrain boasted two high British officials who drove around the island with Union Jacks on their car bonnets. The Foreign Office had had no alternative but to build their own blocks of flats and houses for the staff. The Political Residency, whose writ covered all the other states in the Gulf as well as Bahrain, had found a home in the small Royal Navy depot in Jufair, at the north end of the main island, where the senior naval officer, Persian Gulf (a Captain, RN) was based. When he was afloat, the resident naval officer (a Commander) was left in charge of HMS *Jufair*, technically known in the Navy as a 'stone frigate' with all the flagpoles, sentries, bugle calls, Naafi canteens and other amenities corresponding to these establishments. The Political Resident had temporarily taken over the senior naval officer's shore accommodation (a modest, rambling bungalow with verandahs and a corrugated-tin roof), and this had in turn created any number of displaced persons and cuckoos in other peoples' nests. A new, fully air-conditioned Residency with comprehensive office accommodation and staff houses and flats, swimming pools, and tennis courts was to be built within the Jufair site, but all this was still in the planning stage when I arrived, except for a block of flats for junior staff and female London-based secretaries, neither of whom had existed under the previous administration.

The final straw had come shortly before my arrival, when the roof of the Political Agency collapsed one morning when the incumbent was having his breakfast. This was a fine old single-storied house on the seashore, with a spacious flat above the offices on the ground floor and ample verandahs with ceiling fans facing the sea. There was a private jetty and a mature garden, with the then customary swimming pool and tennis court. The tallest flagpole on the island was set at the end of the driveway in front of the house. In the end, the yearly accretions of mud liberally spread on the flat roof just before the annual rains finally proved too much for the old wooden beams, and only luck prevented the Political Agent from ending up with his breakfast under several tons of broken beams, masonry, and rubble. The Ministry of Works condemned the whole structure and undertook to build a new Political Agency on the site. In the meantime, temporary offices were rented in town and a European-style house was found on the Jufair road, which is where I was staying during his absence. The house had four bedrooms upstairs and a hall, dining-room, sitting-room, and study on the ground floor. It was well furnished with good-quality English furniture (including a new dining-room table), chintzy curtains and fabrics, and Persian rugs. Each bedroom had an air-conditioning unit which was a great boon. There was also a Goanese cook and an elderly Iranian houseboy, who did not appear to be on speaking terms with each other. A sweeper also came to clean during the day but disappeared in the evenings.

The cook was good and produced good meals with the very limited resources then available. Fish was plentiful but meat was at a premium, especially beef. At the time Bahrain produced (other than petroleum) not very much of anything except dates and, in sadly diminishing quantities, the pearls from the neighbouring oyster beds for which the island had originally been famed. As a result meals tended to be rather monotonous; the ubiquitous chickens on which the cook rang the changes all had massive thighs and meagre breasts, probably the result of their free-ranging upbringing and their strenuous efforts to escape their predetermined destiny. Some pernickety tea-drinkers refused fresh milk because this was said to have a strong fishy flavour from the diet of sun-dried fish which was used to supplement the few dairy cows' rationed alfalfa. When a commercial cold store was inaugurated towards the end of my time by an enterprising local merchant, the quality of life in Bahrain suddenly acquired a new meaning, every variety of frozen delicacy becoming available overnight. Corned beef and tinned peas were banished from every dinner table; hostesses competed with each other in presenting to their guests meals which would have been a voluptuary's impossible dream during my first two years in Bahrain.

In spite of the abundance of natural springs on the island the domestic water supply had a strong and unpleasant brackish flavour and most Europeans purchased large jars of distilled water from a local plant. Fruit juices, cordials and minerals were all imported in bottles and were therefore expensive. Sparklet bulbs and siphons were used to make soda water and, although Bahrain was a Muslim state and the import and sale of alcoholic drinks was forbidden, Europeans and some non-Bahraini nationals were permitted to purchase limited quantities of drink from a controlled store after obtaining the corresponding permit from the Political Agency.

The oil company had its headquarters in an artificial town called Awali, situated in the desert more or less in the middle of the island, where the American and mostly British inhabitants led a cloistered life behind wire. They had every modern (American) amenity including, of course, their own libraries, cinemas, hospitals, churches, tennis clubs, swimming pools, squash courts, and a nine-hole golf course with carefully tended 'browns', instead of greens. Some of the older, more permanent houses occupied by the senior management boasted surprising gardens painstakingly created over many years. Most of the other houses were rather like air-conditioned Portakabins, with two or three bedrooms depending on status and family requirements. Everyone was very status conscious, and the accommodation occupied and the area in which it was situated was determined by the grade and scale of pay. Bachelors were housed in unmarried quarters, rather like a barracks with individual bedrooms and communal sitting-rooms. Food was available at any time in the various messes, for which a nominal charge was deducted from the company employees. European women were heavily outnumbered by the men, the oil company's hospital nurses being regularly replaced on marriage after a few months, sometimes weeks. The record was then held by a nurse who was led to the altar after only two weeks on the island, and one or two of our own female secretaries from London were happy to refund the Foreign Office the cost of their outward fares on resigning within the year, for the best of all reasons.

There were then few amusements to be found on Bahrain. Only one or two cinemas showed Indian or Egyptian films; there were virtually no restaurants and no concerts or theatres. But there were amateur dramatic societies which flourished among different groups on the island. Close to the racecourse on the Jufair road, the Gymkhana Club with its attractive gardens, tennis courts and swimming pool, attracted most of the European and British residents of Manama. It held frequent dances, and tennis and darts tournaments, though sporting facilities were widely available and relatively inexpensive. Football was popular, hockey was played by a number of local teams, there were squash and tennis courts in Jufair, and fishing and swimming took place almost anywhere off the islands' fine beaches. The shallow waters of the Gulf and the gentle tidal flows accounted for the characteristic fish traps which were such a notable feature of the sea round the islands on any approach by aeroplane to the islands' airport in Muharraq, which was the other main island, linked to Manama by a causeway for motor traffic and pedestrians. This had a swing bridge which opened twice a day to allow vessels to use the deep-water channel between the two islands as a short cut. Some of the arrow-shaped fish traps were visible from the causeway, the arrowhead with its circular trap pointing in the direction taken by the outgoing tides, which daily left a rich harvest of fish for their proprietors.

All this I learnt from the other temporary occupant of the house when, after a decent afternoon's rest, we met again in the comfortable sitting-room of our temporary quarters. Bill Maudsley was the recently appointed Registrar of Her Majesty's Court for Bahrain where any European, American and some other non-Bahraini transgressors were tried and sentenced when they breached the laws of the land, of which there were providentially few recorded instances. There was, however, much civil litigation between defaulting landlords and shopkeepers and philandering husbands and errant wives, mainly among those non-European communities which were neither Muslim nor as yet under the jurisdiction of the Bahrain Government, whose own judicial administration was then being reinforced to deal with the additional groups of foreign nationals we were keen to see transferred from British jurisdiction to the local courts. The partial prohibition of liquor caused many problems, as I soon discovered. Maudsley was legally qualified and had first practised on the northern circuit in the United Kingdom. A broken marriage after wartime service on the Judge Advocate General's staff in the Middle East led to a legal appointment with the Bahrain Oil Company, based in Awali, in the centre of the island. The reorganization of the British administration in the Gulf and the assumption by the Foreign Office of those responsibilities previously discharged by the Indian Political and Civil Services at first obliged the Foreign Office to engage contract staff to undertake duties of which diplomats had had little experience since the Consular Courts in pre-war Egypt and, more recently, the regime of foreign capitulations in Tangier. In due course the post of Registrar of the Court was advertised and Bill Maudsley, not entirely satisfied with his legal duties in Awali, applied successfully and was employed on contract by the Foreign Office. He was nominally on the staff of the Residency in Jufair and was yet another whose housing problem had not been solved.

In the meantime he was doing his best to answer all my questions against the intrusive sound of throbbing drums, which created an exotic background to our conversation. The noise was coming from an Iranian *barasti* village in some date gardens opposite the house just across the Jufair road. Maudsley had kindly gone out in the afternoon while I was asleep to get some supplies for my use and I found my bathroom newly provided with soap and towels, toothpaste, bath salts, and aftershave lotion. Downstairs he produced a tin of olives and a packet of nuts (both imported) to have with our sundowners and slapped his forehead when I grimaced after splashing some soda from a Sparklet siphon into my first whisky. 'Oh, my God,' he said, 'I forgot to get some distilled water,' and rushed across the room to the desk where he kept a pad and pencil. 'It really tastes quite awful, doesn't it? But I'm afraid I've got used to it and don't really notice it any more.' He was right. The good whisky was given an acrid taste by the salty water and ice and I sipped it gingerly while I plied him with more questions.

Bill Maudsley was then about fifty. He had an engaging if slightly eccentric personality with a lively and inquisitive mind. He had few interests apart from his work, except for classical music about which he was very knowledgeable. He was an accomplished pianist and much enjoyed the opportunity to practice given him by our temporary residence which boasted one of the few pianos on the island. He played tennis rather perfunctorily, but later surprised and delighted all his friends by a tardy blossoming in amateur theatricals. He was of medium height with gingerish colouring and sparse, carroty hair, with eyes almost the same colour. He had a prominent jawline and a curious habit of laughing nervously through clenched teeth. He was a careless dresser, usually wearing a shirt until this was destroyed by the *dhobi*, and a jacket or trousers until all the buttons fell off. Then he would buy a replacement. While reading a book or writing a letter he would get up for no apparent reason and stride rapidly across the room, head well down and chin tucked into his chest while rubbing the knuckles of one fist vigorously against the palm of the other hand. Unless brought to a halt by the wall or screen which unexpectedly materialized in his path, low-lying stools or nests of tables were liable to be scattered to the four winds on these occasions. This usually broke his concentration and, with a word of apology while he picked up the pieces, his pace returned to normal as he walked back to his letter. One occasion when his concentration was not broken took place the very day after my arrival.

The elderly Iranian houseboy, smart in his white tunic and brass buttons, was kneeling in the hall at the bottom of the main staircase adjusting the carpet runner on the bottom rung. Bill had just come in from tennis. The office hours were from 8.0 a.m. till 2.0 p.m., after which one was free to pursue one's own inclinations unless drawn back to a blissfully peaceful office by too many urgent papers, which was not frequently the case. Late nights and early rising made an after-lunch siesta almost inevitable, and even phone calls were taboo until about 4.30 or 5.0 p.m. Then the idle ones read newspapers or had tea until it was time to have a bath and change for the first social event of the evening, whether a first call by a newcomer or a full-scale cocktail party or dinner. The more energetic went swimming, riding, or played squash and tennis. Bill and I were in the hall discussing the evening arrangements (my car had not arrived and I was largely dependent on other people for transport). Bill was idly swinging his racquet, prior to making for his bathroom and a long shower, when I saw his concentration begin to wander as he began rubbing one fist (racquet and all) against his other palm. He turned abruptly and lunged on his first stride across the normally uncluttered hall, oblivious of the hapless Mohammed who, below Bill's line of sight, was kneeling at his feet fiddling with the stair rod. Maudsley had achieved sufficient momentum to make his flight quite spectacular; he landed spread-eagled on a small Persian rug in the centre of the highly polished floor which took him smoothly across the rest of the hall until he collided with a Chinese screen which masked the swing door at the entrance to the kitchen quarters. This promptly collapsed on him and, with the malevolence of inanimate objects, neatly enfolded his body in a four-leaved embrace, looking for all the world like a coffin of oriental design. For his part, Mohammed was also flat on his back, not far from where he had been kneeling. By this time I could hardly stand myself, but I did not wish to appear to be rude to either and quickly sought to disappear up the staircase. I paused to peer over the first landing and saw both bodies slowly gathering themselves, sitting on the floor with hands and arms behind their backs, Mohammed with an expression of pained bewilderment and reproachful eyes, Mausdley's face showing in turn suspicion, irritation and, with dawning comprehension, regret. As there was clearly nothing either could say which would convey their emotions or redress the situation, they picked themselves up in silence, jointly replaced the screen, and withdrew, without a word, to their respective quarters, while I collapsed on my bed upstairs.

In common with most junior arrivals on the island I was given a list of nearly two hundred people I was expected to call on. The list included senior government officials, heads of British firms, some leading merchants, and a sprinkling of more senior colleagues. This was an agreeable Anglo-Indian custom which had, of course, prevailed on the island while under the tutelage of Indian Political and Civil Service officials. It had a number of advantages, the main being that it enabled one to meet the people one would be dealing with, at an early stage and in the informality of their homes. No prior appointments were necessary; if the persons being called upon were out a bent card left on the tray on the verandah would suffice. If the hosts were at home, a maximum of two drinks was the norm; it was not done to stay for a third, no matter how much one was pressed. On the other hand, an early departure on the grounds that one had another call to make was accepted without question; this enabled some enterprising callers to strike three names off their list in one evening, depending on the previously planned geography.

All this meant that a bachelor (married couples were called upon by bachelors, regardless of the pecking order) could happily spend the first three or four months after his arrival having drinks out every evening (except Fridays). Towards the end of the first month one began to receive return calls, but as one was known to be mostly out calling, this was a relatively painless performance involving the checking of the card found on return against the list of names, if only to ensure that this was a return call and not a new arrival making his first call. Some senior businessmen were punctilious about returning calls on even the most junior callers; in my case they invariably appeared resplendent in black shoes and socks, black cummerbund, and starched white slacks and shirt, while I was having a shower after tennis. But this was no disgrace; more than once I was received by a bachelor in a bath towel and by married couples in instalments, their wet hair and other evidence of hasty dressing being eloquent of the frenetic pace of sporting and other activity most of the large British community seemed to thrive on. This made no difference to the warmth of their welcome. If one wore a black cummerbund this advertised the fact that one was going on to a dinner engagement, usually for 8.30 p.m. The black cummerbund was the only difference between formal and informal wear; white slacks, open-necked shirts and short sleeves (but *not* rolled-up long sleeves) were acceptable for black-tie dinners during the summer months. Many a socially popular bachelor lacking sleep put on a black cummerbund for his first evening engagement; this enabled him, after a decent interval and without question, to slink off home to bed and an early night.

The evening of the day following my arrival I was taken to call on the Political Resident in his compound at Jufair. Colonel Sir Rupert Hay was a distinguished member of the Indian Political Service who had already served as Political Resident in the Gulf for eleven years. After Indian independence he had been retained by the Foreign Office on contract, together with many of his brother officers in the Gulf who were gradually to be replaced by Foreign Office officials. Sir Rupert was himself due to retire in a few months on reaching the age of sixty, but in the meantime he continued to provide Bahrain and the other British protected states with a presence redolent of quasi-imperial pomp and tradition. This, together with the imprint of his strong personality, made of Bahrain a microcosm of the Raj which appreciative visitors found to be alive and well and thriving in the Persian Gulf; five years after Indian independence and partition of the subcontinent. Sir Rupert was then a large, imposing figure who looked every inch the image of the stereotyped Indian Army colonel. His beetling brows and bristling moustache were white, as was the horse-shoe of sparse hair over his ears. His jowly complexion was pink, which soon turned red when exposed to the sun and no doubt purple in moments of emotion. His eyes were well set and bright blue, his nose a shade Roman above his partly veiled mouth. His gaze was level and penetrating, his portly bearing authoritative and dignified. In appearance he was, in short, the personification of all my childhood visions of an imperial proconsul, whose ceremonial arrival was attended by nineteen-gun salutes and fixed bayonets, whose presence caused everyone to stand and whose final departure took place amid universal regret.

When in residence in Bahrain, it was Sir Rupert's custom to receive callers in the garden at Jufair in a wide semicircle of chairs arranged on both sides of a sort of throne covered in rugs and leopard skins. Sir Rupert sat on the throne with a large black labrador and an even larger near-alsatian at his feet. Behind him there were two or three imposing personal retainers with bearded countenances and gleaming eyes beneath their Arab head-dress. They were the formal coffee-pourers and cupbearers, their bejewelled daggers and curved scimitars glinting in the folds of their ceremonial robes. Other uniformed bearers would bring round trays of whiskies and soft drinks, which were always offered first to the persons seated on either side of Sir Rupert. This was because it was customary for the last person to arrive at the 'Majlis', as it was still called, to be invited to a seat on Sir Rupert's right or left, the rest of the assembled company moving along one place away from the throne. New arrivals had to walk across the wide carpet-covered area in the centre and stand in front of Sir Rupert, who would put his drink down on an adjacent table and stand ceremoniously to greet the new caller. This was the signal for everyone else to rise also and move one place down towards the end of the horseshoes, leaving a vacant chair next to the Resident for the newcomer, Sir Rupert would then sit down and engage the new arrival in conversation until another caller arrived nervously at the edge of the carpet, before advancing to stand in front of Sir Rupert, who would then rise again thereby giving the signal for the musical chairs. Convention had it that you could stay for either two whiskies or until you reached the last occupied chair at your end of the horseshoe, whichever came first. This went on from about 6.30 p.m. to 8.30 p.m., when the retainers would begin to take away the chairs at the ends of the semicircle. Sir Rupert would then withdraw into the nearby house and prepare to meet his dinner guests who had in the meantime been received by his wife Sybil and their daughter Mary, who acted as their indefatigable social secretary.

The advantages of the Majlis over the more usual cocktail party were mainfest. The system was useful in a number of ways. It enabled the Political Resident to meet new arrivals and talk in relative privacy, without interruptions, at least until the next caller arrived. Devout Muslims could help themselves to coffee, served by Sir Rupert's imposing personal coffee-pourers, or soft drinks from the trays circulated by the bearers. Less devout Muslims had been known to pour a glass of Coca-Cola from the tray into another one containing whisky and pick up the wrong one by mistake. The assembled company, steadily being eased down the line, had a good view of all callers and new arrivals, on whose identity they could speculate with their neighbours unless, as was frequently the case, the name, martial status, parent company or department and precise rank and seniority therein were all already known to some of the persons bobbing up and down, who would obligingly and rapidly pass the information along the line. The new arrivals would meet at least two other callers with whom they could talk as they sat and stood in the semicircle once they had been parted from Sir Rupert's side. Nobody was obliged to stay longer than he or she wanted. No one had to wait until the Resident withdrew. If they had not already signed the visitor's book, the efficient Mary would be hovering on hand ready to take down name, address, and other relevant details as the caller was on his way out.

The Majlis was conducted efficiently and with expediency. There was another aspect of the ceremony which also had value. The Resident left Bahrain at least half a dozen times a year, to visit Kuwait, the Trucial States, Qatar, or Muscat and Oman. He also went on leave, much less frequently. Many of the old hands punctiliously called on Sir Rupert every time he returned to Bahrain. They also called on him before they themselves left Bahrain, or when they returned from leave. They kept the Resident abreast of all news and developments in their own particular fields. Visitors were taken to call as a matter of course, no prior telephone calls or appointments being necessary. As Bahrain was then classified as an 'unhealthy post' for the purpose of home leave, and most commercial company employees (as well as the numerous Bahrain Government British officials) enjoyed fare-paid leave yearly in the United Kingdom, this meant that an awful lot of people had one reason or another to call at the Residency any weekday evening. When well into the third month of making my calls an irreverent colleague of mine, who years later was himself to become Ambassador to Bahrain, reflected that when we came to the end of our list and we had nothing to do one evening, we could always go up to the Residency for a drink, where it would be naturally assumed that we were either going on leave or had recently come back, or that we were calling because Sir Rupert had just returned from touring his parish or was due to go off shortly.

My work in the Political Agency ranged over most of the consular work with which I was already familiar, plus a number of other duties which were at the time unique to posts in the Gulf. I was mildly surprised to find myself invited to numerous dinners, buffets and cocktail parties almost from the day of my arrival. At first I put this down to the hospitality generously offered to new arrivals in isolated posts, far from family, friends, and home. But when I continued to receive invitations even from people I had scarcely met (or, should I say, on whom I had not called) I discovered that the reason for my popularity was the fact that one of my new duties was to sign the liquor permits which enabled the holder to purchase whisky, gin, and other alcoholic drinks from the commercial store which was the only outlet on the island licensed to sell retail.

Bahrain was then technically a 'dry' Muslim state, but in fact only a partial prohibition was enforced. The theory was that all persons not under the jurisdiction of the Ruler of Bahrain were, in principle, entitled to a liquor permit; but there were also a large number of persons who fell into no easy category. In addition to the well-known Bahraini trading families, other prominent local merchants were Indian or Pakistani (including some who were also, of course, Muslims). Yet other prominent merchants were Bahraini Jews. There were many engineers, builders, mechanics, and other qualified and important members of the local labour force who still possessed brown British Palestinian passports. Most were Arabs; some were Muslims but others were Christians. Yet other denizens of Bahrain still held (mostly expired) ordinary blue British passports which described them as British protected persons, subjects of Bahrain (or Kuwait or Qatar) even though Bahrain had issued its own passports since 1929. As far as liquor permits were concerned, many such persons defied any attempt to classify them into existing categories. Ancient precedents, former exceptions, prior rulings, and special cases were legion, and new ones were created all the time. The possibilities and permutations were virtually un-limited. A further complicating factor was provided by the quantities of liquor stipulated in each monthly permit. Company managers and heads of firms were allowed virtually unlimited quantities, but eligible junior staff in firms or government departments could almost double their salaries by selling their monthly entitlement on the black market. If they had a wedding anniversary or birthday party they naturally applied for a special issue. As we tried to administer the law in different ways when our regulations came into conflict with religion, we found that in many cases the law was an ass. All this meant that nearly every application had to be the subject of individual consideration. Fortunately, the oil company in Awali rigorously administered the liquor regulations and controls for their own two thousand employees, and any transgressor was liable to find himself on the next plane out of the island. There was only one case in my time when a serious breach of the regulations took place in Awali and had to be brought to the attention of Her Majesty's Court in Bahrain.

But in Manama this complex situation meant that there were many possibilities for malpractice and abuse; it was impossible to plug all the loopholes even though we all did our best to apply the spirit (if that is the right word) if not the letter of the obligation we had assumed with the Ruler of Bahrain, himself a devout Muslim to whom alcohol was anathema. Part of the problem was caused by the rich variety of races and nationalities at the time living in Bahrain. This created a stimulating and colourful presence of many cultures and ethnic groups, in which Indians and Pakistanis predominated. Many Anglo-Indians with Anglo-Saxon names and black faces were to be found in most government departments and commercial firms. The Political Agency could not have functioned without our loyal Indian and Pakistani assistants; for good measure we also had Anglo-Indians, Arabs from other Gulf states and a Bahraini Head *Munshi*, or head interpreter who subsequently became a high official in their embassy in London. The Bahrain police with their red turbans and coxcomb *pagris* consisted mostly of Baluchi recruits (with a memorable Sikh bandmaster), and Iranians, Somalis, Egyptians, Lebanese, and many others provided Bahrain for many years with economic immigrants, all attracted by the prospect of work and a better living in oil-rich and prosperous Bahrain, under the benevolent if autocratic rule of the Al-Khalifa family. At this time Kuwait was only just beginning to develop its own oil industry and, apart from promising indications in Qatar, no oil had yet been found elsewhere in the Trucial States or Muscat and Oman.

Bahrain was a place where people had little recourse but to make their own amusements. As a result the pace of everyday life was fast and crowded. Sporting activities and social engagements followed each other without pause, and most people eventually went on leave exhausted but having had a generally enjoyable and amusing time. Shortly after my arrival I was introduced to some of the old Indian service customs which had been imported into the Gulf by the Government of India administrators that we were gradually replacing. A week or two after my first call on the Political Resident I was kindly invited to dine at the Residency, where Sir Rupert and Lady Sybil (as she was known) nightly presided over formal dinners for up to twenty or more people. The late nights, early rising, hard work, pink gins, afternoon exercise, and sundowners all combined to make some of the more mature guests at dinner parties doze off before dinner or even enjoy a brief, refreshing nap in between courses. In the middle of a convivial dinner-table conversation, someone's eyes would glaze, and their dinner partners knew that they had lost their audience. But some conversations were resumed after a few minutes as though no interruption had taken place, except perhaps when unmistakable snores became increasingly audible and ulti-mately caused vigilant wives to take action. The customary, 'Isn't that right, *darling*?' shrieked across the table when the husband's snores could no longer be ignored brought all the conversation to a momentary halt, as well as immediate agreement from the snoozer thus rudely awakened.

The facilities in the Political Resident's modest, makeshift residency bungalow were limited. After dinner Lady Sybil would gather up the ladies and lead the way to her private quarters were they powdered noses and repaired any ravages caused by the heat or whatever. As soon as the ladies had left the dining-room and sometimes even before the port was handed round, Sir Rupert would rise and invite the gentlemen to join him in the garden, where a row of hardy bushes traditionally served as an open-air *pissoir*, behind which gentlemen were able subsequently to adjust their dress in relative privacy before re-entering the house, where the conversation was resumed with animation while the brandy and the cigars circulated. Shortly after, the ladies would reappear, the whole essential operation having been carried out with expediency and the efficiency born of long practice. The only complications were caused at the annual Christmas fancy-dress party to which many guests and friends were generously invited. As this was a stand-up, buffet affair and large quantities of liquid refreshment were consumed, the garden and the discreet row of laurel bushes were much in demand by the male guests; I found it disconcerting to be joined behind the hedge by a large, rouged and heavily made-up Widow Twanky who, after hoisting up her skirts, revealed himself as the director of the Public Works Department, or some such other exalted official in fancy dress.

A week or two later Mary Hay rang to ask if I would make up a tennis foursome with her father at the Jufair tennis court. Did I have my racquet and gear? Good. Five o'clock sharp on Wednesday afternoon, please. When I arrived I found that I had been drawn to partner Brigadier Baird, the Political Resident's Military Adviser, against Sir Rupert and his partner, an American naval officer from the *Greenwich Bay*, one of the US naval frigates then stationed in the Gulf. Having won the toss Sir Rupert chose to serve first. The sun was still high in the sky and it was rather hot. We were all perspiring freely and Sir Rupert was mopping his brow. He was dressed in a long-sleeved white shirt (to protect his arms from the sun), voluminous white shorts and stockings. He wore a small towel round his neck. His considerable girth and portly bearing made his tennis rather special. Having thrown the ball into the air from his baseline, he served an easy lob which landed two or three feet outside the service line in front of me. I hit the ball deliberately out of the court while Sir Rupert chanted, 'Hard luck!' As I braced myself for the second service I was surprised to see Sir Rupert march purposefully across to the other side of the court calling out, 'Fifteen love!' I stared in frank disbelief at the Brigadier who studiously avoided my eyes. Sir Rupert's next service landed within the service area in front of my partner, who sent back a splendid drive down the tramlines on Sir Rupert's far right. 'Out!' sang the invincible Sir Rupert, as he mopped his unfurrowed brow with his towel while walking across and preparing to serve again.

When it became our turn to serve the Brigadier, who played rather well, served a couple of aces. The first one was to Sir Rupert's partner, who could not refrain from calling out 'Good shot!' But this was greeted with, 'What was that? A bit doubtful, I think,' from Sir Rupert, who added generously, 'Why don't you play it again?' The next time round my partner served to Sir Rupert, who gazed without emotion at the ball as it whizzed past him after a near-perfect service, well within the service area in front of him. 'Hm!' I don't know. Difficult to see in this light! But you'd better have it, I suppose,' he concluded magnanimously, with a twinkle in his eye. I had the opportunity to play tennis at the Residency on several occasions before Sir Rupert left, and never failed to admire the manner in which he dominated every match, long before the term 'gamesmanship' was invented. Some of us called the PR's game 'real tennis', the practice of which endured and continued long after Sir Rupert had, sadly, left Bahrain.

There were, of course, many who pined for concerts, theatres, opera, art galleries and all the sophisticated amenities which were totally lacking in Bahrain, but in addition to the normal games and sports there were some less usual occasions which were equally available to all. Twice a year there were race meetings at the racecourse. These were animated and popular events undertaken with all the proper regard for tradition and pagentry. On the course there was the equivalent of the Royal Enclosure, complete with the judges' box, pavilions, a totalizator, buglers, stewards with lapel badges and the ceremonial arrival by the Ruler in a dignified Rolls-

Royce which drove slowly along the racecourse preceded by motor-cycle outriders and followed by a mounted escort of the Bahrain Police, complete with bamboo lances and pennants. This was a very grand occasion with a lot of European wives in unusual hats and colourful Indian ladies in their beautiful saris and gold ornaments. Two years running I was invited to ride one of the horses owned by the wife of the BOAC station manager, the other jockeys (with the exception of a girl from Awali and an Irishman called Ryan) being employed in the stables of the Ruler, who also bred and owned most of the horses taking part. The first time, I was entered for the Spring Meeting in 1954. According to the official race card (price one rupee) I sported Mrs Parker's green colours on a mare called Amira in the third race at 3.30 p.m. This was called the Manama Handicap, a distance handicap race for all horses over approximately five furlongs.

Handicapping was by distance and not weight, some of the local jockeys riding bareback. There were eight starters and Amira was favoured by a handicap of plus ten yards. There were only three scratch entries. The start for this race was on the far side of the right-handed racecourse. As soon as the flag came down, two or three of the handicap jockeys, obviously well versed in racing tactics and local practice, moved *en masse* to the rails on the right, not only to choose the shortest route but to block the scratch starters from behind, who were by this time rocketing past me on all sides. As a result there was a monumental pile-up just in front of me, with no less than four horses and riders coming to grief. Fortunately nobody was injured, even though an interesting fist fight between two of the dismounted jockeys was beginning as Amira daintily picked her way through the bodies. After that we had an easy, clear canter to arrive in an honourable fourth position, being overtaken only by a riderless horse (which didn't count) just before we reached the post.

Not long after my arrival, I joined some of my new friends on a pearling expedition, for which we embarked on a Bahraini dhow which sailed all night to the oyster beds not far from the Saudi mainland. I had quickly made friends with two or three bachelors of my own age who seemed to share some of my interests. Robin Huntingdon was an army captain on the staff of the Military Adviser, my erstwhile tennis partner. Like many of us at the time, Robin also was keen on diving and underwater fishing. We had both devoured all the literature on the subject, of which the best-known exponents at the time were Hans and Lotte Hass, whose books and films complemented, in a different dimension, the new frontiers then being excitingly explored by Commander Jacques-Yves Cousteau and his crew on the good ship *Calypso*, which was to visit the Gulf later that year. Robin and I were the proud owners of some of the latest underwater gear then available, and in the right season we frequently joined forces to try our luck off different parts of the island. The fishing was excellent by any standards, and the prospect of meeting a stray shark or barracuda always lent an added element of excitement to our expeditions, although the generally shallow waters kept the larger predators away from the shores. But there were always large rays and numerous sea snakes to lend spice to our expeditions off the three-mile, deep-water oil jetty at Sitra island or even from the shores of the Bahrain Government's experimental agricultural farm at Budeyah, where Nora and Aubrey Van Ollenbach (the Bahrain Government's Agriculture Director) hospitably kept open house.

The pearling dhow had rudimentary accommodation; most of us slept on deck on inflatable Lilos, surrounded by Thermos flasks with iced drinks and insulated food boxes. There was an open-ended thunder box rather like a cage lashed to the high stern of the boat in which one perched perilously over the propeller with no privacy. The crew were mostly members of the same family; the pearl-diving industry was traditionally organized on an extraordinarily complicated basis providing for the apportioning of expenses and benefits between owner, outfitter, master, mate, and crew of the vessels on a pro-rata basis. Sometimes the corresponding shares (of earnings and debts) had been inherited from another generation. Understandably, in self-defence there had developed a tendency to limit membership of the club to the family, even though this sometimes created more problems than it solved. We had two or three hand lines and spoons out while we motored to the oyster beds, but we were going too fast and caught only one suicidal *shanad* or king mackerel, which made delicious eating. It was lovely fish with a blue-grey back and tigerish vertical stripes. It had virtually no scales or bones except the dorsal, central spine. A three-foot king mackerel had six inches of head and six inches of gut. The rest was tender flesh best eaten sliced in round filets, first boiled in sea water and then cooked over an open fire on deck with lots of rice and curry.

But this was not until lunch the following day, by which time we had helped to bring up what looked like several tons of large, fleshy, unappetizing oysters, which had been left on deck overnight in order to be opened more easily next morning by relays of deft oyster-openers who, together with the divers, seemed to be the most important people on board. I was surprised to find that the divers, contrary to my expectations, were mainly small, wizened-looking men who were, I was told, younger than they looked. Most of the waters in the Gulf are quite shallow, and when we anchored over the oyster beds we were in no more than about forty feet of water. When the divers slipped over the side each one held on to a weighted rope which had been let down to the sea bed from a number of poles or oars sticking out horizontally from the side of the dhow. The divers used a large stone or heavy weight to get down to the bottom with the minimum exertion, conserving their energy for the task of collecting oysters and putting them into a basket lowered with them. They wore nothing but curious half gloves made of raw leather which protected their fingers from the coral and the sharp edges of the oysters. Robin and I splashed around trying to follow them down to the sea bed. Even with my new flippers, the air in my goggles, and the deep breath which I sucked into my lungs before diving enabled me at best to watch them at work fifteen or twenty feet beneath me. They stayed down for between a minute and a half to two minutes, while I broke the surface every few seconds. But what Robin and I found astonishing was that the divers, after resting on the surface for ten or fifteen minutes after each dive, actually exhaled all the air from their lungs before plunging to the bottom with the heavy weight. Thus they had virtually no body buoyancy, which certainly helped them to go down; but this also prevented them from coming up for air unaided unless physically hauled up by their helpers on deck, on whom they had to rely for their very life to react promptly as soon as the diver gave the signal. Under water they made a strange sight, the small, naked bodies with a clothes peg on their noses and screwed-up faces being hauled up like corpses from the murky depths, clutching a basket full of oyster shells. I was told that two or three of them could not swim.

On other fishing trips we sometimes caught a large, vicious-looking barracuda or a smallish sand shark, neither of which made good eating. There was also a curious fish called a *halavi* in Arabic (it is called a 'guitar fish' in the Caribbean, where it is also found), which was a sort of cross between a shark and a ray, with a shark-like tail and body widening gradually to a triangular flat head, and a shark-like mouth on the lower surface. I discovered that these fish were viviparous when one day we boated one which promptly produced two little *halavis* on the spot. But the most remarkable fish was the *sikken*, a large, dark-grey and tasty fish which was taken mainly with a weighted line and groundbait. Although people claimed to have caught thirty- and forty-pounders, most of those we landed weighed between eight and fifteen pounds. Its peculiarity was that a hooked *sikken* brought up to the surface was usually accompanied by its mate, swimming freely around the struggling victim in the water. The first time it happened to me, the fish on my line must have weighed about ten pounds. As I looked around for a net or a gaff, one of my Bahraini companions saw my plight and shouted to me not to try to haul in the fish. I thought this was because I had a fine line on my rod and our freeboard was high out of the water. But as I played the fish on the surface close to the side of the boat I was surprised by the appearance of a second *sikken*, about the same size as the first one, which emerged from the depths and swam in agitated circles round its hooked companion. My friend hastened across with a long gaff, with which he unhesitatingly and deftly gaffed and pulled in the free-swimming fish. He then handed me the gaff with a smile, saying, 'Always keep the first one in the water, then you get two!' This was not an isolated instance, the second *sikken* appearing virtually every time we brought one to the surface. I felt rather sorry for the *sikken*, never before having come across a fish which behaved so faithfully to the end. On other occasions we caught *hamour* of various sizes. These were members of the numerous (and tasty) sea bass or grouper species which are normally bottom- or rock-dwellers. In Bahrain waters they surprised me by rising to take a spoon trolled three or four feet beneath the surface. Needless to say, fresh fish made a welcome supplement to our monotonous diet of chicken and tinned peas, at least until the cold store was inaugurated during my last year in Bahrain.

Not all was tennis and diving and fishing, however. Posts in the Gulf were all classified as 'unhealthy' by the Foreign Office for the purposes of leave; this meant that we were entitled to longer leave more frequently than our colleagues in, say, Rome. The inevitable corollary was that those who stayed behind had to work harder. The approved route for leave journeys was originally by sea; to Bombay by British India steamer and then home through the Suez canal by P. & O. Travelling time did not count as leave. These agreeable arrangements were changed while I was in Bahrain, where a new age of air travel was introduced by the beautiful Comets which included Bahrain on their routes to and from the Far East and offered previously unattainable levels of comfort and speed. But, at first, the original surface route arrangements meant that somebody or other was on leave almost all the time, and that people were frequently away for several months. For obvious reasons most tried to get away during the torrid summer months. When the Political Agent was on leave (as when I first arrived) the assistant Political Agent acted in his place. When the Political Resident went on leave, the Political Agent replaced him in the Residency in Jufair. They avoided being away at the same time, but the system created a chain reaction which had officials standing in for their superiors for months on end. The situation was naturally aggravated by sickness or transfers without immediate replacements. As a result, leave absences, transfers, illnesses and premature departures meant that for much of my time in Bahrain I acted as assistant Political Agent and, indeed, as Political Agent for several months in my last year there. All this brought additional responsibilities. I was first appointed a Marriage Registrar, licensed to perform marriages and unite couples who established the necessary residential qualifications under the provisions of the Indian Christian Marriages Act of 1876. Shortly after I was made an assistant Judge of Her Majesty's Court, in which role I was empowered to impose penalties for breaches of the law up to a maximum of 2000 rupees in fines or six months in gaol. In the case of Europeans or Americans, whenever possible or essential, deportation took the place of gaol, mainly because we had no gaol of our own. Jiddah, the

Bahrain prison island, was reserved for Bahraini prisoners sentenced to hard labour. Unlike the other, mainly flat and featureless islands of the group, this was an attractive, rocky island with uncharacteristic cliffs, off which the fishing was very good. Although it was out of bounds to the general public I was invited once or twice by the Ruler's British adviser, who had built himself a weekend cottage on a small cliff on the other side of the penal settlement, where convicted murderers and others wore belts with fearsome-looking chains connected to leather straps on their ankles. This was the hard labour. Belts and ankle straps (and chains) were removed for sleeping and ablutions.

Most of the laws then applicable in Bahrain derived from the relevant Indian legislation as applied to Bahrain by Queen's Regulations or Orders in Council, added to which we had our own regulations governing liquor and residence permits, (two highly contentious issues). At the time, those concerned at the Residency were trying to create a corpus of Gulf law more suited to the peculiar needs of the area. Ivor Lucas, a friend then serving as a third secretary at the Residency and a graduate of the Middle East Centre for Arab Studies, was one of the officials whose task it was to reconcile complex legal texts prepared in London with the realities of unsophisticated life in the Gulf states. For the local administration of justice we had in the meantime to make do with the Indian Code of Civil Procedure, an imposing tome about eight inches thick, and with its complementary Indian Code of Criminal Procedure, which was only slightly slimmer. As a judge of Her Majesty's Court my job was comparable to that of a magistrate's, and I was usually able to hand down decisions in accordance with well-established precedents. On other, more complex, occasions close study of the corresponding Indian volume was unavoidable; but any problems were usually solved under the guidance of Bill Maudsley who, as Registrar of the Court, was always on hand to prevent any miscarriage of justice. As an additional safeguard, the judge of the Chief Court in the Gulf came from London twice a year to review cases and sentences and hear appeals. But there were never any problems. Even at the beginning I found that if I got into deep water all I had to do was to stand up and adjourn the court for ten minutes. In the privacy of the adjoining disrobing room I could then ask Bill

Maudsley for guidance and advice. The large courtroom was at the top of our temporary agency offices, across the landing from the Political Agent's room. One or more members of the Bahrain police were always on hand to stamp their boots when the judge entered or left the room and lend dignity and support to the court when in session. Charges were presented by English-speaking members of the Bahrain police, principally by Chief Superintendent Jim Hyde, an amiable former London Metropolitan policeman, originally recruited by the Ruler many years previously, who had pursued his career mainly in the traffic department of the Bahrain police force.

The judge sat at a high bench on a dais with the royal coat of arms on the wall behind him. Seated immediately below was the Registrar, who was also empowered to rule on cases involving civil offences and litigation and indeed dealt by himself with 90 per cent of the cases brought to our court. But liquor offenders and illegal residents were liable to be expelled from the island and therefore required sentence by higher authority. In particular, many Iranians and Somalis were at the time making determined attempts to seek employment in the oil industry. Some would jump overboard from passing dhows and swim ashore in order to avoid port and passport controls. They were usually successful in establishing themselves on the island until, months later, authority inexorably caught up with them and obliged them, much to their own and their employers' annoyance, to leave. Several were expelled two or three times while I was there, but they always found their way back. Somalis in particular could prove troublesome. A tall, almost blue-black, handsome race of Hamitic people, sometimes with aquiline features and always a proud bearing, they did not take kindly to the prospect of compulsory expulsion. Two Somalis once threatened our Head Munshi with knives when told they would have to leave, and we had to call out our Bahrain police guard.

Other cases which involved me were inquests on seamen who had died on ships in Bahrain waters, of which there were unhappily too many, particularly in the summer when the temperatures on ships without air-conditioning reached unbearable levels. Prior to an inquest the court always had to view the body, which required prompt action in the case of vessels which arrived several days after the death had taken place. One unusual murder case was heard by the special Court of Assizes stipulated by the Indian Code of Criminal Procedure. This involved the summons of half a dozen worthy citizens from different national communities to serve as Assessors to the Court. They did not act as a jury but rather sat on the bench with the Judge who was nevertheless ultimately not bound by their decisions, thereby opening up a number of interesting possibilities. But on this occasion everything went smoothly and happily we all agreed on a verdict of not guilty.

In the same way that Somalis and others tried to swim ashore undetected, slaves from other countries in the area sometimes escaped to Bahrain. Tradition had it that if a slave reached the Agency grounds and embraced the imposing flagstaff at the end of the drive, with its outsize twelve-breadths Union Jack at the masthead, no man could henceforth interfere with him. This constraint was recognized and respected throughout the Gulf, it being no doubt left over from the days when a Political Agent with the power to summon up a gunboat and a whiff of grapeshot had a salutary effect on warring tribes bent on conquest, pillage, and loot. At the Agency we kept a register of manumitted slaves going back to 1861 when the first 'Perpetual Treaty of Peace and Friendship' with Britain was signed. By the time I arrived first applications were mercifully rare, even though a manumission certificate was almost the first document I was called upon to issue the day after my arrival to a man from another country who had made his way to the Agency in fear for his life. He was about forty and told us he had been born a slave. His reaction to the piece of paper we gave him, to which he had aspired for so many years, was a moving experience for which I was unprepared and which left me thoughtful and perturbed. We issued no more than seven or eight new manumission certificates in my three years there, but many more times I was called upon to sign a replacement certificate for a man who, having been previously manumitted, produced a small fragment of worn and shiny cardboard which had been issued to him many years before. The blank certificates in my office cupboard were headed with a picture of the Queen and crossed Union Jacks in the centre. The page below was divided into two halves with the corresponding legend and bearer's names in Arabic from centre to left and in English on the right. Every

New Year's Day in the morning all manumitted slaves still resident on the island came to the old Agency and made manifest their appreciation and recognition with drums, rattles and strings of shells while performing complicated and monotonous gyrations round the Agency flagpole, which was dressed overall for the occasion, after which the Political Agent distributed bags of sweets and sticky fruit drinks to the dancers.

New Year's Day was a busy one for the Political Agent and his staff. Having greeted the New Year the previous night in the traditional manner, some of us barely got to bed in time to get up for the first of the official functions, known as the Maypole dancing at the old Agency. Immediately after we hastened to the Political Agent's house in the Jufair Road, where a formal honour guard of the Bahrain Police was drawn up on the road outside, complete with band and the Sikh bandmaster with his imposing white beard, all nervously awaiting the arrival of the Ruler. As not one of the ten or twelve members of the band could read a single note of music, the bandmaster first had to intone, loudly if rather nasally, the first half-dozen bars of whatever was to be played, be this a national anthem or any other of the pieces in their surprisingly large repertoire. Opposite the new block of flats in the Awal Road where I eventually shared quarters with another member of the staff of the Agency there was a pretty municipal park, laid out with ornamental flower-beds and a small artificial lake, complete with a bandstand where for three or four hours on fine Friday afternoons during the winter, the police band and its gifted bandmaster played for the benefit of general public and passers-by. At the Political Agent's temporary house in the Jufair Road, however, only the national anthem was played when the Ruler arrived in his Rolls with mounted police escort.

His Highness Shaikh Sir Sulman bin Hamed Al-Khalifa, K.C.M.G., K.C.I.E., was not very tall, but made up for his lack of inches by his handsome, bearded appearance and dignified bearing. Then aged about sixty, he was a kindly and courteous man who had ruled Bahrain since 1942 when he succeeded his father. As was usual on his public appearances he was attired in his ceremonial robes, belted and buckled with his bejewelled dagger, on the handle of which he habitually wore his wrist-watch. After the customary exchange of lengthy courtesies and having bidden the Political Agent the compliments of the season the Ruler would then re-embark in his Rolls and proceed at a stately pace up the Jufair Road to the Residency. The stately pace was doubly necessary, both because of the mounted escort and to give the Political Agent time to nip into his car and bolt up the Jufair Road, unceremoniously overtaking the cavalry and the Rolls on the shoulder of the narrow road, in order to be at the Residency with the Political Resident and his senior staff in time to receive the Ruler – this time with a full Royal Air Force guard of honour and band, gun salutes by the Royal Navy, bugles and other marks of respect. This was a colourful ceremony which was much enjoyed by all. The last time I attended, the new Residency buildings and approaches had been virtually completed and ornamental gardens and driveways laid out. The flagpole was dressed overall, and the Political Resident and his senior staff were all in uniforms, medals, and their best finery. By this time the Political Resident was Sir Bernard Burrows, a tall, distinguished and imposing figure, with decorations, white feathers on his hat, and ceremonial sword. The representatives of the armed services were, of course, also in uniform with lots of gold braid, red tabs, medals, and swords Martin Le Quesne, who had been Sir Rupert's Head of Chancery at the Residency when I first arrived, had been replaced by Brooks Richards, who was the possessor of a pre-war 'real' Diplomatic Service uniform with much ornamental braid and a regulation bicorne hat adorned with elegant but by then unusual black feathers. Even in the rank of first secretary, this outshone the Political Agent's and Resident's senior but more austere, post-war, Foreign Service uniforms. It so happened that Brooks Richards also had an outstanding service record with the Royal Navy during the war, and the impressive chestful of medals (which included French and Greek decorations) on his glamourous diplomatic uniform almost put all the others in the shade. The Ruler was accompanied by his adviser, Sir Charles Belgrave, who had served him faithfully for many years. He also was a tall, handsome figure, originally a member of the Sudan Political Service, who followed local traditions and created one or two of his own. On this occasion it was his custom to wear a grey morning suit of impeccable cut, with a light-grey waistcoat and matching spats, the whole edifice crowned by a white pith helmet or 'Bombay bowler' of the sort much worn at the time by Anglo-Indian employees of local companies.

After the Ruler had left as ceremonially as he had arrived, the Political Resident's New Year's reception took place on the Residency lawns at the back of the house overlooking the sea. Until Sir Rupert left Bahrain this was known as his 'Durbar'. It remained a colourful occasion none the less, with European wives in unexpected hats and gloves, officers in smart uniforms, beautiful Asian ladies in elegant and attractive saris, turbans and astrakhan caps mingling with the *thaubs* and *abas* and black *aghals* worn by Bahraini civilians, and here and there a gold-bound head-dress proclaiming the presence of a member of the ruling family. Derek Anderson, the popular information officer at the Residency, was another who turned up resplendent in morning coat and striped trousers, cravat and a grey topper. As the non-Muslim guests increasingly benefited from the many hairs of the dog available (Pimms was a favourite drink after a late night and such a busy morning) the party tended to go on for a long time, until different groups joined forces to continue the celebrations elsewhere. A favourite destination for the more privileged was one of the Royal Navy frigates at anchor in the bay, whose commanding officers had wisely made arrangements to cope with the influx of guests who invited themselves, among whom were also some of the American officers from the US frigates, whose otherwise generous hospitality was marred on such a special day by their inability to offer (or obtain) suitable refreshments on board their own ships were prohibition reigned supreme.

Bahrain was then one of the few places where the pre-dominantly Shiah population were still permitted to perform their Muharram processions and passion play commemor-ating the deaths of Ali, the Prophet's son-in-law and his younger son Hussein. In Bahrain there was a long history of communal strife until the Al-Khalifa family, originally settled in Zubairah on the coast of Qatar, established their rule on the island. The Persian purchase of Bahrain from Oman in the early part of the eighteenth century was followed by a confused period during which the Al-Khalifa gradually consolidated their hold on Bahrain against first Persian, then Muscati, Wahabi, and even Qatari attempts to expel them. They eventually left Zubairah altogether in favour of their island

99

home, where their independence was 'guaranteed' by the British East India Company early in the nineteenth century. But even this form of recognition was followed by further Persian, Omani, Wahabi, and Qatari efforts to overthrow the Al-Khalifa. The situation was not improved by inter-family disputes, in which different pretenders enlisted the help of some of their former foes to overthrow the ruling member of the family. It was not until the late nineteenth century that a British man-of-war appeared with the British Resident in Bushire who speedily imposed the *pax Britannica* on the warring factions of the family and appointed a new ruler of Bahrain, who reigned for over fifty years until the 1920s. Even during this period, claims to sovereignty over the island were occasionally advanced by Persia, Saudi Arabia, Qatar, and Oman until a convention was signed between the British and Ottoman Governments in 1913 formally recognizing the independence of Bahrain. All of this may go some way to explain the extraordinary mixture of races and creeds which made up the population of Bahrain. No doubt partly because of this, the Shiahs' annual self-inflicted blood-letting in the middle of the month of Muharram, the first month of the Islamic year, was still wisely tolerated by their Sunni rulers, even though as a religious manifestation it had been already banned in other Shiah communities elsewhere.

This was the only occasion when we advised Europeans and Americans to keep off the streets; and in no circumstances should they be seen watching from windows or, worse still, trying to take photographs. I found it a fearsome spectacle, reminiscent of a medieval Holy Week procession in Seville, of which it was no doubt a direct ancestor. The glow of the torches, the flagellants in their gory shrouds, the clanking of chains and the hoarse, co-ordinated cries of 'Ali' and 'Hussein' from a thousand throats impressed me deeply. Many participants had froth on their mouths and others were in a self-induced cataleptic state. Together with the flashing swords and bloody faces, the rhythmic drumming of thousands of fists on raw, bare chests, all seemed to be part of the seldom-revealed, unacceptable face of a religious fundamentalism of disturbing intensity which had frequently turned ugly in bygone years. The route of the procession was lined with Bahraini spectators, some of whom were Sunnis, and known to

100

be such. In the past, this uninhibited proximity had led to riots and disturbances, but on my first Muharram procession the situation appeared to be admirably supervised by a smartly uniformed and imperturbable Chief Superintendent Jim Hyde who, known to be neither Sunni nor Shiah, was single-handedly pacing up and down the route of the procession with his unmistakable policeman's walk, a swagger stick under his arm and his hands behind his back – uncontrollable displays of communal religious emotion apparently coming within the jurisdiction of the Bahrain police traffic department.

The Political Agent's official driver, Sayed Amin, was one of the leading members of his religious fraternity. For eleven months of the (Christian) year he was a polite, helpful, and urbane driver, who had learned a little English and was proud of his position behind the wheel of one of the two cars which flew the Union Jack on the island. Shortly after my arrival I learnt that Sayed Amin was one of the principal Shiah preachers in his community. His oratory and eloquence had brought him local renown. It also brought him trouble. After the Muharram celebrations my first year Sayed Amin appeared for work covered in sticking plaster and bandages. The second year he sported an arm in a sling and a foot and ankle in plaster. The third year he was hospitalized for three weeks. When we met again I asked him with a smile what had happened. He looked at me levelly for a long time, before answering me in English, without emotion. 'Sa'ahb,' he said politely, 'You would not understand.'

Years later, shortly after we had arrived in Iraq, I drove with my wife one afternoon to see the mosque at Khadhamain, in one of the northern suburbs of Baghdad, not much frequented by Europeans. The mosque, with its fabled, onion-shaped golden domes and four golden-topped minarets, was at the centre of what I was told was the principal Shiah quarter of Baghdad. I was warned about taking photographs too ostentatiously and advised not to enter the mosque, although this was in theory open to suitably attired and respectful visitors. With memories of the Muharram processions in Bahrain uppermost in my mind I hardly needed cautioning. But I lost my way and we spent half an hour driving around, trying to find our destination. Eventually I decided to ask for directions. I drove up to a corner where there were a couple of itinerant vendors, with their mobile kitchens on wheels, from which there issued the smell of boiling oil and one or two other less recognizable fragrances. There were also five or six men and youths loitering aimlessly, leaning against the wall or squatting on the kerb. My approach was greeted without interest, but as soon as I had made myself understood one of the men detached himself from the group and addressed me in English. 'You'd better go home,' he said, 'This place is no good for you. This morning they threw stones at some European women who wanted to enter the mosque. There is still a crowd round the entrance. They are very angry. You go home,' he concluded, I hardly needed persuading. I turned the car round and, to my relief, I soon found myself on the broad double-carriageway approach to Khadhamain which I should have followed in the first place. There were no other cars on the road, and we seemed unduly to attract the attention of the few pedestrians on the street. Having driven some way, I stopped again and hurriedly took a couple of distant photographs of the golden domes and minarets on the skyline. As I climbed in again behind the wheel a sizeable stone hit the side of my car.

The internal situation in Bahrain did not cause many problems in spite of the potential for intercommunity strife. This was before the Suez intervention, while Egyptian efforts to destabilize some of the traditional regimes in the Middle East were conducted with vigour and imagination. One of the effective instruments for this policy was the powerful Saut al-Arab radio station broadcasting from Cairo. In the absence of any domestic newspapers and before the coming of television, these broadcasts were the principal purveyors of news and views to all possessors of transistor radios in the Gulf. There were also numerous Egyptian schoolteachers (some of whom were subsequently thought to have exceeded their brief) employed by the Bahrain Government and other Gulf states. But, in general, political turmoil was limited to other areas such as the Buraimi oasis and, later, Oman, though even in Bahrain we had one unusual experience which deserves to be recorded. The nascent domestic political stresses and the deep-rooted Sunni/Shiah feeling both played a significant role in a bizarre episode which could have had far-reaching consequences, at the time difficult to foresee.

Stimulated by the foreign broadcasts and always conscious

of the traditional Shiah grievances against their Sunni rulers, a group of dissatisfied Bahraini intellectuals and theorists formed a self-styled 'Higher Executive Committee' which held a number of rallies, political meetings, and related activities. These were tolerated by the authorities until the policies and premises preached from the rostrum came close to sedition and became unacceptable. During a general strike, nails and tacks were put on the roads, public transport was disrupted, and people were kept away from work. In July 1954 the Bahrain Government was at last obliged to take action against the Higher Executive Committee. Two or three of the Committee's leading members were arrested and confined in the Qalat ad-Diwan, another picturesque foreign legion fort (similar to that which had so impressed me at Rutba in Iraq on my way to Bahrain), originally built by the Persians in the eighteenth century. This was used as their headquarters by the Bahrain police. These arrests caused much disquiet and communal agitation which culminated in demonstrations by crowds of Shiah sympathizers of the Higher Executive Committee, which marched on the Bahrain police fort to demand the release of their imprisoned leaders. The Baluchi policemen, after firing warning shots in the air which did nothing to pacify the crowds, opened fire in self-defence against the excited mob and unfortunately killed four of the demonstrators. Initially, the Higher Executive Committee's demands for political reform were rather retrograde, even by the standards of the period. They wanted the Al-Khalifa family banished, the state police replaced by British troops, and Bahrain to become a British colony. As a measure of their dedication to these demands they collected up their dead, wrapped the bodies reverently in large Union flags and brought them to the Political Agency, where they wished to lay them physically and symbolically at the feet of the British Political Agent as (they said) tangible evidence of the tyranny and oppression of their Al-Khalifa rulers and their brutal, mercenary police myrmidons.

The Political Agent at the time was John Wall, who had narrowly escaped being buried with his breakfast when the roof of the old Agency building collapsed. He was a noted oriental scholar and linguist who had originally joined the Levant Consular Service in which he served at many posts in the Near and Middle East. Before coming to Bahrain he had been Head of the British Middle East Office and Oriental Counsellor at the embassy in Cairo. He was generally respected and much admired in Bahrain for his exceptional knowledge of Islamic customs and history and, particularly, for his command of the ritual and complex exchange of lengthy greetings and compliments which always preceded any Arabic conversation (in which exchanges, I was told, he always outclassed his Arab interlocutors, much to their delighted surprise). He was then a studious-looking man in his early forties, although he looked older. Of average height, he had a slight stoop, usually smoked a pipe, wore steel-rimmed glasses, and had a lively and inquisitive mind, with a rather sardonic sense of humour. A routine circular had recently been received from the Foreign Office, in which we were for some reason urged to consider giving blood on our next leave in London. No doubt inspired by the torrid heat of Bahrain and having put his name down as a potential donor, John Wall minuted on the margin: 'First, toil and sweat; now blood. What next?' The answer was not long in coming.

Bahrain was a place were rumour and gossip spread like wildfire. As soon as we heard about the shooting at the police fort we knew that the next port of call was likely to be the Political Agency. But we also had a permanent guard of Bahrain policemen complete with rifles and bayonets, mainly used on those ceremonial occasions when US admirals and other notable visitors called. It was clearly essential to prevent any appeal to the Political Agent for protection being greeted by a hail of hostile bullets from the hapless Baluchis. Dick Giddens and I were despatched immediately with the Head *Munshi* to disarm our nervous police guards. Leaving Dick and the Head *Munshi* arguing with the policemen, I humped half a dozen rifles and the corresponding ammunition to my office upstairs where I locked everything up in a steel cupboard. I raced downstairs again to find Dick herding the policemen into a small storeroom on the ground floor, where they were to be concealed. The Head *Munshi* would stay around down below to protect them (if found) and to ensure that they did not lose their nerve and try to make a run for it.

As anticipated, a few nervous minutes later we saw groups of shouting men running down the three streets which led to the public square in front of the Agency building. The first groups instinctively paused at our gates, until the square filled up and the pressure of the crowds behind pushed those in front into the Agency compound, which rapidly filled with an excited crowd of shouting and jostling people. By this time the square in front of our building and the adjoining streets were a sea of faces and fists. A few minutes later, the noise subsided into a sullen, truculent silence, while the crowd parted to allow the bodies and their bearers to pass through their midst; first into the compound and then to the main entrance, where the appearance of the small procession was greeted with much weeping and wailing and other expressions of public grief. They then climbed awkwardly with the bodies up the narrow staircase to the second-floor office of the Political Agent, even though he had offered to come down. Several self-appointed spokesmen had by this time forced their way through the crowd and up the stairs to his office, where John Wall listened to their accusations and grievances and patiently dealt with their questions and demands, with the corpses dramatically displayed on the floor in front of his desk. Finally, his eloquence and powers of persuasion prevailed, and the spokesmen took up their dead. The temperature was in the lower forties, the humidity was high. The Political Agent's offices, like the rest of the compound, the square, and the streets outside, were filled with milling throngs in a volatile, ugly mood.

On their way out, the reappearance of the bodies in the Union Jacks at the main entrance, this time escorted also by the Political Agent, was greeted by a roar from the crowd, which surged towards us. Inevitably, more furious questions and demands were angrily put forward. John Wall perforce had to begin all over again, addressing an excited and angry audience, while fists were brandished in his face and abuse was hurled at us from all quarters. Dick Giddens and I stood close behind him at the main entrance for what seemed to me like hours, until the Political Agent's calm reasoning, wisdom, and fluency slowly and gradually began to tell on his furious audience. Dick was a tall young man, well above average height, of good presence and appearance. He had for some reason done his military service in the Palestine Police. He was then on the threshold of a promising career, which was to be cut short by a tragically early death. When we coincided in London some time later, I found (to my secret envy) that he was usually given a smart salute by the dismounted guardsmen on duty at the Whitehall entrance of the Horse Guards whenever we walked past in our bowler hats, trench coats and furled umbrellas. But I like to think that his bearing and impassive mien contributed something to the situation while we stood behind John Wall and saw the back of his light-grey suit slowly grow dark with perspiration from collar to the back of his knees until, much later, his impressive oratory and patient arguments finally won the day and the crowds began to leave, reluctantly and sullenly, but peacefully.

This unusual episode set the scene for later developments which neither impressive oratory nor patient arguments alone managed to solve. But other, less dramatic, occasions also remain vivid in my mind, for no better reason than the friends or personalities involved. Shortly after my arrival in 1953 we all trooped out to the airport to welcome Sir John Hunt and the victorious Everest expedition members, whose aircraft was making a brief refuelling stop at Muharraq on their way back to Britain. Amid the excited crowds and photographers at the airport I contrived to include myself in a group photograph of the expedition members taken by Peter Doherty, then Residency Medical Adviser. In addition to Sir John Hunt the group, of course, included Sir Edmund Hillary and the smiling Sherpa Tensing Norkay, also travelling to London with his wife and daughter. I dined out on this photograph for many months, to the unbelieving perplexity of family, friends, and other sceptics. Many years later in Lima I was delighted to welcome to my house Lord Hunt who, in the company of a cousin of Peter Doherty, was on his way to a 'walking' tour in the Peruvian Andes, which was to include the notorious Huascarán peak, the second highest in South America. I could not resist fishing out a copy of the old group photograph taken in Bahrain and asking Lord Hunt if he recognized all the members of his Everest expedition.

Later in the year I was sent on temporary duty to Doha in Qatar. In the absence of any hotels or alternative accommodation, and much to the undisguised speculation and amusement of the local British community, I lived perforce in the absent Political Officer's house, also occupied by his young and attractive wife who had stayed behind. We were all happy to meet again, years after, as colleagues in Baghdad. In Qatar there were also convivial evenings with Pat and David Brown in the oil company's luxurious and formal club mess in Dukhan, which usually concluded with exciting drives far out into the desert to watch the oil flares pale before the approaching dawn, the men incongruously dressed in black ties and boiled shirts. I remember with undiminished pleasure the always memorable fishing expeditions with James Belgrave, Robin Huntingdon, Dick Giddens and Dennis Wilkins, all prematurely dead but not forgotten by their many friends; the fast and furious games of squash at Awali with Malcolm Dennison who, after a long career in the Muscat and Oman armed forces, is now happily retired and installed in his native Orkney as Her Majesty's Lord Lieutenant; the Scottish dancing at the Residency in Jufair which continued to gather all and sundry under Sir Bernard and Lady Burrows' hospitable roof. But I cannot refrain from including one final vignette which was probably symptomatic of the place, the time, and the people.

After my brief sojourn in the Political Agent's temporary house, I moved in with Frank Trew to a dilapidated bungalow, also in the Jufair Road. But when he left, I cast covetous eyes on one of the new flats in the two blocks built by the Bahrain Government on the Awal Road. This flat was occupied by two colleagues in the Agency, Leslie Taylor and Dick Giddens. When I heard that Leslie was leaving I staked my claim successfully, and was invited to co-host his farewell party, to which we contributed in kind. I provided one case of whisky, one case of gin, and four cartons of beer, as well as my two sparklet siphons to help with the making of soda with the distilled water purchased in demijohns for this purpose. Some old-timers drank their whisky with the brackish Bahrain water and claimed not to be able to tell the difference, but in well-ordered households with efficient wives, the distilled water was first decanted into the square gin bottles which had been scrubbed and cleaned and had their labels removed, before being put in the fridge. Other households were less particular. In self-defence, we had invited the other occupants of the block, and they also lent glasses, plates, and even houseboys, as was customary among friends and neighbours. In the event, the party was a crowded, noisy, and convivial affair with people coming and going all the time, moving on to another party or returning after a dinner, until a sizeable hard core settled down to the serious business of the evening. The following morning we left Leslie counting the empties in the kitchen, to ensure that all were present and accounted for. At lunch a worried Leslie reported that a case of gin appeared to have gone missing. This was serious. We, of all people, were bound to conduct a thorough investigation to ensure that there had been no theft. This was all very unpleasant as it involved all the neighbours' houseboys who had helped us. But everything had been counted repeatedly; there was no question about it, twelve litre bottles of Gordon's gin had disappeared. We left an anxious Leslie surrounded by empty cartons and bottles as well as agitated houseboys and cooks, who all knew full well that this could lead to appearances in court and fines or dismissals.

In the evening I went round to wish Leslie *bon voyage*. I found a relaxed Leslie, who had finished his packing and was to catch a plane the next morning. When asked about the missing gin, Leslie shook his head in wonder and said 'You'll never believe this!' His enquiries had established beyond any doubt that, in accordance with local custom, early on the evening of the party a new houseboy, employed for the first time in a European household, had thoughtfully placed the bottles of clear liquid in the fridge, whence they were extracted as and when needed by relays of harried bearers hurriedly making up another Sparklet siphon of soda. I was given my Sparklet siphons to smell. There was no mistaking the aromatic scent clearly distinguishable in the dregs of all the siphons. It seemed impossible, but there could be no doubt. For the latter part of the evening all our guests had been drinking their whiskies mixed with carbonated gin instead of soda. 'And do you know what?' marvelled Leslie, 'Nobody said a word!'

7

The African Department, 1957–1960

When I returned to the Foreign Office in August 1957 I was hoping to be appointed to one of the geographical departments. With the exception of Asunción, where I had done a bit of everything, and Bahrain, where I had acquired some unusual legal and judicial experience, my appointments abroad had involved me in miscellaneous but mainly consular work. I wanted to be involved in doing the sort of job for which the Foreign Office was invented. I was also anxious to avoid being posted to one of the administrative departments, even then beginning to increase in numbers and importance, to which most people of my grade and seniority where then appointed. Before leaving Panama with my bride of six months I had recorded in a letter to the Personnel Department a preference for political work in the office, in which I had served only briefly during an attachment in the Consular Department prior to going abroad to perform the general consular functions which had hitherto been my principal specialization.

I heard nothing more until I called on the Personnel Department, then at Carlton House Terrace where I reported hotfoot from Plymouth where the old *Reina del Mar* had brought us home after a delightful honeymoon crossing from Panama. Great was my joy when I was told that I had been appointed to the African Department on probation, that they were very hard-pressed and wanted me soon, that I would probably be allowed to take some of the leave due to me, and that I was to have one day's overlap with my departing predecessor. But first would I go round straight away to call on the head of the African Department in the main Foreign Office block in Downing Street.

My joy was slightly abated when this august official, having greeted me affably, added that he hoped I had enjoyed my leave and would I please start work the following Monday. My feeble references to leave entitlements and house hunting were waved aside. The department needed my services. My predecessor would be gone on Tuesday. I would be dealing with a particularly sensitive area. One of my new colleagues had been away on sick leave for several weeks (He was, unhappily, never to return to his work). The pressures on the department were increasing. The aftermath of Suez had created many problems. The Secretary of State was considering some new initiatives. The whole of Africa was in turmoil. The Prime Minister— In short, leave was out of the question. If I really insisted I could have some later in the year, when things had quietened down a bit. But in the meantime . . . Needless to say I rushed off to give my wife the good news, while contriving to suggest that my company in seeking accommodation in London would be nothing but a hindrance and that I was quite certain she would find suitable quarters for the next three years or so without the benefit of my assistance. So after a penitential lunch at Wheeler's off Jermyn Street I left her (alas, not for the last time) to find a place to live in a strange capital of which she had no previous experience, but where she made enduring friendships among all those who so generously helped her during what was then a difficult time, without the official facilities and assistance now available for the homeless in London.

In the African Department I found myself dealing with the Maghreb countries. This meant that I took all papers and telegrams on Morocco, Algeria, and Tunisia in the first instance, submitting to higher authority those papers I judged to be of sufficient importance together with my comments or a suggested reply if one was required. At the time the African Department dealt with the whole of Africa (including Egypt) except, of course, those bits coloured red on the map which were dealt with by the Colonial Office and, later, the Commonwealth Relations Office. I found that our otherwise traditional departmental third room had six or seven first secretaries employed as desk officers for their respective countries. I was surprised to find so many first secretaries working as desk officers when the assistant Heads of Department (of whom we had two) were themselves of first secretary rank, albeit with longer service and wider experience.

At first I shared a desk in a large room on the first floor of Downing Street with four other colleagues. This was an elegant room with a high ceiling and an open fireplace at one end, for which we were permitted two scuttlefulls of coal a day. The tall windows directly overlooked 10 Downing Street. We each had two telephones on our desks, most of which seemed to me to be ringing incessantly. At irregular intervals an ominous crescendo of metallic thumps and crashes shook the walls of our room and rattled the stacked teacups and saucers on the small table by the main door. This culminated in a loud explosion which heralded the successful transit through a particularly tight corner of a compressed-air tube containing urgent material on its way from the Cabinet Offices or wherever to the News Department on the ground floor of Downing Street immediately beneath us. Sometimes a tube got stuck in our corner and the unseen operators of the vacuum system had to wrestle with the recalcitrant missile to the accompaniment of much throttled wheezing, sharp reports and, finally, lingering metallic sighs.

Messengers kept coming in with variously coloured boxes and tubes which were deposited with a thump on the large central table which also had a rack with pigeonholes for each desk. From time to time someone who was not on the phone would find the departmental bunch of keys, open up the boxes and distribute the papers and telegrams accordingly. If there was something particularly urgent he would bring it straight to the corresponding desk where it would be quickly seen if the occupant was temporarily out of the room. Absences were frequent, mainly because the rest of the department, including its head and two assistants, were inconveniently housed in a suite of rooms upstairs on the second floor of Downing Street. Our Superintending Under-Secretary of State was also on the second floor of Downing Street, but for some reason his office was at the King Charles Street end of the building. When summoned upstairs by our superiors we had considerable distances to cover. It was only after I had been in the department for some weeks that I learned of the existence of a back staircase leading upstairs which much reduced the distance one had to travel. In the fullness of time a new Middle East Department was formed which absorbed those in the African Department who had dealt with Egyptian affairs; we

111

then moved upstairs into the rooms they had vacated, which was a great improvement. In the meantime, I galloped along the corridors and up the stairs several times a day in response to requests from my superiors, who then had to curb their impatience as I stood in front of their desk panting for breath after my exertions and quite unable to speak. It was only after a kindly Assistant Under-Secretary pointed out plaintively that if I stopped running to his office we would both save a lot of time that I learned to linger outside his door until I regained my breath even if the urgency of his telephoned request had caused me to react too impulsively and bolt up the stairs yet again.

In the meantime, I had much cause to appreciate the guidance and advice of several of the more senior members of the third room who took me in hand and showed me how to deal with the unexpected. Most of the time every occupant of the room concentrated on his papers or telephone calls as though from behind invisible walls. It was simply not done to talk to one another across the room while phones were off the hooks or messengers awaited boxes to be dispatched with a red 'Immediate' label. In the morning one made straight for one's desk in apprehensive silence, wondering what might be contained within the box with the 'Immediate' label which sat in the centre of one's desk. When Christopher Audland joined us from Washington six months later he made a welcome break with tradition by bidding everyone good morning when he came in. I found telephone calls particularly disconcerting during the first few days. The disembodied voice at the other end would bark: 'What are we doing about Washington telegram No. 2534?' I could only say that I would find out and call him back, to which reasonable proposal the voice acquiesced with bad grace and rang off before I could ask for his name or number. In particular, Mervyn Brown gave me much valuable advice and instruction during my first months. He was then one of the elder statesmen in the third room, having previously served in Buenos Aires and at the United Nations in New York. He was a gifted musician and a tennis player of repute. Cheerful, personable, and amusing, he was always ready to answer questions, offer advice, or suggest a solution, quite apart from being a mine of information on such things as the shortest route to the office of the Minister of State or to the canteen in the basement of King Charles Street. Almost all had done at least one earlier tour of duty in a political department and were therefore already well equipped with much of the recondite and self-accumulated expertise which rewarded previous service in geographical departments of the Foreign Office and clearly separated the men from the boys. Yet another helpful elder statesman was Francis MacGinnis, a tall, stooping figure with pockets full of pipes and tobacco pouches. He had already served in Washington and Paris. He had appropriated the only armchair in the room and was thus able to receive selected visitors at his desk by the fireplace, while the rest of us had to make do with the overblown settees in the main corridor outside our office.

Lunch was a rather perfunctory meal, sometimes taken at the desk from a packet of sandwiches during the blissful hour or so in which the telephones would stop ringing and telegrams could be drafted in relative peace. Some who felt like a walk or a breath of fresh air took their sandwiches to the park or walked across Whitehall to the Red Lion where a sausage and a glass of beer would keep body and soul together until teatime. It was several weeks before I discovered the existence of a canteen in the basement of the King Charles Street block. It had separate tables with clean white cloths and waitresses in black dresses and white aprons. The main course (fish and chips or sausage and mash) followed by dessert (apple crumble or cheese and biscuits) and coffee were all served at your table and cost two shillings and ninepence. The only problem was finding the canteen in the first place, the lower regions of King Charles Street being a veritable warren of passageways and staircases which led to the most unexpected places. At first I tried following discreetly somebody I knew habitually lunched there, walking great distances along corridors past the dreadful plasterboard cubicles in the Locarno room with its splendid ceiling, through holes in the walls, into the old India Office, past the impressive portraits of maharajas and sultans and down unexpected staircases only to find that my quarry was going out for a breath of fresh air in the park.

One or two of my more senior colleagues in the department were members of a club in Pall Mall. The nearest one was the Travellers', to which Mervyn Brown generously invited me shortly after I joined the department. They used to run a quick, help-yourself lunch room downstairs, with a communal round table in the centre, frequently patronized by several heads of departments and one or two under-secretaries, all always in a hurry. But in the main, club, or restaurant lunches were limited to those red-letter days when a bank or an oil company with a particular interest in a country took the trouble to seek out the desk officer actually responsible for shuffling the relevant papers, rather than the Head of the Department or the Under-Secretary. On these occasions it was permissible to return to your desk long after the normal time, breathing brandy and cigars over everybody, only to be brought back to earth by a reminder that it was time to make the tea (a weekly chore undertaken by all members of the third room in strict rotation) and that we had run out of the favourite chocolate-covered digestive biscuits, which meant going out again to the shop in Parliament Street. The teapot and the kettle had to be replenished from distant water taps and heated on gas rings concealed in unexpected nooks and crannies in corridors and stairwells usually close to the messengers' cubby-holes.

The departmental tea break was something of an occasion, even though it seldom lasted more than fifteen minutes. The Head of Department would come into the third room where the teapot and the chipped teacups and saucers were available on the table by the door. Having splashed some tea and milk into his cup and taken a biscuit he would then address himself in social conversation with the nearest occupant of the room who had been, like all the others, until that moment bent over his desk in studiously silent concentration. This was taken as a general signal to rise and make for the tea table, where the conversation became animated and general though, inevitably, there was a lot of shop. Those of us who at first hovered on the fringes of the group would hear snippets of conversation ranging from gossip about the identity of the next French Ambassador in Washington to the time taken on the train to do that morning's crossword puzzle. The assistant Heads of Department would take the opportunity to return to their originators drafts or telegrams they had approved, adding reminders about the need to copy them to Paris or Tunis or wherever. We would listen with rapt attention to a casual account of an exalted conversation when walking across the park with the Permanent Under-Secretary of State, even though this might be about growing watercress on blotting paper. Someone would reveal that a new arrival called Downing was in Security Department, where he sat across the desk from a man called Street. This was capped by someone who knew both a Marshall and a Snellgrove in United Nations Department, and produced the latest office directory to prove it. Another turned up another section of the office with both a Comfort and a Joy. We concluded that it was all a game played by the Personnel Department. (Some years later, no less than three Halls were all appointed to the same post in South America). A few more desultory remarks and the animation would subside as suddenly as it had begun. The visitors would make for their own rooms and we would return to our respective corners. One or two whose tea had been interrupted by ringing telephones were already bent over their files. As the evening wore on the phone calls became more infrequent, until they fizzled out altogether. But even in those days the lights burned late over Downing Street, although one tried hard to avoid being the last man out if only to avoid the interminable locking-up process. Steel cupboards and filing cabinets were in short supply and our room had one wall lined with shelves with wooden folding doors which had to be shuttered, barred and padlocked in several places before the departmental bunch of keys could be deposited overnight in our combination key box of which the setting was changed at regular intervals. On the mantelpiece above the open fireplace there were copies of the usual out-of-date reference books; a five-year-old *Who's Who*, old Civil Service lists, the Foreign Office list, and a Bible, which last was used mainly the provide the sort of *memoria technica* which enabled us to avoid covertly writing down the combination on the back of driving licences or in the telephone sections of pocket diaries. Dueteronomy, the fifth book of the Old Testament, seemed to be a favourite source of inspiration.

Although the African Department of the Foreign Office was responsible for the formulation of advice to ministers on matters and policies affecting our relations with the countries in our geographical area, I found that there were also many other ministries, departments, committees, working parties and other organizations in Whitehall which had a finger in our pie. It was therefore important to keep closely in touch with them all and inform them how any situation was developing, if only to prevent later objections or surprises. This was achieved by interdepartmental meetings which sometimes took place in the Treasury, the Cabinet Office, or in the offices of the department which had called the meeting in the first place, either because they wished to register an interest or had some development to divulge.

Most of the time, however, information was conveyed and consultation took place on the telephone. I found it essential to compile a personal telephone directory of departments, and names and extension numbers of those officials who were also involved in our affairs and were in a position to help, usually by either giving or getting a quick decision when one was necessary. Every day there were draft telegrams, Parliamentary Questions, position papers, submissions, paragraphs and even sentences which had to be cleared with half a dozen other departments, both inside the Foreign Office and out of it, before papers could be submitted to higher authority and approved for action. As a result it was usual to develop friendly relations with a number of contacts in other Whitehall departments whose amiable but disembodied voices dispensed advice, opinions, and decisions daily over the phone. Sometimes we subsequently attended a meeting where we identified each other with pleasure, like old friends, but usually our telephone contacts sufficed and there was never, in any event, the opportunity to put a face to the voice. Months or years later, having been moved to another job, we parted, on close and cordial telephone terms, without ever having met. It was not long after I joined the department that I discovered the very real importance of the Whitehall telephone network if things had to be done in a hurry and some of the more ponderous machinery circumvented.

Morocco, Tunisia, and Algeria were the countries for which I was responsible in the first instance. Morocco, newly independent and unified in 1956, had sent the Khalifa of the former Spanish zone of Morocco (and a cousin of the King) to the Court of St James's as its first ambassador. Prince Moulay Hassan and his wife, Princess Fatima Zahara, were an engaging and attractive couple with a large embassy in Wilton Crescent which they had partly redecorated in Moroccan style. I first met him when I was called upon to interpret when he called on the Secretary of State. At the time Prince Moulay

Hassan had little English but, having spent most of his life in the former Spanish (northern) zone of Morocco he spoke perfect Spanish with a strong Andalusian accent. It seems that an earlier interpreter provided by the Foreign Office on an even more ceremonial occasion had only recently returned from the Middle East Centre for Arab Studies in the Lebanon, with the result that his ear was as yet unattuned to some of the regional inflections in the westernmost parts of the Arab world. It being known that I spoke Spanish and had also served in Arabic-speaking countries, I was detailed to stand by for the arrival of the Ambassador and escort him to the Secretary of State's waiting room where the assistant Head of my department would be waiting to take part in the meeting. When I received him at the steps in the courtyard, the Ambassador addressed me in Arabic, but after the initial exchange of greetings I firmly steered him into Spanish with all the tact and diplomacy I could muster. To my relief he responded readily and by the time we reached the Ambassadors' waiting room at the end of the corridor, the language in which the ensuing conversation was to be carried out had been clearly established.

The meeting with the Secretary of State passed without incident, but it also served to enable Prince Moulay Hassan to identify somebody in the Foreign Office with whom he could communicate about his embassy's affairs and problems. From that moment until I left the department three years later he frequently called me when he thought I might be able to help, even on matters not directly the concern of the African Department. The Ambassador and his wife became a popular and respected couple in London's political, social, and diplomatic circles. They entertained generously and in considerable style and I was called upon to accompany the Secretary of State on one or two occasions when he attended Moroccan Embassy functions. In order to save time Mr Selwyn Lloyd had the habit of taking off his overcoat and leaving it in his car before entering the premises where a reception or dinner was taking place. This avoided the need for tickets and queues at cloakrooms while a reception line waited to greet the principal guest. As my task was to interpret I could not leave the Secretary of State unattended, so the first time I accompanied him I also disrobed in the car before following him briskly through the ballroom entrance of the Savoy Hotel. Half an hour later I stood politely on the kerb and watched the tail lights of Mr Lloyd's car disappearing down the foggy Embankment with my overcoat neatly folded on the back seat. The next time my wife had also been invited, and we planned to stay later than the Secretary of State. I thought I would therefore keep my overcoat with me and give it to an attendant who might get me a cloakroom ticket in exchange; unfortunately, all were bearing trays with drinks or canapés and my intervention was almost immediately required when the Ambassador engaged Mr Lloyd in conversation and presented several Moroccan personalities who were visiting London for the occasion. I thus had no recourse but to spend the next half-hour with my overcoat draped casually over my left arm. As the Ambassador had told me that he wanted a private word with the Secretary of State before he left, I simply did not dare leave his side. Eventually I spotted my wife at the other end of the room; my furtive signals and grimaces over Mr Lloyd's left shoulder in the intervals in my translating must have distracted several of his interlocutors until I succeeded in shedding my burden.

But there were more weighty matters in the office which kept the lights on in the African Department long after normal hours. The rebellion in Algeria was then at its height, the Front de Libération National waging what was virtually an all-out war against the French forces. In metropolitan France, which had recently seen the granting of independence to its former protectorates in Morocco and Tunisia, there was a strong reaction to the prospect of any further withdrawals from overseas territories. Feelings were running high, and the situation was further exacerbated by the humiliating defeat suffered by the French armed forces at Dien Bien Phu in 1954. Many veterans of the campaigns in what had been French Indochina, including a number of crack parachute units as well as the Foreign Legion, were now fighting in Algeria, and the central Government in Paris was determined to pursue a hard line and put down the rebellion, even at a high cost in human and economic terms. The Algerian independence movement naturally had the sympathy, if not the active support, of the other Arab countries in the area, even though the French claimed, with some justification, that unlike Morocco and Tunisia there had never existed an Algerian nation and that even the Turkish Ottoman rule in the sixteenth century had been largely nominal. French colonists had settled and developed the northern provinces of the country, which had become part of metropolitan France in the nineteenth century. They were determined to stay; the armed forces were equally determined to win by fair means or foul, and popular opinion in France was solidly behind them. The FLN guerrilla forces were mainly active in the country districts and the inland mountainous regions, areas inhabited by the Kabyles and the Berbers who had for long continued the war against the French after the coastal plains had been settled.

One of the French Government's principal preoccupations was to prevent weapons reaching the FLN who largely depended for arms and ammunition on what they could raid from the French army posts and supply convoys they ambushed. In their perpetual hide-and-seek with the French forces the FLN frequently took refuge across the border of the two limitrophe countries, and there had already been incidents on both the Tunisian and Moroccan borders in which French troops entered non-Algerian territory while in hot pursuit of FLN guerrillas. The French were well aware of the sensitivity of the newly independent former French protectorates on both sides of their war zone, but insisted that the Tunisians and Moroccans should at all times deny sanctuary to FLN forces which might otherwise feel free to mount raids and operations against French forces in Algeria from bases secure in Moroccan or Tunisian territory. All this gave rise to a complex situation with far-reaching implications which were considered at the highest levels in the Foreign Office.

The Tunisian Government in particular felt very vulnerable. The French claimed that the FLN had actually established a number of training camps in the desert just within the Tunisian frontier with Algeria. The Tunisians at the time had an ill-equipped fledgling army with obsolete weapons and a few left-over museum pieces of French artillery. They were greatly outnumbered by the better armed and trained FLN forces whose incursions from Tunisian bases the French had complained about. The Tunisians were hardly in a position to control the borders of their own country, and feared that if things got worse either the French or the FLN would virtually take over parts of Tunisia. They asked the French for modern weapons with which to arm their soldiers and control their frontiers. The French declined, on the grounds that any weapons sent to the Tunisians would find their way into the hands of the FLN. The Tunisian Government then turned to us.

The issues were clear cut. The Tunisians needed arms to prevent the escalation of an unstable and potentially dangerous situation, not of their own making and over which they had no control. The French were totally opposed to the prospect of facilitating the procurement of modern weapons by the FLN (as they put it) via Tunisia. For our part we were concerned to maintain the principle that arms could be purchased from Western countries in reasonable quantities where there was a genuine need. The Tunisians had made it clear that if we refused they would take their shopping list elsewhere, and we were anxious to avoid any excuse for the introduction of Eastern bloc experts, advisers, or weapons in such a sensitive area. Our conditions were uncomplicated. There was to be no military aid, no soft loans, no credit terms, no government-to-government assistance. The initial shopping list was modest: the Tunisians wanted Sterling sub-machine-guns, which were then the last word in personal automatic weaponry. The UK manufacturers were in a position to supply against payment in cash, and the British Government's role would be limited simply to the grant of the corresponding export licence. These terms had been conveyed to the Tunisian Government by the British Ambassador in Tunis. It was on this basis that the arguments for and against were comprehensively analysed, the corresponding recommendations drafted and the policy considerations submitted to ministers for approval. Throughout this period the French Government raised the strongest possible objections; our ambassador in Paris intervened at the highest levels and our departmental submissions and arguments had to overcome the objections and counter-arguments of all those departments in Whitehall which were intent on not disrupting our good relations with the French Government at the time.

One of the two assistant heads of the African Department was Howard Smith. Under his supervision I had been heavily engaged throughout this period in the preparation of the relevant drafts and submissions, which I then delivered hotfoot along the corridors and up and down the staircases to the offices of under-secretaries, ministers of state and private secretaries to the Secretary of State himself. At the same time I was also carefully making all the detailed arrangements for the physical delivery of the weapons. I had been in touch with the manufacturers of the Sterling machine-guns and these were now crated and ready for delivery to the RAF at Lyneham, where a transport aircraft was fuelled up and ready to take off for Tunis as soon as we got the green light. I had a pro-forma invoice for the sub-machine-guns on my desk. The price and conditions had been conveyed to the Tunisian authorities who had expressed their gratitude and raised no objections. The last fulminations from Paris had been overruled. As a gesture of good faith we had agreed to give the French the serial numbers of the weapons, so that they would know if they found any on captured FLN prisoners, and we had so informed the Tunisians. There seemed to be no loose ends anywhere; I had the name, rank and telephone number of the RAF duty officer at Lyneham so that the aircraft could take off the moment we gave the signal. It was then that my troubles began.

When I got to the office the following morning Howard greeted me with an advance copy of a telegram from Tunis. Although one of the last to leave at night, he was always first in the department in the mornings. No matter how early I arrived he was always there before me. He was one of those who daily completed *The Times* crossword puzzle in record time long before his arrival. He supervised the work of five or six desk officers and his burden was considerable, but he was always accessible and ready with guidance and advice. He was then in his late thirties, of medium height, usually with an unruly lock of hair over his forehead and normally dressed in the sombre black coat and striped trousers then customary in the Foreign Office. He was patient and quietly spoken, with a ready smile and, when amused by something, an infectious giggle. He had a reputation for being a gifted mathematician and having a prodigious memory. No drafting slip or wrong reference escaped his scrutiny; his neat left-handed writing invariably added to my drafts anything I had omitted. No superfluous sentence, word, or even comma passed unchallenged. Any draft he approved without alteration was regarded as a measure of excellence by the originator. Some achieved this as a matter of routine; those of us who more frequently failed benefited from the exercise. He usually had a pipe between his teeth and also smoked cigarettes, but he was then trying hard to give up smoking. Thus he would some days bring no tobacco or cigarettes to the office, where he resisted temptation until it became irresistible after lunch when, if the pressure of paper had prevented me from leaving my desk, he would search me out in my corner of an otherwise empty room and ask me for a cigarette with a straight face. I found this an engaging human frailty in such an otherwise formidably efficient perfectionist.

The telegram from Tunis reported a request from the Tunisian Government for an additional supply of rifles and ammunition. Having got agreement for the Sterling sub-machine-guns they had reconsidered their requirements and felt that their purchase should be complemented by an adequate supply of less sophisticated weapons. After further discussion within Whitehall, consultations with all concerned, and more submissions to the Secretary of State, it as agreed to maintain the principle established by the earlier decision to supply weapons to Tunisia and to comply also with the new request.

In the meantime I was trying hard through my telephone network to find out who had any spare rifles and ammunition. My first call to the War Office drew a blank. The army had no spare rifles available, although they did say that if I found any of the appropriate model, they might be able to provide some of the ammunition. My friends in the Air Ministry could not help either, but as an afterthought they said that if I wanted them and the eventual rifles were of a suitable type, I could have any number of bayonets an scabbards, of which they had a large quantity surplus to requirements. Surprisingly, it was the Admiralty which was able to oblige. They said they had plenty of second-hand rifles available but, alas, no ammunition. I quickly made a deal for the modest quantity of rifles we had decided to supply and obtained what I thought was a reasonable price per unit. No sooner had I put the phone down but the War Office rang through to say they also had a quantity of new webbing shoulder slings they would be glad to make available. After several hours on the phone I as able to make up a package consisting of rifles from the Admiralty, 9 mm ammunition from the War Office, bayonets and scabbards from the Air Ministry and, finally, brand new webbing slings from the War Office again. The prices quoted were so many pounds, shillings, and pence for every thousand rounds of ammunition; so many pounds per unit/rifle; a special offer for the job lot of bayonets and scabbards, and, for the sake of variety, the War Office quoted a figure for each unit/parcel containing a dozen webbing slings.

I had carefully noted on separate sheets of paper the number of items, figures and quantities corresponding to each ministry. After clearing my lines in the office I quickly made arrangements to have the lot packed and crated and delivered to the RAF at Lyneham, to join the Sterlings already loaded on the waiting aircraft. Having got agreement at the highest level for the token shipment of arms for Tunisia we were anxious to get the aircraft off and away, before anybody raised new objections or had second thoughts. Our intention was to present the bill for the shipment of weapons as soon as possible after their delivery, and my calculations of pounds, shillings, and pence for the different items and different ministries by now covered my desk, one or two adjacent tables, and part of the floor. The pocket calculator not having been invented I had no recourse but to do my sums the old-fashioned way, though admittedly with the aid of one of the admirable Post Office ready reckoners containing tables of the multiples of pounds, shillings, and pence, halfpennies and farthings which I had thoughtfully borrowed from a friend in Finance Department. When I finally reduced my figures to a single sum I drafted the corresponding telegram to the Ambassador in Tunis requiring him to obtain full payment as soon as possible after delivery. I submitted my draft to Howard Smith in the customary way and, feeling I had something to celebrate, went down to the canteen in the basement for my first lunch in a week. I was half-way through my sausages and mash when I saw Howard making his way through the tables towards me. The final green light had been given, Paris and Washington had been informed. The Private Office (the holy of holies where the Private Secretaries to the Secretary of State toiled and troubled) had just been on the phone and the aircraft could take off.

It was about 2.15 p.m., a time when many people are away from their desks, however briefly. My normal contact at Lyneham was unavailable, and his assistant did not reply, but

I got through to the station duty officer, who said he would find the pilot and crew straight away. I begged him to get them and the aircraft off the ground without delay and to let me know immediately the estimated time of arrival in Tunis. I put down the phone nervously and began drafting another telegram. To my relief the phone rang a few minutes later to confirm that the aircraft was airborne. But the preflight briefing had thrown up a small point. The load had been increased since the original arrangements had been made. The aircraft's fuel capacity and operational range had been reduced and it would have to refuel somewhere on the way. How about putting down at Marseilles? With their customary efficiency the RAF managed to re-route the aircraft in mid-air in order to avoid French air space altogether and refuel in another country. It was clearly best not to risk the possibility that aircraft and cargo might be confiscated within French jurisdiction. In the event the plane landed in Tunis without mishap, the crates were unloaded, the Tunisians were delighted, and our ambassador was instructed the following day to present the bill I had worked out for the combined package. Cash on delivery, as agreed.

After a couple of days' silence the telegram we had been expecting arrived. It explained that Tunisia was still in the franc zone, that its reserves of foreign exchange were limited, that there was clearly no hope of releasing French reserves for this particular payment; and that with the best will in the world there was no prospect of paying the full amount. Would we therefore accept a down payment of 10 per cent straight away, the balance to be paid on mutually agreed terms over a reasonable period of time? None of this came as much of a surprise to us. We had known about the depleted foreign exchange reserves, the franc zone arrangements, and the economic situation, and had for some time been expecting a request for soft terms. But it was important to maintain the principle we had established. All we had undertaken was to permit the purchase of arms from UK sources in the face of French refusals to supply. The terms of the transaction had been clearly explained to all concerned. These could not be changed unilaterally after the event. We therefore regretted . . . etc . . . etc. I was settling down to draft a telegram to the Ambassador in Tunis when Howard walked into the room. He had a sheaf of papers in his hand and a pipe between his teeth. 'Let's have a look at some of these figures, shall we? Bring your papers into my room.'

I followed clutching my bundle of files with my sums and multiplications for ammunition, scabbards, rifles, Sterlings, and all. A few minutes later my scribbled, much corrected totals had been reduced to some semblance of order. I watched with admiration as the numbers were set out systematically into neat columns which were divided, multiplied and added up with consummate ease. As subtotal followed subtotal I began to realize with increasing apprehension that there was something very wrong with my original calculations. 'It rather looks as though you've got an extra nought in somewhere along the line,' said Howard, mildly. 'I think you've charged the Tunisians ten times the actual cost of the shipment.' I was horrified to see the neat rows of figures which left no doubt about my mistake. But I was given little time to marshall my addled thinking. 'Let's send this off to Tunis straight away,' he added, pointing to a short telegram which I noticed for the first time already drafted on the table in front of me. This offered sympathy and understanding for Tunisia's difficulties, promised our unfailing support at all times and tendered our apologies for a clerical error in the earlier telegram which had unintentionally increased tenfold the price of the weapons. In the circumstances there was clearly no need for deferred terms and we would gladly accept the ten per cent down payment already proffered in full and final settlement for the whole shipment.

I sent off the telegram to Tunis and sat back to await reactions with some misgivings. After all, our exchanges of telegrams on this particular subject were customarily given a wide circulation in Whitehall because of the many departments involved in the operation, and I did not have to wait long before getting the first ribald phone call from one of my friends in the Air Ministry. 'It's Siberia for your next post, my lad,' the voice at the other end chuckled insensitively. 'What's the equivalent of a court martial in the Foreign Office?' I sat biting my fingernails for two days but nothing happened. On the evening of the third day a telegram from Tunis was handed to me by an expressionless Howard. It reported that the Ambassador's explanations, conveyed at the highest level, had been received with courteous attention and increasingly respectful silence. The Ambassador's disclaimers and apologies had been brushed aside in polite disbelief. Without rancour, his interlocutor had said that his opinion and regard for Britain's traditional diplomatic skills had always been high, but there were levels of excellence which none could surpass and would always remain beyond compare. The telegram added that a Tunisian treasury draft for the full amount due would follow in the next bag.

Weeks followed days and the excitement and speculation about my little saga gradually subsided to be overtaken and submerged by succeeding waves of telegrams and drafts on other issues of the moment. I had half expected to be carpeted for my carelessness, and confided that I had not even been reprimanded when one day I met one of my friends from the Admiralty lunching in the Treasury canteen. 'Reprimanded?' he said, 'What d'you mean, reprimanded?' He laughed. 'Don't you know that your boss spotted the mistake in the first telegram and deliberately let it go?'

Curiously, my first, rather oblique, contact with Peru took place while I was in the African Department. Apart from the fact that I had a sister-in-law who then lived in Lima with her American husband, I knew little of the country which many years later was to provide me with one of the more stimulating and challenging of my professional experiences. One morning I had a phone call from the Personnel Department. The voice at the other end said that President Manuel Prado of Peru was paying an official visit to Britain and would be offered dinner by the Prime Minister the following evening. The Prime Minister had no Spanish. Would I please be at number 10 Downing Street at 8.00 p.m. for 8.15 p.m. and make myself available to interpret between President and Prime Minister. Oh, and by the way, white tie and tails please, even though I would not be expected to sit at the table. My place would be in a small chair between but behind the Prime Minister and President. So perhaps I'd better have something to eat beforehand. OK?

At lunch-time I raced up to Moss Bros in Covent Garden, where I was competently fitted out with everything down to the last collar stud. I took the bandbox back to the office where I opened it just enough to reveal interesting glimpses of satin lapels and starched shirt-fronts. To any enquiries thus provoked I replied casually that I had been asked to attend a dinner at Number 10 the following evening, which was true, but not quite as it turned out. That night I took my box home, where I wanted my wife to check that everything was in order. The following morning, instead of taking my usual Circle Line underground, I decided to drive in my car to the Foreign Office, as I would not be free until late that night. In those days we habitually drove through Downing Street and into the main courtyard of the Foreign Office where I parked my car. There was a gentlemen's agreement that one half of the courtyard was ours and the other the Commonwealth Relations Office's, but all cars were parked there without permits, prior checks, or other hindrances, and there was always plenty of space. The only reserved parking places were on the Foreign Office Green (facing St James's Park) for heads of department and under-secretaries. They were also authorized to use the small entrance door on the corner, known as the ambassadors' entrance. The Whitehall turning into Downing Street was open and unguarded. Depending on the weather, most mornings there would be half a dozen sightseers (more in the summer months) watching the people who came in and out of Number 10, including the milkman. A solitary policeman paced methodically from the Foreign Office Green steps to the Whitehall end of Downing Street and back. In the middle of the group of sightseers there was a middle-aged man with long grey hair and a large grey beard. Every morning, come rain or shine, he would be kneeling on the pavement on our side of the road facing Number 10. His lips moved constantly and he seemed to be praying devoutly. Nobody knew who he was. By the time I looked out of my office windows overlooking Downing Street after the first telegram distribution an hour later, the sightseers had increased and the kneeling gentleman had gone.

That afternoon we had some sort of a crisis in the Ogaden or the Horn of Africa or the Katanga pedicle, none of which had anything to do with me. Providentially, one or two other members of the department stayed very late; when I adjourned in good time to one of the gents' lavatories in the corridor to change into my evening finery I found that I could not tie the bow in my white tie. Looking apprehensively at my watch I rushed back into our room where I was relieved to find David Mitchell with a telephone at each ear, drafting telegrams with both hands. He was a quiet, balding, softly spoken Scot, clearly more experienced than most of us. With effortless confidence he deftly and smartly did up my bow tie while the affairs of the Katanga pedicle (or whatever) were momentarily relegated. In my white tie I ran down to the front hall, past the messengers at the desk and out to Downing Street where I walked across to the unguarded door of Number 10 and rang the bell just as Big Ben struck eight.

The door was opened by a gentleman in a blue suit with crowns on the lapels. I gave him my name, said I was from the Foreign Office, and that I had come to interpret for the Prime Minister. He asked me to wait a moment, left me alone in the red-carpeted hall and came back after a few minutes with a tall good-looking man in evening dress who said he was Tim Bligh, the Prime Minister's Private Secretary, and shook me warmly by the hand. He added that it was very good of me to come and invited me up to the first floor to meet the Prime Minister. I followed him up the stairs with the portraits on the wall into a large drawing-room where, standing close to the entrance reading some notes through his glasses, stood Mr Harold Macmillan, resplendent in white tie and many decorations. Tim Bligh walked up to him and interrupted his reading to introduce me. Mr Macmillan took off his glasses, folded and pocketed his notes, looked down at me with his hooded eyes and shook my hand with the limp handshake (caused by one of his war wounds) which was to become famous. He also said that it was very good of me to come. Turning to an attentive waiter with a tray of drinks he waved vaguely in my direction. He then pulled at his watch-chain, looked at his pocket watch, and addressed me again, murmuring that they should be appearing any minute. While I made myself scarce with my drink other people began to arrive and greet the Prime Minister. There were ladies wearing tiaras and most of the men seemed to have orders and medals. A few minutes later President Prado and his entourage came up the stairs preceeded by Tim Bligh who seemed to be making signals of some sort in my direction. As I moved forward to do my stuff President Prado, also beribboned and much bemedalled, paused in the doorway and, with a cordial smile and both hands extended, walked in to greet the Prime Minister effusively. In French.

I stayed in the African Department for nearly three years. In the normal course of events several of my colleagues who had been there when I first joined it were moved or posted abroad, to be replaced by new arrivals; thus it became my turn to indoctrinate some of the new boys into the mysteries of locking up in the evening and looking up the right verse of Deuteronomy in the mornings. James Craig joined us in May 1958 from the Middle East Centre for Arab Studies, where he had been principal instructor. He was a gifted Arabic scholar who had been enticed by the Foreign Office away from a promising academic career to teach Arabic at MECAS, then functioning in the pleasant village of Shemlan, in the hills above Beirut in the Lebanon. After a spell teaching Arabic and Islamic history to the students he had been smoothly translated into the Foreign Service and eventually came home to roost in the African Department, where he was to be initiated into the more specialized aspects of political work in Whitehall, with the concomitant drafts, ideal minutes, records of conversations, *tours d'horizon*, telegram distributions, and flagged submissions.

In those days there were no introductory courses (other than on security) for those serving in geographical departments for the first time. But there was the departmental order book, a slim volume setting out those basic principles considered necessary for the proper submission of papers to higher authority, with a few pages of advice on the use of plain English (never use 'regarding' instead of 'about', and eschew jargon). There were also notes on the more esoteric intricacies of 'flagging' references in: for instance, draft replies to Parliamentary Questions or submissions to ministers (the bottom of the cardboard flag to be behind the top of the paper it was attached to, and the pin used to fasten the two always with the point buried in between). Departments had been known to have submissions returned with an icy annotation (on an 'ephemeral slip') requiring the papers to be submitted in 'the proper manner' – perhaps because the top of the file was bristling with uninterred pin points which had drawn blood from an exasperated Under-Secretary of State. Other departments had their submissions returned by the Private Office simply because there were too many flagged references. Although a solicitous Stationery Office supplied departments with the red-lettered tabs which went through the alphabet from *A* to *Z*, references beyond flag *D* on submissions were frowned upon, and anyone finding it necessary to refer to flag *G* was usually asked to reconstruct his draft. It also happened that flags *A* to *F* neatly took up the whole of the available space (beginning from right to left) at the top of a page of foolscap (pins and all) and life became altogether too complicated if one had to start a second row of flags.

In the meantime, James Craig's wholly exceptional knowledge of the Arabic language and Islamic history, his experience and background, his knowledge of Latin and classical Greek, together with his well-rooted academic interest in etymology and phonetics, lent our department an exotic touch of distinction, made the more manifest when swarthy oriental gentlemen began to queue up to see him in the passage or take him out to lunch. I remember that his lively intellectual curiosity led him to question the then current use of French expressions for certain conventional diplomatic exchanges; years before it became standard practice to do so, he preferred to use less precious English phrases, and was indignant when more pedantic colleagues abandoned plain English for whatever elegant gallicism was traditionally *de rigueur* for the particular situation. It was not long before our departmental tea break conversations, which had previously ranged widely over ships and shoes and sealing wax (in daily use at the time), sometimes acquired a tutorial flavour, with much talk of labial fricatives, glottal stops and palatal sibilants, if there really be such things. He was sometimes intrigued by my kitchen Arabic colloquialisms from the Persian Gulf, an area he had not yet visited. As the only other member of the department with Middle Eastern experience, I used to boast about the real 'unspoilt Arabs of the desert', a phrase then much in vogue among the young, starry-eyed, would-be Lawrences of Arabia then being produced in increasing quantities by the very centre for Arab studies over which James had presided. Tuition at the centre for a year (lower standard examination) or eighteen months' (intermediate) included the long break, during which candidates hoping for a career in the Arab world were encouraged to get away from the fleshpots of the Lebanon and visit such of the more remote parts of the Islamic world as were accessible on the limited funds made available. In the early 1950s the stories about the journeys in the long break sometimes achieved epic proportions. One unsubstantiated report had an enterprising Foreign Office student travelling through most countries in the Middle East and central Asia before being repatriated as a distressed British subject to Shemlan from Singapore; another, perhaps with even greater enterprise, spent the whole of his break in a nightclub in Beirut and was incensed when his claim to have been studying local customs in depth was rejected by the authorities. I know that one of the two attained high rank in the service, but I could never remember which.

I must have been an awful bore with my stories of the fearsome Muharram processions in Bahrain and my anecdotes of other occasions and personalities in the Gulf. These were all calculated to flaunt my acquaintance with those parts of the Arab world in which there was then virtually no Foreign Office tradition of service. As other members of the department moved on, my assurance and aplomb had grown with the passage of time. On those occasions when we shared a table in one of the Whitehall canteens I could usually engage the attention of my more tolerant colleagues by a careless reference to the Buraimi oasis; or to the propensity of the Saudi Governor of the Eastern Provinces to decree the chopping off of a hand or, more occasionally, a head. With little prompting I spoke about my experiences when acting as Political Officer in Qatar or, even more exotically, as an assistant Judge of the Court in Bahrain, this last a card few of my interlocutors were then able to trump. When, in the fullness of time, I called on my former department while on leave from Baghdad, I found James still there, by then the third room's elder statesman. But his undisguised pleasure, as well as the brand-new ceremonial sword and elastic-sided, patent-leather boots casually displayed among the files and papers on his table, all heralded his forthcoming appointment as Political Agent in Dubai, deep in the 'real' Arab world.

Years later we met in the office from time to time. Our geographical paths had diverged widely and we never again served together anywhere. We both recalled our time in the African Department and the manner in which one was encouraged to became an instant expert overnight, having been dropped in at the deep end and not only being expected to swim but to match existing records in terms of both speed and endurance. We shook our greying heads and grudgingly concluded that there should have been an easier way, but that, having survived the experience (some, alas, did not), we had benefited from the process and emerged as wiser and worthier citizens. I certainly felt a sense of achievement when, having for some time been the oldest inhabitant of the departmental third room, I was promoted and transferred to Baghdad in 1960.

PART

3

Only the insane take themselves quite seriously.
Lord David Cecil, *Max* (1964)

8

Mexico, 1973–1975

Early in 1973, after three and a half busy years promoting British exports as Commercial Counsellor in Italy, I heard that I had been appointed Consul General in São Paulo, Brazil, where we were about to initiate a major export drive which would include an ambitious British industrial exhibition and fair, with all the concomitant missions and ministerial and other visits.

I received this news with mixed feelings. I had for years been putting Mexico at the top of my list of posts where I wanted to serve. I was disappointed (again) at not going to Mexico City and had also been looking forward to a change from commercial work which in Italy, a major and sophisticated market within our 'area of concentration', had been challenging and enjoyable, but also taxing and exhausting (mainly as a result of complex arrangements which had the Commercial Counsellor of the embassy in Rome sitting with most of his staff in the office of the Consul General in Milan, with one foot in Rome and another in the rest of Italy). These hybrid arrangements were intended to reflect the realities of commercial, financial, and industrial life in Italy, but in practice it was not always possible to be in the right place all the time, and the arrangements called for a great deal of forbearance on the part of the Ambassador in Rome, the Consul General in Milan, and many others concerned. But despite my initial reservations about São Paulo I was pleased with the prospect of getting my own post, particularly in such a large, economically and industrially significant city, in what must be one of the most fascinating countries in the world. I found myself a number of books on Brazil and São Paulo and started my reading on the subjects which were to concern me in my next job.

Three weeks later I went to London on business and while there ran into George Hall, a friend and colleague whose career abroad had been spent mainly in Latin America. His first post had been Mexico City where he remained an unusually long time, having arrived as a Third Secretary and not left until five years later as a First Secretary. He had subsequently served in London and in Lima, and had most recently completed a tour of duty in Lisbon. He spoke Portuguese and Spanish fluently. I thought he looked a little glum, and when I asked him whither he was bound he confided that he had been chosen for the post of Counsellor and deputy Head of Mission in Mexico City but that, having already spent five years there, he had asked to be excused. In those days this was not a step to be undertaken lightly and he was, understandably, worried about the consequences of his decision. He knew that I had for long wanted to go to Mexico and asked me casually how much longer I was due to stay in Italy; whereupon I, in turn, confided that I was bound for São Paulo. At that stage, the same thought clearly entered our heads and we eyed each other with renewed interest. The following day I was called out of a meeting and asked to get in touch with the Personnel Department straight away. Not unexpectedly, I was told that if I wanted Mexico City instead of São Paulo, now was my chance; but the original arrangements would stand if I preferred São Paulo. Could I reply yesterday, please?

What a decision to have to make. Hitherto I had simply been told where I was going. For the first time I had been offered a choice, and between two highly desirable posts. I called my wife on the phone and after an expensive international consultation we decided on Mexico. I dutifully conveyed our preference to the Foreign Office before leaving London the following day, and my friend was immediately and formally appointed Consul General in São Paulo. Back in Italy I waited for a couple of weeks while making a new choice of books to read on Mexico until, no longer able to bear the suspense, I rang London for news. I was then told that the embassy in Mexico City could not wait until I was released from Italy. Somebody else would have to go sooner. Pity about that, but not to worry; I was now bound for Washington. Reflecting soberly on the results of my attempt to interfere with destiny, I looked up the Washington Embassy list where I found no less than twenty-two counsellors on the staff, where each 'shadowed' a Whitehall department in liaison with the US authorities. My job was to be Latin American affairs. In a chastened mood I decided to wait before again changing my reading list. A week or two later, however, a phone call from London told me that Mexico City was back on the cards and that Washington had too many counsellors anyway. The Ambassador in Mexico City had been prevailed upon to wait, even though he had already been without a deputy for several months, there were other transfers and replacements pending and a heavy programme of visits and other commitments was in the offing. Feeling by this time rather insecure, I went back to my Mexican reading, having been transferred from Italy to Brazil, then to Mexico, then to Washington and back to Mexico City all within the space of a month.

All travellers in Mexico have found it a beautiful country of many contrasts, and I was no exception. Mexico has also been the subject of countless books which also reveal something of the manner in which the country, its history, and its people have fascinated numerous gifted writers. My reading list included books by Mexican authors who were themselves as conscious as any others of the contradictions and paradoxes which are such notable features of modern Mexico and its collective character. This narrative does not aspire to emulate any of those who have written so perceptively and comprehensively on different periods of Mexican history, Mexican culture and customs or, most complex and varied of all, the Mexican people. But I cannot avoid offering some personal observations, if only to illustrate something of the situation in which I found myself operating after my arrival in June 1973, long before anybody dreamt that thriving, dynamic, democratic, oil-rich, colourful, and exciting Mexico would ever have to renegotiate the loans which foreign bankers were then queuing up to offer.

The President of Mexico had made a highly successful state visit to Britain earlier in the year and the political momentum generated by his visit over a wide field was considerable. Bilateral economic and commercial relations were increasing notably; new investment and financial agreements had been announced; technical co-operation had been augmented; cultural exchanges were multiplying in both directions; additional scholarships had been created. There were also, of course, many important personalities who had accepted the invitations generously made by the President while in Britain. The first of these was only a few weeks away. The Lord Mayor of London, institutionally a frequent visitor to countries in Latin America during his crowded year in office, was due to arrive in August. The Ambassador told me that one of my first tasks was to initiate the planning for the Lord Mayor's official visit. This gave me the opportunity to acquire experience in the working methods of our Mexican hosts, which was to stand me in good stead in the many visits which were to follow, and which culminated memorably and spectacularly with the state visit by the Queen and the Duke of Edinburgh in February 1975.

Mexico City, then already a vast and sprawling, almost uncontrollable, megatropolis with a population then estimated at between eight and ten million, was a federal district presided over by a *Regente* (a historic Spanish denomination for the ruler of the capital), who had the rank of a minister in the Government and the biggest headache in the cabinet. I called on him soon after my arrival and was surprised when invited to his office at 9.30 am. When I arrived he had clearly been at his desk for some time. He received me with the natural courtesy which was such a notable feature of high-ranking Mexican officialdom and, after concluding our immediate business on the Lord Mayor's forthcoming visit, he asked me about myself; how long I had been in Mexico, where I had served before, and so forth. Encouraged by his manner I asked him about his job and how he coped with the impossible task of managing and administering the federal capital's unending problems. New housing, drainage, road and rail schemes were announced daily, the demands of new traffic and transport were unceasing, the population pressures even then almost unmanageable. The *Regente* sighed gently and thought for a moment. Then he got up and went to a door on the far wall behind his desk. He invited me to see a bare, small, monastic room, with an as yet unmade bed, on which he had clearly slept the previous night. There was also a small bathroom with a shower. 'I seldom go home at night,' he confessed, with a smile, 'and some evenings I feel there is not enough time. But the next day I am inspired and encouraged while I shave and look out of that window and I remember that, every morning, there are ten thousand more Mexicans living in Mexico City.'

Like Greater London, Mexico City had many district councils and mayors. It was decided that the Lord Mayor's formal host in Mexico should be the Mayor of Cuauhtémoc, a district named after the last of the Aztec emperors, whose statue graced one of the intersections in the Paseo de la Reforma. The district of Cuauhtémoc was also that part of Mexico City in which the offices of the British Embassy were situated, in a busy and crowded part of the city just off the Paseo de la Reforma. Our premises occupied what had been the town house of Sir Weetman Pearson, later the first Lord Cowdray, whose splendid full-sized portrait still adorned the wall of the first landing of the staircase in the tiled main hall. The detailed planning for the Lord Mayor's visit was accordingly arranged, less monastically, with the official who was government delegate (equivalent to mayor) for the district of Cuauhtémoc. When I rang for an appointment I was invited to lunch, in order best to discuss the arrangements in peace and privacy. My host suggested a fashionable restaurant in the trendy Zona Rosa district. On the phone he gave me the address of the restaurant and told me to ask for his table. Would three o'clock be too soon for me? Good. He much looked forward to meeting me.

I had already heard something of Mexican working lunches. In fact, most Mexican meals, although always delicious and varied, provided me with serious problems, mainly in gaining access to my office during any part of the day in which it was possible to communicate with London. In Mexico City we were on the wrong side of the clock; while telegrams from London always reached us during office hours, we only had until 11.00 a.m. to answer London's queries before Whitehall closed down for the day. As most Mexican public offices were not manned until 10.30 a.m. at the earliest, our difficulties were compounded by local practice and conditions. Sometimes I also attended working breakfasts (a useful American custom) which sometimes lasted until 10.30 or 11.00 a.m. As Mexican business lunches frequently finished at 6.00 or 7.00 p.m. my difficulties in getting to the office at all become clear. When Robert Stimson became the Commercial Secretary at the Embassy he held the record for a business lunch, which lasted nine hours. Mexican politicians and bureaucrats worked late into the night, and European-style cocktail parties and dinners were not popular, but after my first few months in Mexico I was sometimes invited by Mexican officials for an evening meal – at 11.00 p.m., please, or on one or two memorable occasions, even later. Hence the late start in the mornings.

When I reached the restaurant, I was shown to my host's table and invited to have a drink while I waited. He had just telephoned to say that he had been detained for a few minutes. When he arrived I was immediately taken by his character and manner. Lic. Delfín Sanchez Juàrez was a genial and colourful personality who was descended on his mother's side from Benito Juarez, the pure-blooded Zapotec born in Oaxaca in 1806 who graduated as a bachelor of law, drafted the new Mexican constitution which disestablished the Catholic Church in 1857, became President of Mexico in 1861, and ordered the execution of Maximilian of Austria, briefly Emperor of Mexico, after Napoleon III's ill-advised and sterile military intervention in Mexico.

Lic. Sanchez Juárez was a good-looking man, of heavy build, with a full head of dark hair, rimless glasses, and a moustache. He insisted that we should have another aperitif, and began outlining his ideas for the programme methodically and in some detail. 'My dear minister,' he said to me (the incumbent of my job being known locally as minister-counsellor), 'this is no ordinary visit. We must do everything the English way.' He called for the menu at about 4.00 p.m. and asked for further refreshments while I went through the unfamiliar dishes and made my choice under my host's knowledgeable guidance. The orders were taken half an hour later and the exquisite meal was served shortly after. During our conversation over coffee and liqueurs I discovered that in the course of a full and rewarding political career Lic. Sanchez had been Mexican Ambassador to one or two countries in Europe before being appointed mayor of Cuauhtémoc. He was also, providentially, chairman of the National Federation of Charros, in which capacity he was to provide one of the highlights in the programme for the Lord Mayor's visit. At about 6.30 p.m. I went reeling back to my office to compose a telegram with the outline programme which would not be on desks in London until the following afternoon.

This was the first of many working meetings until, the first week in August, the visitors arrived. Lord Mais, then Lord Mayor of London, was declared a guest of honour by the Consultative Council of Mexico City and was given formal lunches by the President, the *Regente* and other officials including the Minister of Foreign Affairs. The Lord Mayor and his party, which included a sheriff and an alderman, the Chief Commoner, their respective wives, and the Swordbearer, visited a number of archaeological remains in and around the city, including the ruins at Teotihuacán and other historical pre-Columbian sites in the company of the state governor. They were taken up in a helicopter for a bird's-eye view of the federal capital and its unending problems, and shown some of the ambitious public works schemes then nearing completion in Mexico City, including the imaginative and spectacular deep-drainage engineering project and the new underground railway. But there was no doubt that one of the most colourful and unmistakably Mexican occasions was provided by the display organized by the National Federation of Charros, under Sr. Sanchez Juárez's personal supervision.

At the Ambassador's behest I had striven to make certain that the programme included nothing, in the exciting displays of cattle-handling and horsemanship, which might cause embarrassment to the visitors. With all the tact and diplomatic skills that I could muster I explained to a bemused Delfin Sanchez Juárez that we had no objection to any of the riders being maimed by wild horses, gored by maddened bulls, kicked by bucking cows or trampled underfoot by stampeding cattle; but it was essential to ensure that none of the animals were hurt. There were bodies of public opinion in the United Kingdom which might be pained to see photographs of a Lord Mayor of London, in a wide-brimmed Mexican hat, applauding enthusiastically while a splendidly attired Mexican *charro* leant from his galloping horse, grasped a fleeing cow by the tail and, with a dexterous twist of his muscular wrist, deftly threw it on its back before bringing his horse to an instant standstill on its haunches while leaping off to kneel on the unhappy cow in a blur of dust and fast, graceful action. In the event Sr. Sanchez Juárez, with some difficulty, persuaded the members of his Federation to arrange what he afterwards called a 'sanitized' spectacle, which subsequently set the pattern for the benefit of all visitors from Britain.

On the great day, a sunny morning on the first Sunday (5 August) following the Lord Mayor's arrival, we all trooped to the Rancho Grande de la Villa which housed the *lienzo*, a sort of open-ended bullring, where the display was to take place. It was, as are most public spectacles in Mexico, a gloriously colourful, exciting, and happy occasion, with brass bands and Mexican *mariachis* in full cry, and richly accoutred horses with ornate silver-studded saddles and bemedalled bridles and martingales, ridden by strikingly dressed horsemen with broad Mexican hats, embossed belts and holsters, pearl-handled revolvers and gold-inlaid spurs. There were also pretty girls in flowery dresses with frilly skirts riding side-saddle on spirited horses on which they performed complicated musical team rides and other remarkable feats in the ring, the whole against a background of large, jubilant, good-humoured crowds and the gay, stirring Mexican music which almost drowned the sound of the thundering hooves and the bellowing of the angry cattle.

My first *charreada* impressed me as being the modern evocation of the superb horsemanship and cattle-handling expertise which played such an important part in rural Mexico after the Spanish conquest until the Revolution. I had already noted that most of the inhabitants of Mexico City drove their motor cars with much the same careless flair and disregard for danger as when their equestrian proficiency was an essential element in their day-to-day activities and, indeed, in the survival of the individual. By the time I arrived in Mexico, the cultivation of the arts and skills of the Mexican horseman had largely become the spare-time pursuit of groups of enthusiastic and dedicated but essentially city-based amateurs. On weekends they left their dental surgeries, legal offices, or industrial boardrooms to perform thrilling feats of horsemanship in the suburban bullrings, all based on the traditional working methods required and developed for the management and breeding of cattle on the *haciendas* and ranches which no longer existed, their extensive pastures having long ago been expropriated and redistributed to agricultural workers. I found that few public occasions took place without a representation of those gaily dressed, richly accoutred and splendidly mounted lawyers and doctors who, in their reincarnation of the Mexican *charro*, embodied everything that was most noble, glamorous, virile, and traditional in the male Mexican ethos.

The Lord Mayor's visit was a great success. Articles and photographs were published in all the newspapers daily recording our activities, and his departure at the airport at the end of his six days' official visit was a memorable occasion, with *mariachi* bands playing *Las Golondrinas*, the Mexican equivalent of *Will ye no' come back again*, as the group boarded the aircraft. There cannot be many countries which contrive to leave their guests with the public and private impression that their visit has been more special than others, and that their friendship is valued and appreciated. Anglo-Mexican relations had been given another useful fillip and the Lord Mayor's hosts had been left in no doubt about the City's preponderance and expertise in all those financial, insurance and commodity markets in which the Mexicans were most interested. But the visit had also been great fun. One memorable day, while the top brass were all having lunch with the President, Alderman Norman Hall and his charming wife Maureen had lunch with those of us who had not been invited; we were joined by Delfin Sanchez and his wife. At the end of a convivial and musical meal enlivened by the playing and singing of a group of strolling *mariachis* whose popular ballads were chorused by the group round the table, Delfin Sanchez delighted our party when he revealed that, in addition to his other attributes, he was also the possessor of a fine, musical baritone.

No sooner were we back in the office than it was time to start planning for the next visit, which was to be a high-level trade mission led by Sir Montague Pritchard and composed of top-level bankers, businessmen, and industrialists representing a wide sector of British enterprise. They were to arrive in Mexico City six or seven weeks later and would also visit Guadalajara and Monterrey, provincial capitals which were important industrial, financial, and commercial centres in their own right. In the middle of our planning it was announced that the Duke and Duchess of Gloucester were to visit Mexico in October, again in response to an invitation made by the President while in Britain. A short time later came the formal announcement that the Queen and the Duke of Edinburgh were to make a return state visit to Mexico in February 1975.

All this meant that in Mexico, Britain was very much in the public eye throughout this period. Obviously, we had to consider all aspects of the situation which might affect our visitors or their movements. At the time the internal political situation was not really a cause for concern; although there was no organized subversion or active opposition to the Government or the ruling Institutional Revolutionary Party, there was a recent history of killings and kidnappings. Several ultra-left, terrorist guerrilla groups claimed, with little justification, to be politically motivated. They specialized in extortion, bank robberies and shooting up police stations; and there were many unpleasant incidents generated by drug traffic. Provincial politicians and state governors were threatened, and prominent businessmen sent their children to school with bodyguards. Even then many ambassadors moved around with escort cars and armed guards, and earlier in the year Mr Terence Leonhardy, US Consul General in Guadalajara, had been kidnapped. He was released unharmed when the authorities conceded all the kidnappers' demands.

In some ways, many of the frequent occasions involving armed violence were hardly more than the external manifestations of a society with a violent past, where violence remained close to the surface, in a country with a violent modern history. After Mexican independence from Spain was formally declared in the Plan of Igualá in 1821, Mexico's road to political stability was paved with foreign and domestic attempts to impose individual rule by violence and the force of arms. For long years preceding the assumption of office of President Lázaro Cárdenas in 1934 Mexican history was one of insurrections, executions, civil wars, assassinations, and revolts. During this period there took place also two notable foreign interventions on Mexican territory: the first, the Mexican war with the United States, which ended in 1848, deprived Mexico of California, Arizona, Nevada, Colorado, Utah, and a large part of New Mexico, approximately half of the original territory of independent Mexico before the war.

The second intervention was less productive. The French, urged by Britain and Spain, invaded Mexico in 1862 for the second time (troops representing England and Spain as well as France had landed at Veracruz in 1838 in order to exact payment for debts). After heavy initial defeats by Juárez's troops and an arduous campaign, a greatly reinforced French army finally captured Puebla and Mexico City in 1863 and in 1864 installed Maximilian of Austria as Emperor of Mexico.

This did not result in the end of Juárez's resistance, which continued for three years, until Napoleon III, wearying of his costly Mexican adventure, decided to cut his losses and ordered the withdrawal of his troops from Mexico without bothering to inform Maximilian.

Having been abandoned by the French, his tragic reign ended with the defeat of his supporters and his execution on the Cerro de las Campanas in Querétaro (about 140 miles north of Mexico City) on 19 July 1867. His last words were 'Long live Mexico!' before being shot by a firing squad, regardless of many international appeals for clemency, by order of Lic. Delfin Sanchez's illustrious ancestor. Benito Juárez's natural death (after a stroke) in 1872 was followed, with but a brief interruption, by General Porfirio Diaz's thirty-eight-years' dictatorship, which gave way in 1911 to another long, confused period of civil war, insurrections and revolts (with yet a further armed intervention by the United States in 1916) now known as the Mexican Revolution. A new constitution in 1917 provided for economic and social reforms; lands were expropriated and redistributed in 1921; and organized labour was brought into the Government in 1925. But political and economic stability eluded the devastated country until 1930, when the National Revolutionary Party, the only precursor of the present-day Institutional Revolutionary Party, was created.

Even in October 1973 local conditions made it advisable to brief new arrivals and visitors on the need to take some elementary personal precautions when moving around Mexico City, by car or on foot. When the Pritchard Mission arrived and we had the customary briefing meeting, one or two of the members who knew Mexico well asked about this aspect of the situation. They had a heavy programme of engagements in Mexico City for the first week, which they fulfilled with all the accompanying publicity which most British activities then seemed to generate. I was not very much involved in their visits and conversations, being by this time engaged in the arrangements for the visit of the Duke and Duchess of Gloucester, the President's personal guests, whose programme was also to take them outside Mexico City.

145

9

Guadalajara, October 1973

I arrived in my office one morning to be told that Douglas Hardinge, the commercial secretary who had accompanied Sir Monty Pritchard and his mission to Guadalajara, had telephoned to say that Dr Anthony Williams, the Honorary British Consul in Guadalajara, had been kidnapped that morning as he left his home. He had met the mission on arrival at Guadalajara airport and during the next few days had accompanied them on many of their calls and meetings. He had attended the mission's farewell reception the previous evening and had arranged to meet them again the next morning, instead of which a message by his kidnappers had been conveyed to the mission at the hotel in which they were staying. There were few other details then available.

Dr Williams was a large, corpulent man with a heavy beard. He had lived and practised medicine for many years in Guadalajara, where he was a popular and well-known figure. He had been appointed Honorary Consul there, in keeping with our traditional practice of choosing prominent local residents in provincial capitals to act in this capacity. After a hurried council of war the Ambassador decided that I should go to Guadalajara immediately to establish contact with the local authorities and ensure that no stone was left unturned in their efforts to find Dr Williams and secure his release.

No sooner had our decision been taken but we were immediately confronted with the sort of petty difficulties which always seem to arise whenever an emergency requires prompt action. Within a few minutes I was told that all flights to Guadalajara were booked solid for the next two days. It was raining hard and I found that, for various good and valid reasons, no car was available to take me to the airport, a

146

Baghdad. The Chancery, British Embassy, 1962.

The gap left by Residence burned down in 1958.

The Political Resident, Lt. Col. Sir Rupert Hay and his Head of Chancery, Martin Le Quesne. (Bahrain)

Bahrain. The Political Agent, (Mr John Wall) and the Shaikh of Bahrain. The Adviser (Sir Charles Belgrave) in the bow tie behind the Ruler.

The Sultan of Muscat and Oman, Said bin Taimur, arrives in Bahrain from London. In addition to the Ruler of Bahrain, he is greeted by the acting Political Resident, the acting Political Agent, the acting Adviser and the acting Commandant of Police.

The British Political Agent and his staff, 1953.

The Ruler of Bahrain receives a visiting US Admiral.

The Everest conquerors at Manamah Airport, Bahrain, 1953.

New Year's Day at the Political Residency in Jufair.

Mexico, 1975. Sanitised 'Charreada' for Royal visitors from Britain.

President Belaunde's inauguration, 1980.

The Lord Mayor of London and the Swordbearer in Lima, 1981.

Sir Ronald Gardner-Thorpe on his way to Machu Picchu.

Mr Cecil Parkinson inaugurates a viaduct at the Majes Project, Arequipa, 1981.

Montevideo, 1984. Defaced walls of British Embassy calling for release of Raul Sendic, imprisoned leader of Tupamaro terrorists who kidnapped Sir Geoffrey Jackson in 1971.

journey that took anything between half an hour and an hour and a quarter, depending on the time of the day, whether or not it was raining, and the density of the traffic. Taxis were unreliable and usually not available when it rained. I also had to get home first to pack a bag as I did not know how long I would be away. In the event, an appeal to higher authority at the airport found an instant and sympathetic response. One or two passengers would be summarily evicted from the midday flight, on which I was guaranteed a seat if I could get there in time. In an impressive display of effective teamwork, within two hours I was taken to the airport in a a borrowed car which was hijacked by the administration officer, my wife having in the meantime been extracted from a wives' meeting at the other end of town and conveyed to our house in Lomas de Barrilaco, where we both arrived at the same time. In the meantime, the embassy informed the Mexican Foreign Ministry and the Governor of Jalisco (the state of which Guadalajara is the capital) that I was on my way.

Douglas Hardinge met me at Guadalajara airport in a hired car and took me back to the hotel where the mission members were staying. On the way he told me that in a further development since Dr Williams's disappearance, Señor Fernando Aranguren, a young and prominent Guadalajara industrialist and a member of a well-known family with extensive business interests in the area, had also been kidnapped. The police thought it had been done by the same gang, as the two kidnap victims lived in the same residential area of Guadalajara and had been seized within half an hour of each other. The chief of police had sent a police patrol car to the hotel to keep tabs on the mission, who were on the last day of their visit and were due to fly to Monterrey two or three hours later. The Governor and the chief of police had been told of my coming and expected me to get in touch.

The hotel was the Guadalajara Camino Real, owned by a prestigious chain which had luxury hotels throughout Mexico. Situated in a mainly residential suburb, it was built in the long, rambling California ranch-house style, with lovely gardens and pools and tennis courts. The lobby was thronged with tourists and holiday-makers and all the public areas on the ground floor were full of people. I followed Douglas upstairs to the suite which the mission was about to vacate. They were all packed and ready to go, and much concerned by the unexpected turn of events. I spoke to Sir Montague Pritchard and to several others who had talked to Dr Williams the previous evening. It was clear that he had had no inkling of any trouble ahead. The main thing was that the kidnappers had so far made known no demands for the release of either of their hostages. In the past few days the newspaper coverage of the mission's activities had again been extensive, and it was generally known that the mission was leaving Guadalajara that same day. It was obviously desirable to place no obstacle in their way which might prevent them from communicating their demands. After some reflection I booked into the same hotel and, having taken my farewell of Douglas and the mission members, I went down to the main hall, feeling rather alone. I walked out to the mission's police escort car which I saw was equipped with the usual VHF radio. The two patrolmen confirmed that their orders were to escort the mission to the airport and wait until they were airborne. I asked the policeman behind the wheel to speak to his central control and ask for another patrol car to take me to see the Governor. The voice at the other end of the radio immediately acquiesced, adding after a pause that a patrol car with two policemen would arrive shortly and would be permanently assigned to me until further notice. Feeling a little less forlorn I then went back into the main hall and asked for the duty manager.

This turned out to be a personable young man who spoke perfect English, and who immediately offered every assistance when I explained myself and the reason for my visit. He thought I would wish to stay under an assumed name or that I might prefer not to register, in which case there would be no problem. Much though I was attracted by this prospect, I thought that as the first message by the kidnappers had been delivered to the hotel (through a nun in a local convent) it was possible that they would again communicate with the hotel if they wished to make their demands to 'the British', it being known that representatives of the embassy had been attached to the mission. Even if, as was more likely, they wanted to impose conditions on the Mexican authorities, they might still try to use the British as interested intermediaries. I had avoided the press on arrival at the airport, but many people already knew (and an item was indeed to appear in the local press the following day) that I had arrived in Guadalajara. I therefore asked the manager if we could make arrangements to ensure that all phone calls to me were monitored and recorded. Would it be too much trouble to change my room every day or two? The rooms at the back of the hotel overlooking the gardens and swimming pool would be perfect. In the meantime, I would leave my bag at the desk and make my call on the Governor.

The manager carefully noted my requirements and undertook to make all the arrangements by the time I got back. I then made a call from one of the booths in the hall to my wife in Mexico City to tell her I had arrived and where I was, and by the time I turned to leave the hall I saw a police patrol car roll up the drive to the hotel. I walked out, identified myself, and was invited to get in the back. When the driver called up his central control to report that he was leaving the hotel, I suggested we asked them to inform the Governor that I was on my way, but the driver said that they also had the radio frequency of the Governor's house. Passing the microphone to me, he invited me to speak direct. A disembodied voice at the other end confirmed they were expecting me and instructed us to approach the house by the gate at the side. I sat back in my seat, placed my feet carefully on either side on the sub-machine-guns which littered the floor, and looked around me, practically for the first time since my arrival.

Guadalajara was Mexico's second-largest city, an important commercial and communications centre about 400 kilometres north-west of Mexico City. Founded by the Spaniards in 1542, it was situated on the fertile highland plains at the foot of the Sierra Madre mountains in western Mexico. It was then a pleasant, bustling city with some attractive residential suburbs and notable colonial architecture in the centre including the fine Cathedral and the Plaza de Armas. There were also some large murals by the noted Mexican artist José Clemente Orozco, which I hoped to see. The climate was almost ideal. The city's parks and plazas always had flowers in bloom, and it was surrounded by some of the richest agricultural lands in the country. The population was then estimated to be about one and a half million, and the overcrowding and pressures of the federal capital were notably absent. There were large numbers of retired Americans living in the pleasant suburbs, including, as it happened, my sister-in-law and her American husband who, after eight years in Lima with W.R. Grace & Co., had retired in Guadalajara, where they lived in an attractive semi-colonial house in one of the suburbs, close to a golf club, where many other retired couples lived. I hoped I would have an opportunity to get in touch with them.

When we drove up to the Governor's house I could not help noticing the police cars parked outside, the armed guards at the gates, and the plain-clothes loiterers smoking cigarettes and chatting to the heavily armed, uniformed policemen. As I walked up to the closed main doors a small spy window in the door opened up and a face was partially framed in the opening. When I identified myself the doors opened and I was ushered into a smallish hall which led to a large sitting-room at the side. There were two men standing in the centre of this room. The Governor of the State of Jalisco came forward with a smile and an outstretched hand and greeted me warmly. He introduced his companion as the deputy director general of the Mexican state security police who, he explained, had also arrived hotfoot from Mexico City to direct and co-ordinate the investigations. He had a couple of assistants with him who would also liaise with the Guadalajara police. There had been no further developments since the kidnapping of Sr Aranguren, but the local police were carrying out searches in various areas where they thought the gang might be holed up. Dr Williams was a large conspicuous figure with his heavy beard, and his presence would not always be easy to conceal. If they moved him, curious neighbours or onlookers were almost certain to notice. They were bound to give themselves away in the fullness of time. The police also had several leads they were actively pursuing. Did I have any ideas or suggestions to put forward?

The Governor was a good-looking man of medium height, then in his late forties, with dark hair greying at the temples and brushed straight back. He had a small moustache and rather striking green eyes. He smiled readily and had an attractive manner. He insisted that I should henceforth regard his house as my headquarters, where I could join him at all times in waiting for news and deciding what to do next. He had a direct telephone line to Mexico City. The police patrol car would stay with me all night at the hotel, and their radio was at my disposal. If there was anything else I needed I had only to ask. We went over what we knew of the manner of the two kidnappings and speculated on the motivation. Dr Williams was not a man of great wealth, which suggested that the kidnappers sought to obtain international publicity on the one hand and funds from the Aranguren family on the other. For his part, the deputy director general of security said he would report at regular intervals to the Governor, and all planning and activities would be co-ordinated at the Governor's residence. My own ideas and advice would be welcome. He asked me how long I planned to stay at the Camino Real, which he though a little isolated in its leafy suburb. He agreed, however, that the kidnappers might ring through to the hotel, and reminded me that if any messages came to me at the Camino Real, the Governor would be able to reach him at all times.

All this seemed to me to be eminently sensible. I was naturally anxious to be close to the centre of things, and this was clearly the best way to achieve this. The deputy director general of security, whose first name was Miguel, was a shortish man, then aged about forty, with fair, wavy hair and pale-blue eyes. He was stocky and looked fit, and moved and spoke very quietly. Later I found that he had a rare smile which transformed his normally saturnine expression. He carried a large automatic pistol tucked into the waistband of his trousers, ill concealed by the elegant short-waisted leather jacket he was wearing. After a few more general remarks we agreed to meet at nine o'clock the next morning, in order to exchange information and consider further moves, including the results of the long night which Miguel clearly had ahead. He said that one or two of the suspects arrested after the kidnapping of the US Consul General some months back were still in gaol in Guadalajara. Some of those also implicated had recently broken out of a gaol in Aguas Calientes, and others had been moved to gaols in other states. He was getting them all together in order to question them thoroughly.

While I was pondering over the precise significance of this, an aide came in to say that the Ambassador had been on the phone, asking if I was there. I was invited to call him back and I made the first of my calls from a small room just off the large sitting-room/study. In those days, operators sometimes took half an hour to put through provincial calls but, having been told that I could dial the Mexico City number direct, I got through to the Ambassador straight away, reported on the latest developments, and outlined the arrangements made. I said that I would henceforth be spending most of my time in the Governor's house. I explained about the private line to Mexico City which was normally used by the Governor to speak to the President and the Minister of the Interior (Gobernación). I would report at least once daily with any news. When I returned to thank the Governor I found that Miguel had been joined by one of his henchmen, another member of the state security police with the rank of *comisario*. He was more typically Mexican in appearance, with thick, black hair brushed straight back and an equally thick, black, Mexican moustache drooping beyond the corners of his mouth. His name was Florentino and he also carried a large gun in his waistband. He was a very quiet, uncommunicative individual of whom I caught rare glimpses from time to time over the next few days.

It had been a long day. By this time it was quite dark and late in the evening. As there seemed to be nothing more that I could do I took my leave from the Governor, confirming that, unless there were any developments during the night, I would report to his house at nine o'clock the next morning. Miguel and Florentino escorted me to the door and, as we paused in the hall to say goodbye, I noticed for the first time an ornamental hat rack and mirror, with coat-hangers and an umbrella stand on the far wall. There were no umbrellas. The umbrella stand was stacked with sub-machine-guns. When he saw the direction of my glance, Miguel asked me if I needed an umbrella.

The patrol car took me back to the Camino Real through the dark, suburban streets. The manager had been as good as his word. When I collected my suitcase at the desk I was also given a note and a small package. The note gave me the number of the room to which my few belongings would be moved in the morning, and went on to explain that there were several telephone operators simultaneously on duty who were changed at intervals. Monitoring and recording might be difficult to arrange downstairs without the risk of missing something important, but the package contained a neat little gadget which I was invited to use instead. This turned out to be a small electronic device with a wire and a suction cup which was to be attached to the base of the telephone by the side of my bed. The accompanying child's cassette recorder did the rest. In my room I fitted it up immediately and asked the operator to call me. It worked perfectly. Then I went down to talk to my police car crew, who confirmed that they were to stay the night parked at the hotel, on duty in their car. A relief car and crew would report at 8.00 a.m. I asked one of them to come up to identify my room, have a look at the road round the back of the hotel, and choose a parking place where I could see them from my balcony overlooking the rear of the hotel grounds. A few minutes later the patrol car was in position. I ordered four large triple-decker American-style sandwiches to be sent out to the policemen and, after a smaller sandwich and a glass of milk, brushed my teeth and stretched out thoughtfully on my bed to spend my first night in the luxurious Camino Real.

Needless to say I could not sleep. Several times I went to the balcony to look at the police patrol car, in which I saw the glow of cigarettes from time to time. For some reason, the telephone rang, once, briefly, which made me knock over the cassette recorder in my agitated scramble in the dark. A couple of owls were hooting menacingly in the neighbourhood, which I naturally assumed to be signals by masked prowlers. The dawn was a long time coming. Eventually I gave up, shaved, showered and dressed and went down to a deserted hall to collect the newspapers, which I read while having coffee and a bun at the bar. There was little of any interest to me, other than the reports of everything I already knew. As soon as it was decently possible I briefly rang my sister-in-law to say hello, adding that I did not know when I would be able to see them. They had a birthday present they wished me to take back to my wife, and they also offered to take me round to see the Orozco murals. They thought the best ones were at the University of Jalisco in Guadalajara, Finally, I went out to find a different police car, scrutinized the faces of the new patrolmen on duty, and was driven to the Governor's house.

Fortunately, we all have a defence mechanism which sooner or later obliterates the memory of pain, anxiety or grief, or simply unpleasant memories. Although I kept a log of calls and developments at the time, I have not had access to it for a long time. My recollection of the days and nights that followed have therefore merged into a blurred, ill-focused series of images with only some episodes which still stand out clearly. I

153

remember I spent long hours talking with the Governor in his sitting-room, jumping up every time a telephone rang. He obviously managed to delegate many of his duties throughout this period, when he clearly devoted most of his time to the kidnappings and to me. The first morning he told me that he had asked for a couple of police helicopters to be sent up from Mexico City. These could be useful in a number of ways, but would initially be kept hovering systematically over selected parts of the city from dawn till dusk. He said that this had a nerve-racking effect on malefactors in hiding, who felt vulnerable to the all-seeing helicopters clattering over their heads and were liable to break cover and run for it when no longer able to stand the strain. More patrol cars and police reinforcements had arrived from Mexico City, and there were roadblocks on all the roads out of Guadalajara. The prisoners in the local gaol were being questioned. He was in close touch with the Aranguren family, and everything possible was being done. In the meantime, I could only wait, while phones rang in various rooms and offices and quiet men came discreetly in and out. Our conversations were frequently interrupted by the helicopters patrolling overhead. When, late in the evening, I found myself nodding off on the Governor's comfortable sofa I rang the Ambassador, signed off for the day, and went back with my patrol car to the Camino Real for another sleepless night, having first sent out the usual sandwiches to the policemen. When I changed rooms I re-connected my telephone tap and cassette recorder, and then spent the rest of the night waiting for it to ring.

The following day Miguel appeared briefly at the Governor's house with a copy of a broadsheet which had been left with a local newspaper. It was addressed to the Mexican authorities. This carried a message from the kidnappers listing their demands for the release of their hostages. These included the publication in the national press of a statement by the Mexican Government admitting culpability in the wrongful imprisonment of political prisoners, breaches of human rights, and repressive police methods; it listed nearly one hundred 'political prisoners' then in various Mexican gaols who were to be released, asked for one (or was it two?) million US dollars in cash, and a safe passage and an aircraft to take the lot to Cuba.

This led to much activity on all fronts. Miguel and his

policemen were intent on keeping up the pressure. They already had some ideas on the identity of the kidnappers, who were thought to include a particularly murderous group of wanted criminals who had broken out of gaol not long previously. The Mexican authorities were disposed to appear to be ready to meet the kidnapper's demands, and arrangements were accordingly made to gather together the 'political prisoners' named in the broadsheet – only to find that the majority of these, being fine, upstanding and straight forward Mexican lawbreakers, wanted no part of the deal and were totally opposed both to the prospect of being handed over to the kidnappers or travelling to Cuba in their company. A temporizing scheme was devised to gain time, while further leads were followed up by Miguel and his men, who managed to put in an appearance once or twice a day.

The Governor was a well-read and much-travelled man. He had been initially intrigued and amused by my Castilian accent when speaking Spanish and spoke to me at length about Mexican history and the *leyenda negra* or conventional myths perpetuated by Mexican and Spanish writers which had distorted history for generations in both countries. The legend of systematic atrocities and unbridled cruelty during the conquest, by the Aztec overlords on one side and the *gachupín* invaders and Inquisitors on the other, had affected generations of historians and even the attitudes of ordinary people. These were slowly changing as more objective writers threw new light on particular episodes or explained incidents against the background of the customs prevailing at the time. But in modern Mexico's search for a historical identity, public attitudes towards Spain had for long been ambivalent. As an example he cited the then current controversy about whether or not a statue of Hernán Cortés should at last be erected somewhere on Mexico City's famed Paseo de la Reforma. He thought it a measure of the gradual readjustment of these attitudes that the issue could at least be ventilated in the correspondence columns of some weekly periodicals and magazines. He told me a joke then current about all the fine statues sited along the Paseo de la Reforma in Mexico City. A common denominator had them all bearing feathers, if not actually on their heads then at least on some part of their raiment (not excluding the statue of Christopher Columbus at the junction of Avenida Benito Juárez and the Paseo de la Reforma, on which there were frequently to be seen feathers, droppings, and even nests constructed there by some of Mexico City's feral pigeons). The graceful effigy of a nude Diana then at one of the junctions in the Paseo de la Reforma was likewise included in the feather-bearing category of statues, even though in her case the feathers flighted the imaginary arrow she was about to discharge from her bow into the massed motor cars milling at her feet.

The famous larger-than-life-sized statue of Charles IV of Spain on an enormous charger was in a category of its own. It had been cast in bronze in 1803 by a Spanish-born architect and sculptor named Manuel Tolsá who arrived in Mexico in 1791 and also built the magnificent Colegio de Mineria in Mexico City. In keeping with the prevailing civic reluctance to have public monuments honouring 'foreign' as distinct from 'national' personages, the municipal authorities had felt bound to attach a plaque to the plinth informing potentially critical passers-by that the statue was not there because of any implied reverence for a foreign monarchy or the person it represented, but simply because it happened to be a rather fine example of equestrian statuary. With characteristic Mexican whimsy the colossal statue of the gigantic horse and rider was known throughout the land as *el caballito*.

The Governor was a witty and entertaining speaker, but his enforced inactivity was beginning to prey on his nerves. One evening he took me out to a garage in the yard at the side of the house and invited me inside. With a smile he confessed he was a motor cycle enthusiast and put the lights on. I blinked at the sight of three or four large and powerful, glossy machines, bristling with radio aerials, mirrors, extra lights and gleaming exhausts. When I expressed admiration for some of the more unusual features, he said rather wistfully that he usually tried to get off for an hour or so early in the mornings to exercise his machines on one of the deserted state highways. Sometimes he played a cassette with the theme music from the film *Lawrence of Arabia*, a great favourite. He found this a good way to recharge his mental batteries. With a mischievous smile he added that his security escort did not approve because he frequently left them out of sight in their following car. Would I like to go out with him one morning?

156

A day or two later, Miguel appeared and conferred with the Governor in a corner of the room. The Governor eventually came over and told me that the police had been tipped off about a large, bearded *gringo* who had been spotted in the back of a pick-up truck in the approaches to an isolated farm in a rural area outside the state capital. A raid on the farm was to take place, with helicopters and police cars. He proposed to go also, and he thought I might welcome an outing. Without further ado, we drove out to the airport at high speed in half a dozen cars, the Governor's official car escorted by two or three patrol cars in position fore and aft, with my patrol car bringing up the rear, all with sirens at full blast and flashing lights. I was told that this was being done deliberately in order to maintain a high police profile throughout the town and make everybody nervous. It was essential to keep up the pressure.

Without pausing on arrival at the airport we drove on to the tarmac where two helicopters were already turning their rotors. One was a large, military-type machine, with two or three rows of belted seats running the width of the main cabin between two alarming doorless openings in the fuselage. The seats were mostly occupied by half a dozen heavily armed men in casual plain clothes. The smaller helicopter was a four-seater machine with a bubble cabin in which the Governor and I took our places. The rendezvous was with an unmarked police vehicle which would bear a red X on its roof, visible only from the air. We took off a minute or two later, gained height, and flew across part of the capital and out into the countryside for about half an hour, while Miguel and the pilot consulted maps and took bearings. A few minutes later Miguel spotted the marked car below us parked on a dirt road between a wooded copse and a field. We landed easily in the field about a hundred yards from the car. More men materialized from a van concealed in the wood and, after a brief conference, the Governor, Miguel and all the armed men got into the van and drove off, followed by more men in the car. With his habitual courtesy the Governor had explained that if there was to be a shoot-out with an armed gang at the farm, he did not want me there. He thought they'd be gone for about an hour. I was therefore left behind with the two pilots, in the middle of a pleasant meadow on a sunny and balmy afternoon. A few minutes later the pilot of the small helicopter received a radio message from the Governor which caused him to take off with a wave. I wandered round the large machine, kicked its tyres and lay down in the long grass in the shade of the fuselage. With only the drone of the bumble-bees in my ears, within seconds I was fast asleep.

The returning helicopter woke me about two hours later, when the shadows were lengthening under the fuselage above me. The Governor was in the bubble with the pilot. He shook his head at me before they landed. 'Nothing,' he said, beckoning me in, 'a false alarm,' I got in beside him, feeling much refreshed by my first carefree sleep in days. But I was doomed not to remain carefree. While we were driving into town from the airport we received a radio message from Miguel arranging to meet us at the Governor's house. When he arrived about an hour later he went into a corner to confer with the Governor. I noticed that they looked once or twice in my direction. Finally, the Governor came across and suggested that I might prefer to move out of the Camino Real. Miguel had received a tip-off to the effect that another kidnapping was being planned and that I was one of the possible targets. The Governor suggested I should move into the central hotel in town where Miguel was himself staying. After all, there was no point in staying on at the Camino Real. The kidnappers had made no effort to get in touch with me there and their requirements were now known. But they also knew I was there, and it might be wiser to move out, in spite of all my changing of rooms and police patrol cars. The Camino Real was virtually out of town and the policemen in the patrol car probably had another, daytime, job and could not be relied upon to keep awake all night. He though I should move straight away.

It would have been foolish not to heed their advice. I drove to the Camino Real, packed by bag, collected the gadget and tape recorder, and returned them to the reception desk downstairs where I asked for my bill. A few seconds later the duty manager came out of the inner office and said there was no bill. No, not even for the policemen's sandwiches. I said I was very grateful for the kind offer, but explained that I was not paying myself, and that the British Government would pay my costs. Surely . . . ? No, nothing. They wished they could have done more. But, at least, no bill.

I then drove to the new hotel in the town centre, in a busy, crowded, shopping area where (no doubt inspired by the Governor's historical musing) I registered under the name Velasquez. The long arm of coincidence resulted in my being given a room on the third floor between the rooms occupied by Miguel and Florentino. I left my bag and drove back to the Governor's house, where I found him in the garage with his motor cycles. I told him what I had done and he said he thought I would sleep better in the new, noisy, hotel, with Florentino next door and Miguel on the other side. I rang through to the Ambassador, reported on the most recent developments and gave him my assumed name and new address and room number. I also asked for assistance from the embassy. The Governor had invited me to see something of the police operations in the suburbs, and my helicopter excursion was likely to be repeated. I had been out of touch most of the day and needed somebody who could man the phone and take messages in my absence. The next day John Blakemore, the assistant information officer at the embassy, joined me on the Governor's settee in Guadalajara.

A day or two later my conversation with the Governor was interrupted when an aide reported to him that a man and a woman insisted on seeing him. They claimed to have news of the kidnapping. Messages were sent immediately to Miguel. The Governor, anxious to leave no stone unturned invited them in. The woman was a medium who claimed to be clairvoyant. Her companion interpreted her utterances while she was in a trance. During a session the previous day she had spoken of a large, bearded man, lying on a bed, blindfolded, in a bare room. The man was called José and the woman Guadalupe. Half and hour later, while we were still talking about the previous day, Miguel hastened in. They agreed to hold a seance straight away, although José was reluctant to put Guadalupe through the renewed strain without adequate preparation. The Governor invited us to follow him to the darkened room they had requested, where Guadalupe sat in an armchair while José chose an upright chair in front of her, the normally inscrutable Miguel sceptically bringing up the rear.

Guadalupe placed her hands over her eyes and, in unison with José, intoned what sounded like a short prayer. Almost immediately she slumped in her chair making small sounds. José snapped his fingers in front of her face and asked her what she saw. Seemingly in a trance, she repeated in a monotonous voice what they had said about the large man on the bed. There were newspapers on the floor, but she could not see the date. There was a window in the room, which gave on to a garden. There was one door into the room, which was closed. The man on the bed seemed to be asleep. Each question was accompanied by a snap of José's fingers, which was apparently necessary to provoke a reply. After a while Miguel took up the questioning, trying to enlarge the range and content of the questions, but this produced mainly negative replies until, with an apparent start but still firmly closed eyes, Guadalupe said that the door into the room had opened. Two men entered bearing some food, but their faces were masked. In reply to questions about their dress and appearance, she said they were wearing jeans, which was greeted by a barely concealed snort from Miguel. After a final snap of José's fingers, Guadalupe regained consciousness and they prepared to take their leave. The Governor thanked them politely and said they had been very helpful. Disappointed, we dispersed in various directions, the Governor and Miguel going off to their corner to confer privately and I to my seat on the sofa where, half an hour later, Miguel woke me with a snap of his fingers under my nose to say that the lifeless body of a *gringo* had been found by a police patrol on an isolated mountain road some distance out of Guadalajara.

Full of anguish and foreboding, I left John Blakemore to report to the Ambassador and followed Miguel to his car, a large, powerful American model with no distinguishing markings but equipped with radios, sirens and other tools of the trade, including the inevitable sub-machine-guns on the floor. To be on the safe side, I was to travel with the policemen in my patrol car. We had a long way to go. The report was that the remains were those of a corpulent man with grey hair and blue eyes. Miguel told me that a car or truck had been used to run over the body repeatedly in order to make identification difficult. There was no mention of a beard, but I did not wish to go into details and, in any case, beards could be shaved off. It would take about two hours to drive there. But half an hour later Miguel was told on the radio that parallel enquiries being made elsewhere had established beyond doubt that the body was that of an American. A group of drug traffickers had been captured two or three days before, and one or two of those arrested were helping the police with their enquiries. They told the police that they had several American associates, one of whom was suspected of having shopped them. Arrangements had therefore been made from within the gaol to have him taken care of. The body had been left on the solitary country road and rendered unrecognisable for good measure. As Miguel had pressing business elsewhere, we parted on the roadside and he took off in a great hurry. I turned round and went back to the Governor's house, while I reflected on the wages of sin and the high cost of virtue. I reported on the phone to the Ambassador in Mexico City and reassembled briefly with the Governor before parting for the night.

A day or two later when I arrived early in the morning at the Governor's house the helicopters were already rattling overhead. The Governor was not around and I wondered if he was out on the state highway thundering into the foothills of the Sierra Madre to the impotent fury of his security escort car. When he came in an hour later he greeted me affably and asked for news. I shook my head. No news is good news, he thought. The longer the captives remained alive the better were their chances. He asked if there was any word from Miguel. Half an hour later, one of the Aranguren brothers called to see the Governor, who introduced me in due course. I found it difficult to think of anything to say. I excused myself on the pretext of having to make a phone call to Mexico City, while John Blakemore entered up my log. Miguel came in later and conferred briefly with the Governor in their usual corner. A couple of hours later John and I went out for a sandwich after which we returned to resume our vigil on the settee. I busied myself checking our log and John Blakemore fiddled with the pocket transitor radio he had brought with him, on which he listened to the news broadcasts. At about 5.00 p.m. he heard a brief news flash on a local station which said that there was an unconfirmed report that Dr Williams had been released close to his home, more or less where he was originally kidnapped. He had been taken there in a car and had then made his way to his house on foot.

Then several things happened at the same time. The Governor, who had clearly heard the same report on his radio, hastened into the room, nodded to me and reached for the

161

nearest phone. I went to another phone and tried to speak to Dr Williams' home but the number was constantly engaged. I asked John Blakemore to go down to the Williams's house in the police car and to call me back from there, either on the phone or on the car radio. A policeman came in to say Miguel wanted to speak to me on one of the patrol car radios. I first went to ring the Ambassador but found the Governor talking on the direct line. Other phones began ringing in different parts of the house. Another message from Miguel came on the radio, saying that he was going straight to Dr Williams's house. Just as I got through to the Ambassador in Mexico City, the efficient John Blakemore rang on the other line to confirm that Dr Williams was indeed in his house, unharmed and in good health. He added that the press and TV crews were beginning to arrive in large numbers, and could he have police reinforcements, please?

After conferring with the Ambassador and the Governor and later, again on the phone, with the Ambassador, it was decided that he should fly to Guadalajara, alone, the following day to see the right people and say all the right things. I was to meet him at the airport with 'my' police patrol car. Nobody was to know about the Ambassador's proposed visit; if any word leaked out in advance of his arrival I would take police reinforcements to the airport, but I hoped the news would break only when he was safely within the Governor's house – I was naturally anxious to avoid running any risk of exchanging one hostage for another. When I finished my phone conversations the Governor told me that he had agreed to hold a press conference later that evening. This gave me food for thought. I had so far managed to escape the attention of the press, no doubt as a result of my departure from the Camino Real and my transmogrification into Sr Velasquez, after which most journalists had assumed that I had left Guadalajara. Most, that is, except one rather persistent newshawk who had spotted me once or twice skulking in the background in the Governor's house.

When the journalists and TV crews began gathering later in the evening, I said to the Governor I was hoping to continue to escape notice, particularly in the light of the ambassadorial visit due on the morrow, which the Governor agreed should in no circumstances be given advance publicity. While we talked, the press, radio and TV journalists began to gather outside, under the vigilant eyes of the police guards. In those days portable TV equipment was large and cumbersome and not, as nowadays, mainly self-contained. Cameras and floodlights were brought in by relays of operators and interviewers until the floors of the Governor's hall and sitting-room were both strewn with electric cables. When the interviews and questions began, the Governor dealt with them comprehensively and effectively, with the ease born of long practice. For many years, Mexico's two-thousand-mile border with the United States had created many bilateral problems. Inevitably, one tendentious questioner asked if he had sought the assistance of the CIA. When the Governor denied this he was pressed about the otherwise unidentified long-term occupant of his sitting-room sofa. The Governor asked me to reply and explain myself. As I rose from my chair, photographers reached for their flashes and pencils were poised over pads. Providentially, someone then plugged a set of extra powerful TV arc lights into a convenient socket in the Governor's sitting-room, and instantly plunged the whole block into total darkness.

Unhappily, this was not the end of the story, which for me culminated the following day in a shocking and tragic manner. When I called next morning at the Governor's house in order to finalize arrangements for the Ambassador's visit I was horrified to learn that the lifeless body of Sr Aranguren had been found earlier that morning in the boot of an abandoned car. He had been shot in the back of the head and his hands were still tied behind his back. I think that more than one of us had feared a violent end to the captives' purgatory, a fear we had steadfastly pushed to the backs of our minds, but the news of Dr Williams's release had been followed by an unbelieving surge of hope and relief. As a result, this cruel and irrational demonstration of evil violence left me numbed and drained. For days and nights I had thought about little but the victims' ordeal and their state of mind. I had met members of their families and in some small way shared their anguish. I could not understand this sickening, final twist in the nightmare. I was deeply affected by the news, as was the Ambassador when I met him later at the airport, and my recollection of the rest of the day is very patchy. I remember that after calling on the Governor we went to the stricken Aranguren family home,

163

where I could hardly fail to be impressed by the sorrow and dignity of his brothers and the courage and grief of the young widow and the small children. There was little we could say and even less that we could do, but at least they knew that we, also, were thinking of them. The elderly father was under medical sedation after a heart attack, which eventually gave the murderers two victims for the price of one. Later (or was it earlier?) we went to see Dr Williams at his house, where he was still besieged by journalists. The Ambassador's unexpected arrival caused a sensation and he was obliged to hold an impromptu press conference which seemed to me to go on for hours; in my apprehension I was anxious to get him back to the airport and away from a blemished Guadalajara which for me had became hostile, ominous and threatening.

When we took our leave of the Governor, we found him troubled and concerned, but otherwise showing few signs of the burden of responsibility he was to continue to bear. When I thanked him for the many facilities and his unfailing courtesy and hospitality he shook his head in silence, put his hands on my shoulders and embraced me warmly, sending me on my way with a final handshake and a lasting memory of a good and sensitive man, of great humanity and kindness.

My umpteenth police patrol car was waiting, with yet a different crew, to take us to the airport. Sr Velasquez had checked out that morning (and paid his bill) and taken his bag to the Governor's house on his way to meet the Ambassador. We therefore had ample time to get to the airport and report for our flight to Mexico City. But I was destined to go through yet another half-hour of tension and agitation when, unbelievably, the patrol car (with the now disregarded sub-machine-guns on the floor) broke down on the way to the airport as a result of some mechanical problem. Was the breakdown some sort of a ruse? Were the two policemen in front (whom I had never seen before) really policemen? Was this a carefully prepared ambush? Why didn't they use their radio? Should I leap out and stop a passing car before it was too late? But after opening the bonnet once and twice and fiddling inside, the patrol car was finally coaxed to trundle the remaining five or six kilometres to deposit us at the main entrance at Guadalajara airport, where both the car and I arrived verging on a state of inner collapse, the car firing on two and a half cylinders, the

Ambassador impassive and urbane, the policemen grinning sheepishly. When at last we fastened our seat-belts, secure in the confined quarters of the aircraft as it was taking off for Mexico City, my last conscious thought before falling asleep on the Ambassador's shoulder was that I should never see the Orozco murals at the University of Jalisco in Guadalajara.

As a footnote to this tragic story it should be recorded that as a result of the Williams and Aranguren kidnappings the Mexican authorities redoubled their efforts to bring to justice the terrorists and guerrillas known to be responsible for the campaign of violence, kidnappings and killings. Army units were deployed against the rural guerrillas in the mountains of Guerrero state. The police authorities in Guadalajara continued their drive against the urban terrorists. A few weeks later it was reported in the local press that one Pedro Orozco Guzman, alias 'Camilo', died after a gun battle with police in Guadalajara on Christmas Eve, 1973. The report added that before 'Camilo' died he confessed in his last moments to the kidnappings and Leonhardy, Williams, and Aranguren.

10

Paraguay, 1947–1949

When we left Mexico City in July 1975 I had been told I was
going back to the Foreign Office. Both my wife and I were
much looking forward to a long stay in London, where, in spite
of the long office hours, it was still possible to lead a more
'normal' life, with fewer social demands and representational
obligations of the sort which take up such a lot of time at some
posts abroad. We took a holiday in the Bahamas on our way
home just in case, and arrived in London to learn that plans
had changed and that I had been appointed ambassador to
Paraguay, where I was expected to arrive in January 1976. In
the meantime, I was to go to the General Assembly of the
United Nations in New York to lobby Latin American
delegations on the Guatemala/Belize dispute.

All this came as a surprise; I had not expected to go abroad
in the first place, and even less as an ambassador. But,
however, reluctant I might be to forego our two or three years
in London, this was an offer I could hardly refuse; and not least
because I already knew Paraguay and had much enjoyed my
first posting to Asunción from 1947 to 1949 as a youthful,
carefree bachelor on my first formal overseas appointment
under the Foreign Office. At the time, I was hoping to enter the
Foreign Service through the back door by means of one of the
various post-war 'reconstruction' schemes. These were intended to make up for the suspension of normal recruitment
during the war years as well as the large numbers of temporary
wartime officials then returning to their own careers and
interests. I was anxious to make my way in life and foolishly did
not relish the prospect of resuming my interrupted education.
As happened to millions of other people, the war had brought
about changes in my family and personal circumstances. In

1946 I found Britain a rather gloomy place and the rest of Europe certainly no better. When the opportunity arose to go to South America on a temporary Foreign Office appointment, I jumped at it. The fact that I was going to what was at the time one of the most backward countries in the whole of Latin America mattered not one bit. What little I knew about Paraguay at the time derived mainly from a book called *Land of Women* by a Baroness von Dombrowsky who had been the wife of the German Minister in Asunción before the First World War. It told an extraordinarily tragic and romantic story about a beautiful and remote land-locked country with an attractive and courageous people and a violent and dramatic history.

Aided by its very remoteness Paraguay was one of the first countries in Latin America to declare its independence from Spain. Nuestra Señora de la Asunción, the Mother of Cities, had been founded in 1537 by Spanish colonists who intended their settlement to be the seat of the Spanish administration for the whole of the southern cone of South America. Paraguay eventually became a province subordinate to the Viceroyalty of Peru, however, and in 1776 part of the Viceroyalty of Buenos Aires. In the meantime, the beauty of the country, the subtropical indolence and the friendliness and hospitality of the original Guarani inhabitants all combined to create a proud and comely race of bilingual people who descended from the original Spanish settlers and today make up the bulk of the population of Paraguay. After independence in 1811, Paraguay was ruled as a personal fief in turn by three remarkable men: Dr José Luis Gaspar Rodríguez de Francia until his death in 1840; his nephew Cárlos Antonio López until he died in 1862; and the latter's more famous son Francisco Solano López, whose death in 1870 also brought to an end the War of the Triple Alliance against Argentina, Brazil and Uruguay, which devastated Paraguay and literally decimated its population during the five years the war lasted. The tragic figure of Eliza Alicia Lynch, López's faithful Anglo-Irish consort, still regarded by some historians as López's principal source of strength and encouragement, provided an element of romantic drama which fired the imagination.

Baroness von Dombrowski, arriving with her husband in Paraguay while the war was still within living memory, could hardly fail to dwell on one of the more enduring results of the bitter conflict. In the last few months of the war, Paraguayan women and children fought in the trenches alongside López's remaining troops. Few able-bodied men were left alive. Out of a population estimated to number over half a million people when the war began in 1865, only about 28,000 men and 200,000 women survived, and several generations were needed to redress the balance. Some of the most comprehensive reports on the war in Paraguay were written by none other than Captain (later to be Sir Richard) Burton* better known for his Arabian chronicles and translations. An extraordinary Victorian explorer, traveller, and consular official, he wrote with perception, insight, and vision of the butchery and violence after visiting the Paraguayan battlefields in 1868 and 1869. Other contemporary accounts have it that merchant ships arriving at the river port of Asunción in the years following the end of the war were greeted by massed crowds of women squatting silently and patiently on the quays, waiting for the sailors to disembark, and some vessels were obliged to cancel shore leave for fear of being stranded in Asunción without a crew – hence the title of the book by the baroness, now sadly out of print for many years. But there have been other books describing this dramatic period, of which one of the most recent and well documented was published in 1975 by Gilbert Phelps, a historian and prolific writer on Latin American and other subjects. His sympathetic treatment of Paraguayan history during the War of the Triple Alliance sheds a new light on the subject and on the individual participants, and suggests that authoritarian rule has provided Paraguay with the only periods of social and economic development in a country which has seen much violence and political instability even when not engaged in full-scale wars.†

Another fascinating look at the same period with a closer British focus is provided by the book engendered by Brian MacDermot, one of my more distinguished predecessors in Asunción who, while Ambassador in Paraguay from 1968 to 1972, persuaded Josefina Plá, then the country's most famous living author, poet, and critic, to compile a history of the remarkable part played by British technicians and artisans in Paraguay between 1850 and 1870. These years included, of

*He had been appointed Consul in Santos (Brazil) in 1864.
†Gilbert Phelps, *The Tragedy of Paraguay*, Charles Knight & Co., 1975.

168

course, the period of the disastrous war. The book was written in Spanish by Josefina Plá and translated into English by Brian MacDermot, whose resurrection of this little-known aspect of individual British personal and technical contributions to Francisco Solano López's Paraguay deserves to be rediscovered.* According to the book jacket, 'Mr MacDermot's interest in the British in Paraguay began on the day he presented his credentials, when President Stroessner recalled the British technicians of the last century, and his interest in the events with which these largely forgotten men were connected gradually developed as the centenary celebrations of the successive events of the National Epic unfolded during his time in Asunción.'

In recent years, Paraguay has been in the news for a variety of reasons, most recently when General Alfredo Stroessner was overthrown in 1989 by a brother officer for long widely regarded as his potential successor; who also happened by this time to be the father in law of Stroessner's younger son. After having helped General Stroessner to rule the country with an iron hand and not much of a velvet glove for thirty-five years, his successor, General Andrés Rodriguez, promised democratic elections after a suitable period of political transition, the traditional opposition parties being in total disarray after forty years of repression. If the promised elections take place they will be virtually the first genuinely democratic elections in Paraguay's history.

When I arrived in Asunción in February 1947 General Stroessner was the colonel commanding the artillery regiment quartered at Paraguarí and, as such, already a political force to be reckoned with. The President at the time was another general, Higinio Moriñigo, who had adroitly stepped into the presidency as a result of the untimely death in an air crash of the former President, Marshall José Félix Estigarribia, hero of the Chaco war against Bolivia in the mid 1930s and a man of integrity and vision. Moriñigo consolidated his position by ingratiating himself with the armed forces and enlisting the support of the Colorado party, which had not been in power in Paraguay since the beginning of the century and was hungry for office. In February 1947, Asunción was a sleepy, sub-

*Josefina Plá, *The British in Paraguay*, Richmond Publishing Co. Ltd. in association with St Antony's College, Oxford, 1976.

tropical town, built on gentle hills sloping down to the river bay, with colonnaded houses and cobbled streets, ancient tramways, a British-owned railway system and a population of about 150,000 of whom the majority went barefoot. The fragrance of luxuriant and rotting vegetation and wet earth was everywhere; colourful *lapacho* and flame trees and jacarandas adorned all the central squares and lined some of the avenues. There was a tiny upper middle class of well-to-do business men, landowners and cattle ranchers with houses in Buenos Aires and holiday flats in Mar del Plata and Punta del Este. There was no municipal drainage system. Most houses had their own cesspools, which had to be emptied at regular intervals. When it rained, which it did frequently and torrentially, some of Asunción's cobbled streets were turned into raging rapids, cars were washed away, and people were drowned in the intersections.

The British Legation was a dilapidated rented house in large grounds on the Avenida Mariscal López, at the time one of the two main avenues in the residential suburbs. The other was the Avenida España where the US Embassy was situated. Our Envoy Extraordinary and Minister Plenipotentiary (to give him his full title) was a cheerful and delightful gentleman, who was enjoying his last post after a long career in the general Consular Service. He had married late in life and was devoted to his young Anglo-Argentine wife and two small daughters. After an energetic start with frequent reports on the political and economic situation in Paraguay he decided, when these failed to elicit any acknowledgement from the corresponding departments in Whitehall, increasingly to devote more time to the large garden and to his unceasing battle against leaf-cutting ants and other equally voracious predators. He was punctilious in fulfilling his representational and social obligations, and he and his wife were popular among both the tiny diplomatic corps and the resident British community. The house was a rambling, neo-Spanish colonial, ground-floor house, with verandahs protected with heavy screening against the rapacious mosquitoes, flying beetles, termites, vampire bats, and other denizens of Asunción's sub-tropical night which made their presence felt in various unpleasant ways every evening at dusk. At the back of the house was a more modest bungalow, built on a low concrete platform, with a sagging roof

170

supported by decaying wooden columns, which consisted of three rooms with peeling paint and flaking plaster, all originally intended to be the servants' quarters. This was the Chancery. One room was the Minister's office, although for reasons which must already be evident he received all his visitors in the house. The outer office was occupied by the vice-consul, a remarkable man called William Chippendale. I was given a desk in the same room. The bathroom and a storeroom completed the facilities. Next door was the kitchen, and dishes for lunch or dinner parties had to be protected from the elements on their journey from the kitchen across the yard to the flight of steps which led up to the dining-room in the rear of the main house. Many a rainy day I was to see Mario Lezcano, the chancery messenger-cum-butler-cum-general factotum set off from the kitchen next door in his smart white jacket with brass buttons bearing a succulent roast on an elegant silver carver, escorted by a giggling housemaid with a black umbrella.

The Minister's office contained the large, gleaming safe. This was a fairly recent arrival and housed the few confidential documents. Legend had it that when its carefully locked predecessor was moved for some reason in the middle of the war years, its back was found to have come away, finally eroded by damp walls, termites, long years of service in Asunción, lack of moral fibre, or what have you. The outer office where Chip(pendale) and I sat had a sort of notice board on the wall behind his desk. But instead of the usual Notices to Mariners and Tables of Consular Fees, it displayed a fearsome collection of the largest spiders, scorpions and centipedes I had ever seen. Each corpse was neatly pinned to the board having previously been preserved in the appropriate fluid, Chip being an expert at this sort of thing. Every one had been captured on the premises. When he saw my expression Chip added casually that he contributed to the collection almost every week. When I brought myself to examine the display more closely I was impressed by a spider, whose outspread, hairy legs must have spanned a full six inches. Chip volunteered that this was a male tarantula, the most recent acquisition, that they were always to be found in pairs, and that we would no doubt come across the female in the next few days. Anywhere.

Chip had been recently elected a fellow of the Royal

171

Geographical Society, but it was for his contributions to the Zoological Society that he was best known at the time. The London Zoo was then exhibiting a rare species of South American maned wolf, the only one in captivity in Europe. This had been sent to London, together with other animals, in Chip's last shipment from Asunción. I went to his home for a drink that evening and he showed me a number of crates in his garden, ready for the next lot of animals to be shipped. There were several exotic birds, a tame South American ostrich, a tapir, a large armadillo, a playful young puma, and other interesting specimens. When I went to his bathroom later in the evening I was not surprised to find that the bathtub with six inches of water was occupied by a three-foot-long Paraguayan cayman which eyed me balefully while I washed my hands.

Chip did not personally capture the birds and animals. Later in the evening he told me that he had originally come out to Paraguay to work for a missionary society which had established a lonely outpost at a place called Makthlawaya, a snake-infested 'island' in swampy ground in the middle of the Paraguayan Chaco, the vast area of rolling plains and scrub land across the river to the west of Asunción. His work among the Tozle, Chulupi, and Lengua Indians had, in the fullness of time, resulted in his being made a blood brother and honorary chief of one or two of these tribes. He explained that, contrary to popular belief, there were no longer any real Guaraní Indians left in Paraguay, although most of the non-Indian population spoke the language, which had its own literature and poetry; this made Paraguay the only truly bilingual country in South America. Only the more educated Paraguayans at the time spoke Spanish as well as reading and writing it. The few remaining Indian tribes in Paraguay had their own languages, and only those who came across the river into Asunción to sell their feather dusters, bows and arrows, and baskets and beads, had learned some Guaraní which they used as the lingua franca in their commerical exchanges with the Paraguayans in the towns. Chip spoke Guaraní fluently, and also had a smattering of Lengua and Tozle, as I was to discover unexpectedly the following morning.

I had been lucky in finding accommodation on the Avenida Mariscal López, within easy walking distance of the Legation. The traffic manager of the British-owned railway was an

Englishman called Winton Irvine. His wife had recently been hospitalized and was thought, sadly, unlikely to recover for some time. There were no children. When offered the prospect of sharing his house, I leapt at the opportunity. He was then about 35 having recently returned to South America from the war, from which he emerged as a major in the 2nd Punjab Regiment of the Indian Army, having originally joined up in 1939 with the Argyll and Sutherland Highlanders with which regiment there was a family connection. When he was demobbed he went back to his pre-war job in one of the British-owned Argentine railways, only to find himself out of work when these were subsequently nationalized by General Perón. He had himself been in Asunción only a short time, but was knowledgeable, friendly, and helpful, and spoke fluent Spanish with an Argentine accent. We were to become fast friends. His house was again a typically single-storied sub-urban house, in a neo-colonial style, standing in its own garden, with separate kitchen facilities and service quarters in the rear. My own bedroom with a ceiling fan, a shared bathroom, a dining-room, sitting-room and verandah leading on to the garden steps and front gate provided ideal accommodation for me at that stage. To get to the Legation I had to walk a couple of hundred yards up to the top of the gentle hill where the headquarters of the army general staff was situated, occupying at the time a large family house which had previously been a rather seedy hotel. Passing the armed sentries lounging outside I picked my way past the rotting windfalls under the bitter-orange trees lining the pavement of Avenida Mariscal López and walked a further two hundred yards down to the corner of Calle Rodo, an unpaved street which turned into a raging torrent during the rainy season. This marked the boundary of the Legation property and I could walk up this side road and go in past the kitchen quarters to the chancery through a wicket gate on the wire fence. This was also used by other visitors.

The following morning I was concentrating on my files at my desk in the outer office. Chip was deciphering a rare telegram in the privacy of the Minister's office while the usual in-cumbent attended a meeting of the diplomatic corps in the Papal Nuncio's house next door. I suddenly became aware of a strange sensation – the proverbial prickling at the back of my neck. I felt I was being observed by hidden, prying eyes. I looked up quickly at the window but there was nothing. I bent again over my files when, out of the corner of my eye, I caught a movement at the fly-screen door to the room. When I looked up, a large, expressionless face which had been peering silently into the relative dusk of the shady room, withdrew shyly and quickly. I got up startled and opened the door. When I stepped outside I found myself standing between four large, half-naked, copper-coloured figures, with feathers and head bands and enormous hands and bare feet who touched my arms and shoulders gently, with nodding and beaming faces, the while pointing silently at the inner office. Squatting on the verandah were half a dozen assorted men, women, and babies all of whom had clearly been there for some time without making the tiniest sound. Their clothing was rudimentary but all wore beads and bangles and other ornaments. The men were tall and well built, muscular and obviously strong. The women were either pregnant, or had babies around their necks. Apart from one toothless old crone, they were not ill-looking, with broad shoulders and slim hips. All wore their long lank hair cut in a straight fringe across their foreheads. Their features were regular and rather Mongolian in appearance, with prominent cheekbones, flat noses, wide mouths, and thick lips. They had clearly travelled a long way, were streaked with dust and sweating profusely. They all smelt to high heaven. Some carried bundles and sacks and I thought I detected some movement under the sacking.

Going back into my office I called out, 'Chip, I think you have some visitors!' to the figure immersed in his addition and subtraction in the inner room. Chip looked up with a start, got up from his papers and, looking out of the window at the assembled company in the yard, picked up the telegram, codebooks, and pads and bundled everything into the safe saying, 'It can wait until tomorrow, it's nothing very important anyway.' When he went out to the verandah, I could not help following. With an expressionless face he exchanged complicated greetings with one or two of the older men he seemed to know, shaking both hands at the elbows, so to speak, while uttering the guttural, monosyllabic, 'Ugh!' which seemed to comprise every third word of the conversation. The women were ignored. The leader of the group spoke in slow, measured words, with an even voice, like a man not accustomed to speak very much, in any language. Turning to one of the women, he reached out for the bag she was carrying and, placing it carefully on the floor of the verandah, tipped out the contents. These turned out to be two anacondas, the acquatic boa constrictor of the South American rivers, which grew to a large size in the jungles close to the Brazilian borders. I was told that at that time of the year the anacondas were in hibernation and therefore torpid and half asleep. Chip picked up one of them and uncoiled it as much as he could. 'Ugh!' he said, 'Not very big.' He was holding it up with one hand grasping the snake behind its head, two or three feet of tail still half coiled on the floor. 'A young one,' he said, passing it to the Indian chief, 'And this one is even smaller,' turning to the other heap of coils on the floor. The first one was about seven or eight feet long, dark greyish brown, almost black in places, and the thickest part of its body no more than about four or five inches in diameter. 'But they look in good condition. What else have they got?' he said, turning to another bundle already being unwrapped by the leader, who was carefully removing a blindfold from a curious-looking, hairy animal with large, hobbled feet and long nose. 'Ugh!' An anteater! Watch out for its claws! This is a good specimen.' Further exchanges with the Indians produced a small fox-like creature and a beautiful toucan with an enormous yellow beak as long as the rest of his body. Having negotiated a fair price, Chip told the Indians to take the animals along to his house and went into the office to telephone his wife warning her to expect company. At that moment the beflagged, official Humber Super Snipe came up the drive bearing the Minister from his meeting. 'Ha!' he sniffed, 'I wish Chip would get his friends to wash a little more frequently!' and, while doffing his tie and jacket added with interest, 'What have they brought this time?' whereupon everything had to be unpacked and exhibited again – and yet again when his two small daughters came out of the house shrieking with excitement in response to their father's calls.

Social life was hectic and bachelors much in demand, both among the foreign diplomatic corps and within the British community. All the Latin American ambassadors seemed to have attractive daughters and, in the absence of any theatre, opera, or other cultural pursuits of the sort taken for granted in

European capitals, the various foreign communities organized regular events, of which some of the most popular were the open-air barbecues in the capacious grounds of private houses, and the Sunday night dances at the Centenario country and social club. The young people managed to have a lot of fun, organizing parties at the drop of a hat, for any reason or excuse. Indulgent parents provided houses and servants (as well as food and drink) and the enchanting Paraguayan harp and guitar music and the balmy Paraguayan nights ensured that almost every evening was memorable in some way.

At weekends there was tennis and picnics and swimming, and, for those so inclined, riding, golf, and fishing. A wealthy counsellor at the Argentine Embassy (the largest mission in Asunción at the time) had sailed his luxury 50-foot cabin cruiser up from Buenos Aires; his three teenage daughters were popular hostesses on moonlight picnics on the river. There were several hospitable Paraguayan families who had ranches and stock-breeding *estancias* quite close to Asunción, where *asados* and parties and dances also took place during the weekends. The British-owned Liebig's Extract of Beef company had a large meat-packing plant at Zeballos-cué, outside the capital, where there lived also the mainly British expatriate management and technical staff, their wives and families, all generous and welcoming people. Altogether, the absence of more sophisticated entertainment ensured that everybody had a lot of fun most of the time, as is so frequently the case when people are thrown into each other's company and have to rely upon their own resources. But all this came to an unexpected and dramatic end, at least temporarily, after I had been there only a few weeks.

By the time I arrived in Asunción, General Moriñigo had alienated most of his original supporters except the Colorado party which was keen to retain power. More seriously, he had also lost the support of several of the army strong men he had originally appointed, including the commander of the first Cavalry Division based at Campo Grande, about eight miles from Asunción, which was then (as now) an important element in any political equation. Early one morning at the beginning of March a group of armed men in a bus drove to Asunción's central police station, seized the building, and wounded the chief of police, subsequently being driven off by the army.

Subsequent rumour had it that the attacking group had been promised support by the navy which, in the event, failed to materialize.

At the time we still had a press and information office in town, which had done sterling work during the war years, but which disappeared together with its staff as a result of the following round of public-spending cuts in the United Kingdom a few months later. I used to spend some mornings at this office in order to gain experience of all aspects of the Legation's work. That morning I had gone into town, heading for the police station where a British seaman was being held. From time to time a rare British-registered vessel was to be found moored in the port of Asunción, having sailed up the river from Buenos Aires. Although generally well behaved, seamen occasionally got into trouble, and when the agents told us that one of the ship's crew had been arrested the previous evening for being drunk and disorderly I was detailed to go and bail him out. As I neared the police station I became aware of unusual activity. The streets were full of army Jeeps and other vehicles, and there were groups of heavily armed soldiers on street corners. I could also hear bursts of firing. I prudently retreated and went back to the press and information office, where I tried to find out what was happening. For good measure I also went to the British Council Institute further up the road where the director, an expatriate Englishman called Duncan Targett-Adams, gave me a cup of tea but no news. A couple of hours later, I heard on the radio that order had been restored and that that the Government was in control of the situation. When, rather gingerly, I again approached the police station, I was invited in by a suspicious policeman who kept his rifle levelled at my back while he escorted me into the premises, where the drunken seaman, now as sober as a judge and as white as a sheet after the fright of his life, was duly handed over. He told me that the attackers had promised to free all prisoners, but when the government troops had driven them off and recaptured the police station the prisoners thought they were all going to be shot out of hand, if only to avoid the possibility of any cases of mistaken identity.

A few days later, we heard that the military garrison in Concepción, Paraguay's second city about 125 miles to the north of the capital, had revolted. A rebel radio station broadcast the rebel officers' intention to free Paraguay from Moriñigo's dictatorship and 'restore liberty and democracy', a claim made many times in Paraguay's brief history. The rebels were soon joined by Colonel Rafael Franco, one of the outstanding commanders of the Chaco war and founder of the Febrerista Party, which had been banned by Moriñigo, Colonel Franco was followed by a number of Moriñigo's political opponents and, more significantly, by the whole of the military garrison in the Chaco, where most of the army's equipment and ammunition was held. The rebels established a Provisional Government in Concepción and waited for Moriñigo's next move which, according to tradition, should have been a dignified exit across the river to the handy Argentine shore on the other side. In the meantime, there was a dusk-to-dawn curfew in Asunción, but the prevalence of trigger-happy patrols of teenaged conscripts kept most people off the streets even outside the curfew hours.

In the first few days, several dead donkeys were found shot every morning on the approaches to the general staff head-quarters near my house. One of the more picturesque aspects of life in Asunción was normally provided by the dozens of peasant women who, smoking their cigars, came into town early each day to sell fruit, vegetables, meat, and other commodities from the back of their long-suffering donkeys, a special breed of hardy grey animals which were habitually turned loose into the streets at night to graze on the succulent clumps of grass which grew high between the cobbles and the tramlines. They occupied a special place in the affection of all Paraguayans and had been the subject of poetry and children's fables. The nervous sentries guarding the general staff head-quarters at the top of the hill sometimes heard surreptitious noises in the darkness. When no reply was forthcoming to their loud challenge (in Guaraní), they unhesitatingly opened fire. A dead donkey was frequently the result.

A few days later, while the government troops were claiming successes in their unopposed march towards the rebel strong-hold in the north, the air force joined the rebels, while the Paraguayan Navy chose to remain neutral, possibly because the navy's two river gunboats were at the time undergoing a refit in Buenos Aires; they were obviously waiting on develop-ments before committing themselves in any way. In the meantime, the experts claimed that the situation could no longer be described as a *golpe* or revolution. In the past these had tended to be quick, incisive initiatives, followed by the crucial 'pronouncement' in support of one side or the other. The First Cavalry Division at Campo Grande was a reliable weather-vane; or, if things really looked serious, the deployment of the Artillery Regiment based at Paraguarí was usually decisive. But this was turning into a full-scale civil war. In fact, it went on for nearly six months, during which period most streets in Asunción were deserted, shops half closed, business at a standstill, and nervous tension evident on all sides. There were some episodes in this tragic period which deserve recording.

The government troops' northward march continued until the radio announced the imminent capture of Concepción, but the following few days' nervous silence suggested that there was something wrong. It turned out that when the government troops entered the city they found that it had been abandoned by the rebels, who had embarked with all their equipment and were even then sailing down the river on boats, barges, rafts, and anything that would float, to besiege a virtually defenceless Asunción which was clearly their objective. While the government troops, outflanked and bypassed by the rebels, were proclaiming their victory in Concepción, most people in the capital thought that the occupation of Asunción by the rebel troops was inevitable. But, having landed in the suburbs, the rebel forces encountered unexpected resistance from the new regiments of conscripts hurriedly formed by the government. As a result the 'front' moved back and forth in the suburbs of Asunción; day and night there was heavy firing just a few blocks away from the Legation. In the middle of one night I was frightened awake when the lights were suddenly turned on in my room where I was asleep. Through the mosquito netting I blinked at the sight of half a dozen soldiers in their olive-green uniforms aiming their rifles at me; they were only partially reassured when Winton rushed in and told them that I was a legitimate occupant of the house. With desultory kicks at the wardrobe and much jabbing of rifles under the bed they continued their search, which ended when a soldier in the street at the corner of the block arrested a man he saw jumping over our back wall. It turned out that our barefooted Paraguayan housemaid in the rear quarters had, in the time-honoured fashion, been entertaining a suitor who had been glimpsed scaling our garden wall after hours by one of the sentries at the general staff headquarters.

A few days later a well-known Lothario on the Brazilian Ambassador's staff drove out one evening to one of the suburbs to visit a young lady of his acquaintance. To their embarrassment, the next morning he found that the front had moved during the night; the rebel lines were between him and his embassy, and it was several days before the tide of war enabled him to emerge from his predicament, during which time his loyal colleagues tried to cover up for his absence while the Brazilian Ambassador clamoured for his presence. Unfortunately, a major with the attacking rebels and an eye for a rainy day sought to ingratiate himself with the Brazilian Ambassador (whose embassy was by this time already full of refugees) by ringing up the Ambassador to say that a safe passage for the errant swain had been arranged.

Throughout this period the sound of rifle and machine-gun fire and the boom of cannon could be heard as the rebels pressed into the outskirts of the capital. One immediate result of this situation was that Asunción suffered its first and last recorded air raid. It must have been a Sunday morning, as Winton Irvine and I were in the garden having a cool drink before lunch, chatting to some neighbours over the fence. Directly across the road from us there lived a colonel in the US military mission (they had all downed tools on the outbreak of hostilities) who was making some mint juleps which he sent us to sample. There was no traffic on the deserted avenue, and the characteristic drone of distant piston-driven engines gradually intruded into our awareness. After a few minutes we saw two biplanes circling lazily in the sky dropping bombs which the pilots heaved over the side of the cockpit from a great height. They were clearly aiming for the general staff headquarters just up the road. Two bombs landed in the Legation garden and did not explode. I must have been one of the few casualties of that historic raid. Having climbed to the roof of the house to get a better view I slipped on a loose tile and in order to save a fall embraced the hot iron pipe of the kitchen chimney-stack, painfully burning my hands and forearms. Meanwhile, many rumours circulated through an apprehensive town of closed shops and empty streets. The Argentine and Brazilian embassies could hardly cope with the influx of political refugees seeking asylum, and a truce was arranged to allow them to ship to Argentine territory across the river several hundred individuals who had reason to fear reprisals, from one side or the other, as a result of the situation.

Even through these abnormal months there was much to keep me busy and occupied. Shortly after my arrival I learnt that in order to get paid I had to submit something called a 'life certificate' to the Foreign Office. This was required at the end of every quarter and included details of the 'advances' I had drawn from legation funds every month in order to exist. The size of these advances was limited by a complicated formula designed to ensure that an adequate balance remained at the end of the quarter to enable the authorities to collect income tax, national insurance contributions, and other deductions made at source. My annual emoluments were made up of a salary of £245, a foreign allowance of £258, and a rent allowance of £145. As most of our correspondence, other than that which was classified and carried by 'safe hand', arrived by sea mail, any exchanges with London about administrative matters were liable to take up to six months to complete the round trip. In practice, this meant that the balance of the salary I had earned in April was not paid to me until my life certificate signed at the end of the June quarter was received at the Foreign Office (probably in August) where they made the proper deductions and paid what was left into my London bank in, say, September. In the fullness of time I then received a foolscap form (confusingly, it was also called a 'life certificate') setting out, in beautiful copperplate handwriting, the corresponding calculations and subtotals and notifying me of the final figure paid into my account. If our certificates from Asunción were delayed for any reason, payment was naturally withheld.

Classified correspondence was collected in a special tray in the safe, in which it reposed until there was enough to justify a special 'safe hand' journey to or from Buenos Aires which was at the receiving end of the regular, scheduled King's messenger run from London and North America. Likewise, classified material from London for Asunción was collected in the registry of the Buenos Aires Embassy until its onward delivery was arranged by 'safe hand'. When I discovered that it was customary to wait for somebody in Buenos Aires (the Service Attachés there were also accredited to Paraguay and each one came to Asunción two or three times a year on other business) to bring our classified bag to Asunción I volunteered to travel to Buenos Aires at any time this might be necessary. As a result of the civil war, I undertook several journeys with confidential despatches (and, in the light of the suspension of normal postal services, also our life certificates) to Buenos Aires, where I was royally entertained by members of the embassy there, all anxious for the latest news from the front. I flew down on a Friday on the Argentine-operated Sunderland passenger flying boats which conveniently landed in the harbour at both ends, and travelled back to Asunción on the Monday. This gave me the opportunity to savour some of the big-city attractions of Buenos Aires.

In 1947 Buenos Aires' well-stocked department stores, wide avenues, clubs, restaurants, parks, and bright lights all made a startling change for anybody fresh from Europe. On my way to Paraguay I had spent a day or two in Buenos Aires before taking passage on the old-fashioned paddle-steamer which took me nearly a thousand miles up the Paraná river to Asunción. On that first occasion there had been little time for anything other than onward travel arrangements for self and luggage, whereas my trips to Buenos Aires from Asunción with the diplomatic bag during the disturbed period which followed my arrival in Paraguay provided many opportunities to see places and meet people. The Naval Attaché took me to lunch at the Jockey Club, then still in its original premises on the Calle Florida where, I was told, about two thousand people lunched every day in its dining-rooms, consuming vast steaks, known locally as *bifes*, among other delicacies. The club facilities were legendary; libraries, gymnasiums, fencing halls and swimming pools were shown to me; the imposing main entrance hall and staircase displayed Carrara marble, rich tapestries, and crystal chandeliers at every turn; and many other imported materials, carpets, and works of art combined to give the club the ostentatiously opulent atmosphere, redolent of wealth, tradition, and breeding which made it such a special target for the Peronist mob which sacked and burnt it down a short time later.

182

Another kind host took me to the Hurlingham Club to watch the polo on Sunday. At the time this club was the quintessential and unabashed concentration of everything that had made Argentina the foreign country with the largest resident British community outside the Commonwealth, although the winds of change were even then beginning to make themselves felt. In a splendid setting, there were several polo grounds, tennis courts, swimming pools and golf courses. Cricket and rugger flourished and proliferated. The cold buffet on Sundays was famed throughout South America. One helped oneself from a central table which seemed to go on for miles, laden with every conceivable delicacy of the sort not seen in England since before the war. Enormous cold cuts, saddles of beef, boned turkeys, sucking pig, fish and prawns were all displayed side by side with game pies, pâtés, hams, partridge and quail's eggs, sausages, different salads, avocado pears, fruits, cheeses, and puddings; after which one drove to the chosen polo ground where one sat in the car parked on the sidelines viewing the exciting matches, with fast ponies and reckless riders who encouraged each other with shouts and strange oaths in a mixture of English and Spanish. When somebody scored a goal the orderly ranks of parked cars tooted their horns politely. Pretty English-looking girls in English school uniforms and gymslips sat on the open sunshine roofs of the family cars and twittered and chattered in 'spanglish', unlike some of their parents or grandparents in the car below who could hardly speak Spanish even though they, also, had been born in Argentina. Neither their birth, nor Argentina's refusal to declare war on the Axis Powers until 1945 prevented many thousands of Anglo-Argentine volunteers from joining the British armed forces on the outbreak of war in 1939; indeed, so numerous were they that in due course a special shoulder flash with the word *Argentina* was authorized, as was the case with the forces of Commonwealth countries.

All the Argentine railways had been British owned, as well as many other public utilities. Wire fencing had originally been imported by the British, and there were vast ranches throughout the country which were owned by British companies or individuals. The meat-canning plants were also foreign owned, as were the banks which financed the meat trade and the refrigerated ships that plied regularly from the River Plate to

European ports with many hundreds of thousands of tons of frozen and chilled beef for devastated and rationed Europe. It was said that an Englishman working in Buenos Aires could leave his home with a copy of the English-language *Buenos Aires Herald* (founded in 1876) under his arm, travel into the commercial centre of the capital on one of the British-owned railways, spend the day in the city working in his British insurance office or bank or whatever, having adjourned for lunch to one of the three English clubs in town, and return home on the evening train while glancing through the English-language *Standard* to the bosom of his wife and family in, say, suburban Temperley. His children went to a nearby English school, one of a dozen or more in greater Buenos Aires, including the prestigious St George's College, at the time the only British Headmasters' Conference school (together with Victoria College in Cairo) outside the Commonwealth. No wonder they never needed to learn Spanish.

When I returned to Asunción after my second such trip to Buenos Aires I found that our official driver, a likeable but monosyllabic Paraguayan of unmistakably close Indian ancestry, had disappeared. It was thought that he had either been conscripted into one of the new regiments hurriedly formed by the Government, or had gone into hiding to avoid this. At all events, this proved to be an unexpected boon for me. Imports had been suspended, commerce was at a standstill, and I had not yet acquired a car. In the prevailing conditions walking was not advisable and, in some areas, unsafe, and neither the minister nor his wife could drive. Even though most social and official activities had come to a halt (with the exception of the heads of missions' regular meetings at the Papal Nuncio's house next door), like everybody else I found my confinement to quarters increasingly irksome; and someone had to go down to the post office in town, if only to see if any sea mail diplomatic bags (containing unclassified correspondence, out-of-date newspapers or private mail) had trickled through. There were other essential chores which entailed a trip to the Ministry of Foreign Affairs in town at least once a week, tasks which I happily undertook driving the official car, feeling more or less secure in the shadow of the largest Union Jack I could fit, which fluttered gallantly from the bonnet of the Minister's Humber.

I was thus indoctrinated into the techniques required for driving on Asunción's cobbled streets, some of which had been eroded by season after season of rains. The cobblestones were uneven and irregular and very uncomfortable (not to speak of what they did to the car's suspension) to drive on. I had previously noted with curiosity the predominance of pre-war-model American cars on Asunción's streets; it turned out that the main reason for their popularity was that their wheels fitted precisely on the tramlines which then existed in Asunción's main streets and avenues. This enabled drivers to mount the tracks and drive in level comfort as far as they could before being obliged to take avoiding action by, for instance, a tram coming in the opposite direction. There was even a rule of the road which gave cars heading into town priority on the tramlines over vehicles (other than trams) coming out. These were obliged to reduce their speed to a crawl and abandon the comfort of the tramlines in favour of the driver coming in the opposite direction. All this was lent additional interest by the fact that the tramlines had, in many places, been exposed to a height of six or eight inches by the seasonal rains which had caused the uneven supporting cobbles to subside. Some of my friends displayed their skill when driving over points by taking the diverging track at over sixty miles an hour in places where a fall from the tramlines at that speed would have seriously damaged the suspension of their cars. The then new-fangled Jeeps were popular in the 'camp' but their wheels did not fit the tramlines in town. Low-slung British (small) cars had to confine themselves to the irregular cobbles, or attempt an even more hazardous balancing act on one set of wheels.

The Humber Super Snipe (a large British car in those days) was precisely the right size and would glide serenely into town and back again as I discovered when I acquired the knack of driving on the tramlines without falling off. One morning I drove into town along the Avenida España, the other main residential avenue which ran more or less parallel to Avenida Mariscal López. Needless to say this also had a single set of tramlines with the corresponding points and a bypass with double track at two or three places along the route, where incoming tram drivers could pass their outward heading colleagues, with much clanging of bells, switching of points and electric flashing from the overhead trolleys. This was always carried out at the leisurely tempo which permitted the conductors to pause for a companionable smoke and exchange news of the traffic in town or whatever, while some of the passengers nipped out for a coffee or Coca-Cola at the roadside stall. It had been raining all night and the streets were full of puddles, which covered the tramlines where these dipped into a pool of water. If travelling at any speed one had to see where the tramline came out and estimate accurately what happened in between. But there was another hazard also, which I discovered when I was passing the US Embassy, just as the ambassadorial Buick, a large, new car of the latest model, emerged from the gates, the driver pausing politely when he saw me coming down the tramlines. I could not see if the Ambassador was within, as I was still some distance away, but with the proper deference to rank and seniority, I waved the driver on and began braking as the Buick acknowledged my signal and lumbered across the uneven road. But the tramlines were wet and the Humber's tyres must have been balding. To my horror the Humber continued sailing down the tramlines as though no brakes had been applied. Fortunately, I was travelling at a moderate speed, but by the time I came off the tramlines the alarmed Buick driver had likewise taken avoiding action and reversed right into my new course. Inevitably, we came together with a gentle crunch as the front of my Super Snipe hit the new Buick in its bulbous rear quarter.

The US Ambassador in Paraguay was then Mr Fletcher Warren, a tall, large, genial man with grey hair brushed straight back, steel-rimmed spectacles, and a ready smile. He towered over any gathering in more senses than one. For their own reasons, the US administration then attached greater importance to Paraguay (as a buffer state between the two giant rivals) than did, for instance, many European governments. As a result their envoys to Paraguay were, with few exceptions, either individuals whose reputations preceded them, or who went on to greater things. Mr Warren fitted into both categories and achieved high office in the Department of State after he left Asunción which, providentially, was not until shortly before I myself was transferred. I was therefore given both the time and some opportunities to get to know and appreciate him. But when I hit his car outside his offices I had only met him once, and when I got out of the Humber I was much relieved to see that he was not in his car. His driver looked aggrieved, pointed to the damaged rear wing, and looked at me enquiringly. After a few moments' helpless reflection I decided that there was nothing to do but to go into the US Embassy and own up. When I walked in nervously I asked for a Third Secretary called Roy Makepeace, who was a friend. When I told him what had happened he hooted with laughter and said I should see the Ambassador straight away. Without further ado he marched me into the ambassadorial suite, past the vigilant marine guard and the secretary in the outer office, opened the door, and addressed the bulky figure at the far desk. 'Good morning, Mr Ambassador,' he said, 'here's someone who has a confession to make!' and with a half-suppressed giggle he left the room and closed the door quickly, leaving me squirming on the carpet in the middle of the room.

Mr Warren looked up in surprise, and got up courteously with a smile, 'Hi, Charlie! What's new?' As soon as the Ambassador got the drift of my incoherent excuses and stammered explanations, he interrupted me with a rambling anecdote about an embarrassing experience he recalled as a young man shortly after joining the Foreign Service, which I suspect he was making up as he went along. With much laughter and heaving shoulders he assured me he had felt terrible. In order to put at ease he then drew my attention to a wholly unremarkable painting on one of the walls and called his secretary to bring us some coffee. He wondered if I was enjoying Paraguay and asked me for my opinion of the latest political developments. Before I left he again cut short my apologies and invited me to dinner the following week, sending me on my way with a cheery wave and an unshakeable conviction that US ambassadors were great and good men, a conviction which was to remain with me for many years.

The civil war continued until August 1947, when General Moriñigo, with the aid of Argentine arms and equipment made freely available by General Perón, was finally successful in defeating the insurgents, mainly as a result of the manifest lack of harmony among the rebel Febrerista, Liberal, and Communist leaders and commanders. Their forces disintegrated into marauding guerrilla bands which for months continued to roam about the countryside with scant regard for the central Government's writ. Ironically, a few months later General

Moriñigo was also obliged to follow the insurgent leaders into exile when the electoral ploy with which he intended to retain influence and control behind the presidency failed. The Colorado party then seized the opportunity to assume power in their own right. This was followed by a period of continuing political instability in which no less than four other presidents, either provisional or elected, assumed office before I left Asunción in September 1949.

During this confused period, most people tried hard to resume their normal lives and work. A friend of mine whose father had extensive ranching interests in the north was on holiday from his American university where he was studying agricultural engineering. He invited me to join him on a trip intended to restock their ranches with horses, most of which had been requisitioned or stolen by one side or the other in the recent hostilities. Throughout the country there was much overdue work in the 'camp' branding or inoculating new calves, moving herds to new pastures, and selecting cattle for slaughter or sale. Little of this could be undertaken without horses. As I had had no leave since my arrival (my trips to Buenos Aires did not count), my kind superiors decided that my selfless dedication and unceasing devotion to duty throughout the civil war merited a reward and I was granted a week's local leave.

I set off at dawn one morning with my friend, four or five cow-hands and a troop of thirty riderless, half-wild horses led by a bell mare. The plan was to leave six or eight horses at each of the four ranches we were to visit on our way to Concepción, the ertswhile rebel capital in the north where, having got rid of the horses, we proposed to embark on a river steamer and return in comfort to Asunción overnight. In the aftermath of the civil war, when conditions in some parts of the country were still very unsettled, our trip was an adventurous and exciting undertaking. For me, it was also a memorable experience. I was prodigally fitted out with a broad-brimmed straw hat, baggy riding trousers and soft leather boots, a Winchester rifle, a Colt .45 revolver, enormous spurs (the large rowels were quite blunt, but they tinkled pleasantly), and a rawhide lasso, as well as a fearsome machete about three feet long which was carried in a leather scabbard attached to the saddle rather like a cavalry sword. The evening before we left I thought that all

188

this was rather theatrical, until the following morning I saw that everybody else was similarly attired and equipped, except for the boots. Some of the cow-hands wore spurs strapped on their bare feet. I rode a well-trained and intelligent cow pony, with a brisk and level walking pace, for up to twelve hours a day while herding the troop of wandering horses behind the lead mare.

At night my bulky but comfortable Paraguayan saddle with its component sheepskins, blankets, leather jerkins, and ponchos disintegrated into an equally comfortable bed on which I slept the sleep of the just under the starry southern skies, my face and head covered by blanket and hat against any wandering, probably rabid, bats. Just in case, one or two sacrificial horses were tethered under a tree close by. One morning we did find one of the horses drenched in its own blood from neck to fetlock. At first sight it looked as though its throat had been slit open. But after we washed the blood away we could scarcely see the tiny orifice in the tough skin, neatly sliced out by the bat's front teeth, which had obviously bled for hours. I was told that the bats did not suck the blood, but that their saliva contained an anti-coagulant which caused the blood to flow freely, thus enabling the vampire to drink without even waking the horse, which continued to bleed after the bat had gorged itself and flitted away. If this happened three or four consecutive nights the horses were much weakened and the constant loss of blood could cause their death. It was therefore essential to move the horses frequently and tether them away from the leafy mango trees frequented by bats.

On the trail we were roused just before dawn with hot coffee or *mate*, which some of the riders brewed squatting on their heels round the small fire. We had brought boiled mandioca and strips of dried meat, but most of the time we lived off the land, shooting wildfowl or partridges for the pot and catching fish in the rivers and lagoons we forded. Many were the strange dishes I savoured on this trip. We ate the tender, white meat of the greater armadillo and the tasty, flaky flesh of the crocodile's tail. Every two or three days we arrived at a ranch where a welcome bath, a change of clothing, an iced drink, and a proper bed for the night were all available in return for the half-dozen horses we had delivered. We had encounters with alligators, pumas, wild boar, jackals, one beautiful ocelot, ostriches, and any number of snakes, and visited Indian villages and isolated farms.

The memory of one incident at one of the ranches we visited remains vivid. Having showered and changed after arriving one evening we were sitting outside in the grassy courtyard of the main house before dinner. Like most of the ranches we visited, this one had a tame donkey which was allowed the run of the yard and played with the dogs and children. One of the cowboys was teasing him, pulling on the short rope round his neck which dragged behind him and was used to tether him whenever necessary. Kicking up his heels the donkey trotted off to a nearby hedge by the wire fence, where his trailing rope caught in one of the bushes. The cow-hand followed the donkey and bent to pick up the rope from the thicket with his left hand. When he straightened up he had the rope in his hand, but hanging from its fangs deep in his index finger there was a small snake, not more than twelve inches long, with a noticeable reddish pattern down its back. Without a second's hesitation he strode across to the nearest wooden post in the fence, placed finger and snake on the block and, with a muttered curse in Guaraní, neatly chopped off the top of his index finger with his machete. As an afterthought he also chopped off the head of the snake, still attached to the finger lying on the post. He drank half a bottle of rum while undergoing some rudimentary cauterization which I declined to watch. When he mounted his horse the next morning with his bandaged hand and a sore head he explained to me that he had recognized the snake as a *jarará*, which I learnt later was a particularly virulent variety of the indigenous coral snake, whose bite was said to be mortal in a few minutes. In those days few ranches had a supply of anti-poison serum to be used in such emergencies, as is now the case, and there was no doubt that this courageous and stoical reaction saved his life. Some months later I was myself bitten by a black widow spider and was quite ill until the Brazilian Air Force mission's aeroplane brought back to Asunción the appropriate antidote from the Brazilian Government's snake and poison farm at Butantan.

My trip, the first of many visits to the attractive and always varied Paraguayan 'camp', gave me my first opportunity to see the country outside the capital and learn something of the character and nature of the friendly and gentle people with such an unusual and violent history. Whether in isolated ranches, remote villages, or modest dwellings in the middle of nowhere, I met men and women of great charm who were welcoming and proud, generous and hospitable, with a natural sense of dignity and courtesy. They made a notable impression on me (admittedly at an impressionable age) and I made a lot of friends. This is perhaps why the events of those far-off years remained so clear in my mind, and why the prospect of returning to Paraguay so many years later was impossible to refuse.

Before I leave those early days at my first post abroad, I must return to the ramshackle chancery offices of the Legation. Just before Chip left Paraguay on transfer his Indian friends began to resume their visits after the civil war. One day, while we were both working in the outer office, Chip hissed at me in a stage whisper, 'Don't look now, but we're surrounded!' I looked up and caught a glimpse of a coppery face peering through the door. There was another face at the window. The usual group had arrived with the usual bags. Having opened one bag on the chancery floor I saw eight or ten baby alligators with protruding eyes wriggling and panting in the bottom of the bag. Chip deftly picked one up, holding it firmly behind its head, studied it and concluded that he was only a few days out of the egg, being no more than about eight or nine inches from nose to tail. When he put it down on his desk, it quickly scuttled for cover under the open cover of the fat government telegraph code book which was on his table. With the familiarity I had by then acquired, I reached out and confidently picked it up by the tail with my thumb and forefinger, rather like a matron daintly holding a cup of tea with the little finger pointing to the ceiling. The indignant little beast promptly reared up on its own tail and bit my extended little finger, which was the only one within range of its tiny but sharp teeth.

Twenty-six years later I presented my credentials to President Alfredo Stroessner on 25 February 1976. General Stroessner was at that time in his early sixties, a corpulent figure above average height, with thinning fair hair, pale-blue eyes, a florid complexion, and a clipped moustache. He did not fit into the popular image of a Latin American dictator, being an indifferent orator who had never been known to deliver a speech without notes or, preferably, a full text. Even after thirty-odd years of accrediting ambassadors he read, with teutonic thoroughness, a printed card with the traditional formula of half a dozen words which acknowledged the new ambassador's speech and recognized him as such. My presentation of credentials had been delayed for a week or so because he had undergone a cosmetic operation on his eyelids, reportedly to remove an excessive upper fold of skin which had given him a hooded, sinister gaze. Normally impassive and undemonstrative, throughout the official ceremony he wore sunglasses while photographers were present. Afterwards, when we sat down for the customary private chat, he removed them to reveal puffy, red-rimmed lids which obviously caused him some discomfort. His Spanish had a strong Guaraní intonation. He was almost monosyllabic and clearly not a conversationalist, being hard put to it to make any small talk at all. When I referred to my earlier sojourn in the 1940s he smiled fleetingly and said, 'That was a bad period, but now all that sort of thing is over.' He changed the subject by asking me about Field Marshal Montgomery, of whom (I learnt subsequently) he was a great admirer, having read every book available in Spanish about the Eighth Army and Second World War campaigns in North Africa and Europe. He referred to one or two notable occasions during Montgomery's North African campaign, with dates and numbers and names, and was clearly unimpressed when I confessed I was a schoolboy at the time. But I think I scored a point when I claimed to be a friend of the field marshal's son, David, who had interests in Latin America.

When I arrived in Paraguay in 1976, there were estimated to be between six hundred and a thousand political prisoners or detainees, some of whom had been many years in captivity. They had been the subject of repeated representations over many years by a number of countries, including the United Kingdom, but it was only when Mr Robert White was appointed US Ambassador that the situation began to improve. Bob White and his attractive wife were close neighbours; our houses shared a common boundary wall. Our physical proximity enabled us to meet frequently and informally and we became friends. As United States Ambassador he was in a good position to bring various pressures to bear and it was not long before his forceful initiatives persuaded the Paraguayan authorities to release some of the longer-serving prisoners. Yet others were exiled or released when the European Community representatives, acting in concert, regularly added the telling weight of our combined represent-ations to the US Ambassador's efforts. By the time I left Paraguay in mid-1979 there were less than half a dozen political prisoners left in gaol, an achievement in which Bob White's determined efforts played a leading role, but which also resulted in a highly organized anti-US demonstration taking place in Asunción for the first time in living memory.

I also found that there were many other, less unpleasant, changes. Happily, neither the country nor the people had lost any of their charm. The population of the capital had grown to over half a million, and the cobblestones and grass had given way to paved streets and broad new avenues. We had a new house and new offices. There were highways to the Iguazú Falls on the Brazilian border and to the principal provincial capitals. The building of the colossal dam at Itaipú gave work and a measure of prosperity to many thousands of Paraguayan workers, to the extent that it became difficult to find a plumber or electrician or carpenter to carry out domestic repairs in Asunción. People no longer went barefoot. The Indians still came into town with feather dusters, baskets and beads, but they wore jeans and sandals and T-shirts. The political instability and economic uncertainties which had been such tragic but constant features of the local scene throughout my first sojourn in Paraguay had ended when, in yet another military coup after my departure, General Stroessner, the erstwhile colonel commanding the Artillery Division in Paraguarí, seized power in 1954. Unexpectedly, his *golpe* was this time to be followed by a period of thirty-five years, wholly unprecedented in the history of Paraguay, of stable and uninterrupted authoritarian rule. Perhaps the country was exhausted by so many years of wars, revolutions, and con-spiracies, or weakened by the loss of almost a third of its population, either in exile or seeking a more promising future elsewhere. Be that as it may, General Stroessner's autocratic and paternalistic regime, with its darker side and grave flaws, presided over many years of significant economic and social development which saw the emergence of a new, broadly based, educated and prosperous middle class of lawyers, doctors, bank managers and businessmen, as well as the more traditional stock breeders and landowners, which also increased and multiplied. Perhaps, as some writers have suggested, Paraguayans have an atavistic empathy and predilection for strong and authoritarian government, rooted in the origins of their unusual history. Perhaps not. In either case, I wish them well.

PART

4

Let observation with extensive view,
Survey mankind, from China to Peru.

Samuel Johnson, *The Vanity of Human Wishes*
(1749).

11

Peru and the Falklands: Lima

The Church of San Pedro in Lima is in a small square adjacent to the Palace of Torre Tagle, the splendid colonial mansion in central Lima which was the home of one of Peru's Spanish viceroys and is now the Ministry of Foreign Affairs. When I arrived in Lima in September 1979 I was met at the airport by the ministry's Director of Protocol and cordially invited to call on his minister a couple of days later, in order to hand over the copies of my letters of credence which I would in due course present ceremonially to the President, General Francisco Morales Bermudez.

Before leaving my office on the appointed day I was warned to make due allowance for the traffic congestion in central Lima and give myself plenty of time in order to avoid, at all costs, the possibility of being late. It was explained to me that this would never do for the British Ambassador in a country where appointments stipulated *hora inglesa* as a matter of course whenever punctuality was expected. The density of the traffic being unpredictable I found myself arriving at the Torre Tagle palace with nearly half an hour to spare. The narrow streets and one-way traffic flow of viceregal Lima made it inadvisable to drive round a couple of blocks without again running the risk of being stuck in a jam and having to abandon the car and hoof it back to one's destination, probably arriving late as a result. I therefore responded with alacrity to my driver's suggestion that I should fill in the time by visiting the Church of San Pedro, whence I could walk the few yards across the square to the Ministry thus ensuring my arrival at the appointed hour, while he went off to find a parking place.

The church is possibly the finest example of Jesuit religious architecture to be found in Peru. I was much impressed by the

197

richness of the wood carvings, the hand-painted tiles, the magnificent paintings, the gilded frames, the latticed balconies, the soaring naves, and the skilful lighting. The arches separating the various chapels are as varied as the chapels themselves. The abundance of religious silverware and the innumerable works of art were prodigally distributed in the three main naves. The chapels in a row on both sides were each different in style and content, the whole producing an impression of artistic splendour and superlative beauty. The church was built and owned by the Jesuits until their expulsion in 1767. Because of its solid structure it had not suffered overmuch from the earthquakes and tremors which were frequent in Lima and was therefore supposed to be in much the same condition as when it was inaugurated in 1638. The wealth of religious paintings alone justified many hours of contemplation, but the architectural excellence and the variety and richness of the decoration made the discovery of new treasures an exciting feature of every visit. One of the chapels by the main entrance to the church was known as the 'penitentiary' because sinners who had been to confession there offered up their paternosters and Ave Marias in private penance at this altar, one of the most attractive in the whole complex.

Needless to say, I did not take in a fraction of all this on my first visit, but the virtually empty church, magically insulated from the prevailing traffic noise and bustle of the streets of central Lima, together with its permanent atmosphere of richly endowed spiritual peace, provided me, when calling at the Ministry in later years, with the often welcome opportunity of a few minutes' solitary reflection in which I could rehearse the terms of my instructions from London or the manner in which my arguments were to be deployed. Then, three or four minutes before the appointed time, I would leave the church and walk across the street to the Ministry of Foreign Affairs where a diligent member of the Protocol Department, who could see no sign of my official car, would be waiting at the main entrance looking anxiously at this watch.

Unlike some of my foreign colleagues I thus managed to uphold the tradition, established by generations of British ambassadors, of arriving precisely at the appointed 'English' hour. I also benefited, both physically and mentally, from the cool and peaceful atmosphere of spiritual solace which enabled me, without going so far as seeking divine inspiration, to marshall my thoughts and reorder my choice of words. My habit was doubly useful whenever English texts hurriedly translated into Spanish did not always succeed in conveying the proper meaning or significance. Even though it was always made clear that the English version was the formal text and most Peruvian officials spoke admirable English, it was clearly desirable to facilitate the task of the Peruvian authorities by ensuring that no possible misinterpretation could impair their understanding of the precise terms of our communication.

Before the Falklands crisis, President Belaúnde Terry's first foreign minister, Dr Javier Arias Stella, by profession a pathologist of eminence and a man of great charm and humour, discovered my retreat in the Church of San Pedro and reproached me for making it appear that I had to do penance every time I went to see him. His jovial personality and informal manner soon enabled us to establish a close and harmonious working relationship which was to endure throughout his tenure of office. Much the same applied to successive secretaries-general (vice-ministers), under-secretaries, departmental directors and other officials at the Ministry, without exception courteous and accessible as well as highly professional and dedicated.

Many of the officials I had dealings with had served in London; one or two had been my 'clients' while I was in the American Department of the Foreign Office. Yet others I had met in New York when I went to the United Nations to do a Latin American lobbying exercise in the autumn of 1975 during a critical period in the Guatemala/Belize dispute. There I found that the head of the Peruvian delegation to the UN had been a close friend many years before during my first tour of duty in Asunción, where the Peruvian Embassy (and the Peruvian Ambassador's charming daughters) provided a hospitable and convivial rallying point for a group of un-attached and carefree bachelors and maidens who nightly danced the hours away to the strains of the imcomparable Paraguayan music under a preposterous Paraguayan moon. When I arrived in Lima in 1979 I found that the Peruvian Ambassador's daughter, whose grace and beauty had so impressed all in Asunción, had in the fullness of time returned with her parents to Peru, where she had married another

Belaúnde, the future President's younger brother. Great was my pleasure when we met again after umpteen years with our respective spouses and much talk of assorted children and grandchildren.

Also at the UN in 1975 I was happy to find that many officials of the Mexican foreign ministry had taken up residence in New York to reinforce their delegation for the General Assembly. Having spent the previous two years at the embassy in Mexico City I was able to resume business with several of my friends and contacts from the Mexican skyscraper on the Plaza of the Three Cultures at Tlatelolco who had sensibly translated themselves for the duration to the corridors and committee rooms of the United Nations skyscraper on the lower east side of Manhattan. It so happened that Mexico that year played a significant role in defusing the Guatemala/Belize situation. My long hours of selfless and dedicated work at the delegate's bar and dining-rooms with my Mexican and other Latin American friends certainly made my task easier and enabled our delegation to pursue our objective (a General Assembly resolution supporting the principle of Belizean independence) in a manner which proved satisfactory to all (except the then Guatemalan Military Government). All of which proves nothing; except possibly that the Latin American 'circuit' is as readily identifiable as any of those in other parts of the world with a common language, and perhaps more so than some.

I regarded myself as fortunate in having been appointed to Peru at that particular time. General Francisco Morales Bermudez had already announced that a return to civilian rule would take place in 1980 and that the armed forces would ensure that the presidential elections were free, fair, and above board. The last democratically elected civilian president, Fernando Belaúnde Terry had been overthrown in a bloodless military coup in 1968 by a group of left-wing military officers led by General Juan Velasco Alvarado who departed from the traditional Latin American model of military intervention and formed a radical Government which embarked on populist and wide-ranging programmes involving agricultural reform, expropriation of land, and nationalization of industry. This led to the massive intervention of the state in a public sector which ranged from oil and mining, through agriculture and fishing to cinemas and supermarkets. Eventually, the results of an inefficient administration, agricultural underemployment, the flight of capital, exorbitant state subsidies, and heavy expenditure on sophisticated military weapons and aircraft contrived to bring about a change of course, which also resulted in the replacement of General Velasco (by this time seriously ill) by General Morales Bermudez, who had himself been a member of President Belaúnde's last cabinet in 1968.

The new government pursued the more conservative and traditional policies usual in a continent where the military tend to regard themselves as the custodians of the established order of things and the declared enemies of communism, this last a legacy from the days when anti-communist postures and pronouncements were calculated to produce unlimited largesse from the United States, together with avuncular encouragement to those authoritarian military regimes which could be trusted to stem the threatening tide of communist infiltration in Uncle Sam's back yard. The Peruvian radical military government of General Velasco was a curious exception to the rule, even in a country where the gap between the haves and the have nots was truly frightening, but the results of his reforms were manifestly disastrous even within the period of his own mandate. His successor adopted more cautious, middle-of-the-road policies, while a constituent assembly redrafted the constitution and legislation was enacted to reform the electoral system.

When I arrived in Lima the decision to hold democratic elections had already been announced, and the political parties were planning their strategy. The odds lay between Victor Raul Haya de la Torre's APRA (Alianza Popular Revolucionaria Americana) and Fernando Belaúnde's Acción Popular, and the betting was that the armed forces would keep their word and permit the formation of a civilian government unless a fearsome last-minute alliance of all the left-wing parties won the elections. This was in itself an advance on the historical attitude of the armed forces towards APRA, an organization they had regarded as dangerous and revolutionary (as evinced by the party's name) and a threat to the armed forces' tradition of entrenched privilege. But Haya's untimely death robbed APRA of the possibility of an electoral landslide in 1980, even though the final outcome, after twelve years without political activity, was by no means easy to predict. There also remained, of course, the persistent question mark over the armed forces' real intentions, after long years of absolute power in a country with a history of reiterated intervention in government.

Having presented my credentials to General Francisco Morales Bermudez I embarked on the inevitable round of visits to foreign ambassadors and ministers of the government. While most of the ambassadors I called on (I was privileged to find a couple of friends from earlier postings elsewhere) freely gave me their impressions of the situation and opinions on the prospects before us, the Peruvian ministers I called on were markedly less communicative. With the exception of the Minister of Foreign Affairs (a retired career diplomat) most were army or air force generals. The navy minister was an admiral. In the main, they saw themselves as administrators and tried to do their best to solve the problems facing their departments. They had no parliament or congress to answer to. If they reached retiring age while in office they were succeeded by the next man on the seniority list. They were always in uniform and most of their senior collaborators were members of their own service. Their philosophy was uncomplicated. They made no pretence at being politically inspired, and contrived to suggest that they were governing only because the civilians had (yet again) demonstrated that they were incapable of doing so. But they were disposed to give the politicians another chance, and hoped that this time things would turn out for the better. My mornings were thus taken up by visits to a succession of courteous, unsmiling, uniformed figures behind large, empty desks, who usually answered my questions with statistics and printed brochures. One notable exception was the Prime Minister, Minster for War, and Chief of Staff of the Armed Forces, General Pedro Richter Prada. On ceremonial occasions his smart uniform, German-style helmet, stern appearance and rimless glasses had earned him the sobriquet 'Der Führer' from Lima's irrepressible political satirists, but he was a genial, impressive and sensitive man whose intellectual stature made him stand out among his peers. His brother was the Archbishop of Ayacucho and he was himself a deeply religious man. I valued his friendship throughout my time in Peru, particularly after he became more accessible when he retired after President Belaúnde assumed office.

My daily calls on government officials and ambassadors continued unabated into the beginning of 1980. I was in something of a hurry; I had been warned by London of the prospect of one or two ministerial visits before the elections and was anxious to work myself into the job well in advance. I arranged meetings with newspaper editors and journalists and also presidential candidates as soon as the dates of the elections had been confirmed and their candidature formally announced. This was a very interesting and exciting period in Lima; political figures began to emerge from the obscurity or exile in which they had existed for the previous decade, and traditional establishment names were joined by a new generation of relatively unknown personalities who were determined to exercise their constitutional rights in an increasingly effervescent political atmosphere. Distinguished personalities who had not deemed it necessary to grace the social scene for many years began to reappear on informal occasions. One such gathering was described by a cynical colleague as having an odour of turned earth about it. But the Peruvians are a gregarious and hospitable people and the social round became more and more frenetic. At this stage all this was hardly reflected in the local press, which had been nationalized by the armed forces in 1974 and did not accurately reflect popular opinions or feeling.

I had therefore taken an early opportunity to call on Fernando Belaúnde, then living quietly in a small flat in a residential suburb of Lima after eight years of exile in the United States, where he taught architecture at various prestigious universities. We had also been in touch with other members of the Belaúnde family which, it so happened, had been known to my wife and her family for many years. As children, my wife, her brother, and sisters lived with their parents in Madrid. In the privileged years between the wars it was customary to abandon the capital during the torrid summer months, and the northern resorts of San Sebastián and Fuenterrabía in Spain, and Hendaye just across the border in France, were among the favourites for parents and children in Madrid, as indeed they were also for many French families. At the time the Belaúnde family was living in Paris, the future President's father, himself, a prominent establishment figure in Peruvian politics, being out of sympathy with the regime then in office in Peru. They also chose to spend their summer holidays at Hendaye, where they struck up a friendship with my future wife's family. The young architectural student was a favourite with the children playing on the beach, and the annual encounter in Hendaye renewed the friendship between the two families for three or four summers. When the Belaúnde family returned eventually to Peru, circumstances contrived to maintain the links when my wife's eldest sister married an American who worked for W.R. Grace & Co. and went with her husband to live in Lima for eight years in the early fifties.

When I went to call on Fernando Belaúnde in his Lima suburban flat we had already been in touch with his sister, a gracious and charming widow, with grown-up sons and daughters-in-law. All had been very kind to my eldest stepson, himself an architectural student in the United States, when he visited Peru during a vacation before graduating. When he came to us in London he told us he had been overwhelmed by the courtesies and hospitality generously extended to him in Lima by the Belaúndes. We had not, therefore, been entirely without news of the births, marriages, and divorces in the respective families through the intervening years. I had also kept abreast of developments in Peru when I was Assistant Head of the American Department in the Foreign Office in the late 60s, and was indeed at my desk in King Charles Street when the news arrived of the military coup in 1968 and the manner in which President Belaúnde had been unceremoniously bundled into an aircraft bound for Bueno Aires. I was keen to meet a personality of whom I had heard so much, both before and since my arrival in Peru. His candidature had already been announced, but the outcome of the elections was anybody's guess; there were many who still doubted if there would be any elections at all. Eventually, one dull and gloomy afternoon, I rang the intercom bell on the street door of the block of flats at the appointed hour. Belaúnde's voice answered and instructed me to take the lift to the appropriate floor. When I stepped out of the lift he opened the front door of the flat himself, greeted me courteously, ushered me into his small study and said, 'Now, ambassador, first of all, tell me; how is little Gloria?'

One of the pleasures of life in Lima as a diplomatic post was the presence of several commonwealth ambassadors who provided a ready and willing pool of experience, friendship, and advice to a newly arrived member of the club. One or two got in touch with me even before I presented my credentials, during the period when a new head of mission has no official existence in the country, although he has already taken charge as far as London is concerned. There were no formal arrangements or regular commonwealth meetings, but our frequent social encounters enabled us to compare views and opinions. The Australian offices were just across the road from our own premises, and the Canadian and Australian official residences were in the same Lima suburb as our house. The Indian and the New Zealand ambassadors lived further away, but golf and tennis on Saturdays, and the Sunday service conducted by the Anglican bishop in Peru, followed by morning coffee for the large congregation, ensured that we were seldom out of touch. Additionally, the numerous 'British' societies, clubs, associations, schools, and assorted groups of which all commonwealth ambassadors were honorary presidents again ensured that few days went by without the opportunity to exchange news.

All these associations reflected the existence of a large, prosperous, well-organized British business community, supported by many Peruvians of British extraction and even more Peruvian ex-scholars who had studied at British institutions either in Peru or in the United Kingdom. Many had married British wives and all were keen to maintain their links with the country which had contributed much to their formative years. When I left Lima in 1983 I was given a farewell dinner by the ex-British scholars association which was attended by six hundred people. The origins of the widespread British involvement originated in the political assistance rendered to Peru during its struggle for independence from Spain and in the substantial British investment and financial participation in Peru's economic development thereafter. My friend Brenda Harriman, the widow of the first British Council representative in Lima (who chose to retire there), published in 1984 a booklet called *The British in Peru*. In it she quoted the following statement by the President of Peru in 1934 when the British envoy at the time presented his credentials:

'Peru will never forget that British subjects tendered the generous support of their arms in the struggle for freedom and that scarcely had our life as a free nation seen its birth than your country was the first with which financial and commercial relations were established. Our mutual commercial relations, first established in the War of Independence, have been more and more strengthened with the passing years. Today we have in our midst a British colony which lends its energy and capital to the progress of Peru and which represents an all-important element in the industrial life of the country.'

Shortly before my final departure from Peru I was presented with a rare copy of a commemorative edition of the 1937 Coronation supplement of the *West Coast Leader*, together with the Coronation supplement published in 1953 by the *Leader*'s successor, the *Peruvian Times*. The first contains 103 pages of advertising by British firms established in Peru. The second has 98 such pages. In addition to the advertisements by the local 'British' firms there are handsome photographs of the Church of the Good Shepherd, the Peruvian-British Cultural Association in Lima, the Phoenix Club, the British Schools in Peru (including Markham College, now the only Headmasters' Conference school in Latin America), the Peruvian Corporation's coffee plantations, the Lima Cricket and Football Club, the Lima Golf Club, and even of Lima's National stadium, which was built on grounds donated to the state in 1931 by the British community in Peru to mark the celebration of the centenary of Peru's declaration of independence, and built at a cost of over three million dollars. It was therefore fitting and proper that Peru should have been included in the itinerary of Mr Michael Stewart when he paid the first-ever visit to Latin America by a British foreign secretary in 1966 during Belaúnde's first presidency.

If successive British governments in modern times appeared to neglect a continent with many countries where early British influence and investment were paramount, this was happily not the case with other travellers of distinction. Members of the Royal Family visited Peru on a number of occasions, the attractions of Cuzco, Machu Picchu, and the other historical sites of pre-Columbian civilizations in Peru being difficult to resist by any traveller with business in any of the neighbouring countries. Thus, when making the preliminary arrangements for the visit of Princess Alexandra in 1982, I found we were virtually retracing the steps taken by her father, Prince George, Duke of Kent, when he accompanied the Prince of Wales (later King Edward VIII) during their visit in February 1931. This visit was recalled by commemorative plaques both in the railway coaches they used to travel from Arequipa to Cuzco and on the steamer still plying on Lake Titicaca. The *Ollanta*, a sturdy vessel of some 2000 tonnes, was put into service in 1930 to complement the *Yavari*, a smaller ship built in Scotland in 1862, then dismantled and carried in pieces by mules up to the lake. The main saloon of the *Ollanta* bears this single commemorative tablet on the wall, even though the vessel has subsequently been used by many other notable visitors to her home port of Puno on the Peruvian side of Lake Titicaca. British visitors to Arequipa are also shown with much pride the distinguished visitors' book in the Arequipa Club, which records the visit on 15 February 1931 of the two Princes and their aides, Viscount Ednam, Majors Aird and Butler, and Mr Hugh Lloyd Thomas, Private Secretary.

We were all therefore doubly distressed when, virtually on the eve of the arrival of Princess Alexandra and Sir Angus Ogilvie, due in April 1982, and after consulations with President Belaúnde, it was my painful duty to recommend the postponement of their visit as a result of the Argentine invasion of the Falklands on 2 April 1982. Public reactions in Peru, skilfully orchestrated by the Argentine Military Government which counted on instant support and encouragement from the Peruvian military, made it evident that such a visit could no longer be a 'popular' event, and that even hostile demonstrations might take place. The degree of spontaneity of such demonstrations might be open to question, but their occurrence would embarrass the visitors, the Peruvian Government, and ourselves, with consequences it was then difficult to foretell. There was really no alternative; it was a decision which both the Peruvian authorities and I had to take with great reluctance and deep disappointment.

Why was it that the tragic and sterile Argentine initiative taken by the unpopular military government of General Galtieri found such a vociferously sympathetic response in newly democratic Peru, a country with so many historical and economic ties with the United Kingdom? What were the reasons which impelled ordinary Peruvians to throw bombs at the British Council offices and at my house? The Lima police chief who talked to me immediately after I had viewed the damage at the Council offices early one morning was vehement in his attempts to dismiss the outrages as the work of a lunatic fringe which could in no circumstances be taken as representatives of 'real' Peruvian opinion, and was at pains to disabuse me of any impression that bombs and anonymous threats had the support of ordinary Peruvians. I think that the real reason is to be found in a combination of circumstances which bear closer examination.

There is hardly a country in continental Latin America which does not have some territorial claim against one or more of its neighbours. The ancestry of some of these claims is complex, but most have their origin in that the boundaries of the newly independent nations were mostly based on the administrative areas over which the Spanish Crown had held sway. These were sometimes ill defined, but no better definition was necessary for a single overlord. Sometimes they overlapped for reasons of what today would be called administrative expediency. Other territorial demarcations were based on ecclesiastical jurisdiction, the area of a Spanish bishop's writ not always coinciding with that of the lay administrators. None of this mattered so long as the whole was under Spanish rule. It was only when the different independence movements gained strength and achieved their regional objectives that the need to establish the national frontiers arose, once it became clear that Simon Bolivar's dream of a united federation of South American states was doomed to failure.

In the event, the former Spanish administrative boundaries defining the areas which had been governed by generations of viceroys, governors, *intendentes, corregidores,* and *adelantados* were initially adopted as international frontiers. Only after independence did the problems arise, and many have persisted until the present day. Thus, Peru fought a six-day war with Ecuador in 1980 as a result of Ecuadorean military infiltration in the Condor mountain ranges over which Peru claims sovereignty. Peru also has a latent territorial dispute with Colombia. More significantly, Peru and Chile fought a disastrous War of the Pacific in the nineteenth century in which Peru lost territories in the south which are still the subject of dispute (and Bolivia lost its own outlet to the sea). Also significantly, Argentina has a history of territorial and frontier problems with Chile, and the two countries nearly went to war in December 1978 over three islands in the Beagle Channel. Argentina also has marginal disputes with Paraguay and Uruguay. All this clearly shows that limitrophe nations in South America frequently have border disputes, that the best relations are likely to exist between countries which do not share a common frontier, and that the old saw 'the enemies of my enemies are my friends' is very relevant in some parts of the world today.

When I arrived in Lima in 1979 the authorities were commemorating the centenary of the War of the Pacific against Chile. In my first conversations when calling on ministers and officials I found that the Peruvian armed forces were deeply resentful of their humiliation by the Chileans one hundred years earlier, and still viewed Chilean attitudes and intentions with suspicion. There were rumours that some sectors of the Peruvian military had advocated an irredentist intervention in Chile's north in support of Argentina when the Beagle Channel dispute in the south nearly led to open hostilities between Argentina and Chile (admittedly at a time when Argentina and Peru were both ruled by military regimes). But there can be little doubt that the historical attitudes of the Peruvian and Argentine military establishments towards Chile reflected wide areas in which their perceived interests and objectives coincided to an extent which would have been difficult, if not impossible, between two limitrophe nations. The fact that Argentina is an 'Atlantic' power and Peru a 'Pacific' nation also helped to concentrate the minds of those who still attached importance to relative spheres of influence and might have had expansionist ambitions.

The history of most Latin American states after independence is short: the emphasis on the pages written during their efforts to overthrow Spanish rule is inevitable. Thus the calendar is peppered with anniversaries of uprisings, proclamations, and battles; and commemorations of victories, defeats, and massacres. A strong bond between Argentina and Peru was forged as a result of their struggle for independence from Spain. Unlike the inhabitants of Bolivia, Colombia, Venezuela, and Ecuador, many Peruvians do not feel theirs is really a 'Bolivarian' country, even though Bolivia itself was originally part of 'Upper Peru' and Bolivar played a decisive role in Peru in the confused period which followed the end of Spanish rule. But many Peruvians revered Argentina's national hero and 'Liberator' General José de San Martín as the principal architect of their own Peruvian independence.

The son of a Spanish military officer, San Martín was born in Yapeyú on the River Uruguay, close to what is now Paraguay. As was frequently the case with the sons of well-to-do families in the colonies, he was sent to Madrid for his education. His military studies there were followed by service with the Spanish forces in the peninsula, first against the Moors and subsequently against the armies of Napoleon. When he returned to Buenos Aires, San Martín was one of the conspirators who realized that in order to shake off the Spanish yoke, it would not suffice merely to overthrow the local Spanish administration. This would simply induce retaliation from Spanish forces in neighbouring garrisons. Historically, the seat of Spanish power and influence was in Lima, where the Viceroy, whose writ had included large parts of what was to become Argentina, represented the might and main of the Spanish Crown in South America.

San Martín, who had been appointed Governor of Mendoza in 1814, raised an army which he led into Chile in January 1817 through the Uspallata Pass across the Andes in what is still regarded as one of the great military epics. His victory over the Spanish forces in the battle of Chacabuco on 12 February 1817 was followed by the liberation of northern Chile including Santiago. Leaving General O'Higgins to assume the government, San Martín set about reconquering the south. His Chilean campaign ended with the battle of Maipú in April, 1818 which brought about the independence of the whole of Chile.

After this victory in Chile, San Martín's assembled a fleet commanded by Lord Cochrane and sailed up the Pacific coast to disembark in Paracas Bay, near Pisco, in southern Peru. His campaign was again successful, and in January 1821 the Spaniards evacuated Lima on the coastal plain and withdrew to the mountains in the hinterland. San Martín entered Lima, proclaimed the independence of Peru, and assumed the government under the title of 'Protector'. Thus, modern Argentina's national hero and 'Liberator' was also Peru's first 'President', albeit not for very long. San Martín's single, mysterious meeting in Guayaquil with the other great liberator, Simon Bolivar, clearly failed to bring about a meeting of minds; disappointed, San Martín retired from Peru in September 1822, having none the less paved the way for the two conclusive victories of Junín in August 1824 and Ayacucho in December of the same year, both in Peru. In this last battle, General Sucre's victory over the Spaniards culminated in the capitulation of all Spanish forces in South America and the end of Spain's American empire.

To the bonds of history briefly outlined above, a more recent dimension may be added to the affinities between Argentina and Peru. Both countries have seen civilian governments succeeded by military regimes which have sometimes remained long years in power. When controlling the purse-strings, the military were substantial purchasers of sophisticated weapons and aircraft. Both countries thus developed strong, well-armed and effective armed forces which frequently played a decisive role in domestic political crises. The absence of a common frontier over which to quarrel and the awareness of shared interests and objectives over many years generated a high level of military co-operation between the armed forces of Argentina and Peru. Training courses and exchange scholarships, reciprocal maintenance and servicing arrangements, and regular consultations within (and without) pan-American defence and military organizations became the norm. Argentine jet engines were regularly serviced at Peruvian Air Force test benches. Generations of Peruvian cadets graduated from Argentine military academies. As luck would have it, when the Argentine invasion of the Falklands took place in April 1982, the Peruvian Minister of War in President Belaúnde's cabinet was a general who as a cadet had graduated from a prestigious Argentine military academy in the same class and the same year as General Galtieri, then President of Argentina's military government.

The links forged between the armed forces during the years when they governed in each country also generated, as a sort of by-product, close connections between the respective political and business classes. Throughout Latin America the right of political asylum is sacrosanct; many nations harboured for years political figures who had sought sanctuary as a result of changes in their own country, where either their continued presence might be unwelcome to the new rulers or their own safety could not be guaranteed. Political exiles existed in almost every capital, where they were kept under loose surveillance by the local authorities but not otherwise interfered with so long as they behaved. When I arrived in Lima in 1979 it was generally known that several Argentine *montonero* leaders, wanted by the Argentine military authorities, had been given asylum in Peru. Other *montonero* groups were in Paraguay. Similarly, many members of the Peruvian political establishment had spent long years of exile in Buenos Aires, until a change of government at home made their return possible. Some had married Argentine wives, and there were several distinguished Argentine surnames which were as well known in Lima as they were in Buenos Aires. When President Belaúnde was overthrown by the Peruvian military radicals in 1968 they unhesitatingly put him on the first aeroplane bound for Buenos Aires.

There were also important links in the business and financial sectors. These were the type of connections which made it possible during the Falklands crisis for the Prime Minister of Peru, in private life a successful businessman with international interests, to pick up the phone and speak to his longstanding friend and legal adviser in Buenos Aires, who also happened to be the Argentine foreign minister at the time. At the other extreme, the reaction of the Lima man in the street was uncomplicated. Appealed to by Argentine television broadcasts beamed every evening into Peruvian homes and stimulated by the undiluted diet of Argentine public hysteria retailed by every transistor radio in the land, the popular reaction was similar to that which prevailed in the streets of Buenos Aires when Argentina won the World Cup. For the general public in Peru the identification between 'us' and 'them' was made even easier by the latent anti-colonial bias which many South American countries, deeply conscious of their own origins resulting from the overthrow of a colonial regime, readily displayed on appropriate occasions.

Such then, were some of the strands which made up the complex fabric woven over many years by history, geography, military appreciations, and political expediency. Outside the military there were few educated Peruvians who were prepared to defend in private the Argentine invasion. But in their public prounouncements and postures, the Peruvian Government could hardly fail to show some support for the futile and desperate Argentine initiative, even though this had been undertaken for self-evident domestic political reasons by a discredited military regime with which Peru's democratic government had little sympathy. The degree of vociferous near-unanimity adroitly generated by Argentina at the meetings of the Organization of American States, together with the local demonstrations of popular support more discreetly orchestrated in Lima by the able and effective Argentine Ambassador, made it impossible for Peru to step out of line, even if the Government had wanted to. Added to which, the Peruvian armed forces provided a further element which had to be taken carefully into account. The Peruvian military had but recently withdrawn to the barracks, undefeated, of their own volition, after twelve years of absolute rule. As a result, they were at full strength, well equipped with sophisticated weaponry and technology, clearly underemployed and keenly aware of their historic capability of making and breaking governments in Peru. It is against this general background that we should view President Belaúnde's intervention in the Falklands crisis when General Alexander Haig finally gave up the United States' attempts at mediation. The Peruvian Government's decision to continue his efforts to bring about a ceasefire and a negotiated settlement between Britain and Argentina was politically hazardous and domestically courageous.

Fernando Belaúnde assumed the Presidency of Peru, for the second time, on 28 July 1980, after an exciting and arduous electoral campaign. When I first met him, Belaúnde was in his late sixties, a man of medium height with a full head of grey hair brushed straight back from his forehead. His regular features, broad brow, slightly acquiline nose, well-set eyes, and firm mouth and chin gave him a handsome, almost patrician appearance. He smiled readily and was an attentive listener. Without flattery he contrived to give his interlocutors the impression that their views and opinions were of paramount importance. An architect by profession, qualified in the United

States, for many years he practised in Lima where he also edited an architectural review and taught at the National University where he eventually became Dean of the Faculty of Architecture. He was elected a deputy in 1945 and in 1956 he founded a new political party, Acción Popular, whose presidential candidate he was in 1956 and again in 1962. He was elected President in 1963 in a three-cornered campaign against Haya de la Torre, founder of APRA, and General Manuel Odria, the former military President. The subsequent parliamentary alliance of his two opponents made his Government's task difficult and complex in his first mandate, during which he was advised and encouraged, but refused, to dissolve Congress and assume personal rule.

My first conversation with Belaúnde in his suburban flat ranged over a wide variety of subjects. I was anxious to improve my knowledge of Peru and learn something of the exciting prospects then before us. His replies to my questions were clear and comprehensive. He spoke with eloquence and the authority of experience. He was articulate and knowledgeable, reasonable and convincing. But more than his grasp of the subject or the nature of his reply, it was his character and personality which seldom failed to impress. I subsequently had many opportunities to continue our exchanges, not only in private conversations but also when I escorted visitors from London who were received by the President, or when I accompanied him on his working trips to distant corners of Peru where, as he put it, there would always be much to be done. He had a prodigious memory for facts and figures, and impressed his collaborators by his total recall, after one reading, of any brief however complex and lengthy. He was a gifted orator and seldom delivered any speeches from prepared texts, preferring to improvise, rationally and coherently, without vehemence or histrionics. He had an encyclopedic knowledge of Peru and was proud of having visited every corner of his vast and contrasting country, once described as 'a combination of the Sahara desert, the Himalayas and the African Congo'. His engineering and architectural training was evident in his readiness to illustrate his explanations with maps and plans. He abhorred violence; his style of government was humane and altruistic, and as a political leader he was magnanimous and forgiving. His critics claimed that he was

214

more of a visionary and less of an administrator, and that his choice of collaborators did not always reflect his better judgement. Although he was twice to hold the highest office in the land, he never lost the common touch which made him such a welcome visitor in the remote hamlets deep in the Amazonian jungles, Andean highlands or coastal deserts. There was a touch of greatness in his genuine concern for the poor and underprivileged. He spoke several European languages well, including English. With his impeccably democratic credentials he stood out among his political contemporaries in Latin America. This had already been made manifest during his first presidency by his memorable intervention at the historic first-ever meeting of American heads of state in Punta del Este (Uruguay) in 1967 when, it so happened, I was on my first spell of duty at the embassy in Montevideo.

Traditionally, a presidential inauguration takes place on Peru's national day, the anniversary of General San Martín's declaration of independence on 28 July. Ironically, in 1980 the armed forces were relinquishing power to the very man they had overthrown in 1968, but the elections and even the preceding campaign had passed without bloodshed or incident and the military had made good their word and withdrawn to the barracks in good time and order. The general feeling in Lima was one of relief and exultation, and throughout the ceremonies and celebrations in the official programme visiting delegations remarked on the festive and joyful atmosphere which they described as almost evocative of a restoration. As we walked across Lima's beautiful Plaza de Armas from the cathedral to the palace in the wake of the official entourage, Lord Trefgarne, the British Government's special envoy to the presidential inauguration, joked that even Lima's normally grey, mid-winter skies had given way to unusual sunshine.

For my part, I was content. I had already visited several provincial capitals in different parts of the vast country, third in size in South America after Brazil and Argentina. I never ceased to marvel at the contrasts in Peru's remarkable geography, having travelled in one day from the barren coastal deserts to oil installations deep in the Amazon rain forest, visiting on the way mining towns in their highland valleys surrounded by mountain peaks covered in eternal snows. A number of initiatives had already been taken. The new democratic Government was certain of international economic and financial support. The level of exports and investment from Britain was set to increase, important visits in both directions were in the offing, and the foundations laid for additional exchanges in productive areas. I was confident that the promotion of British objectives could be successfully pursued, within the ample framework of interests common to both countries, in collaboration with a friendly and well-disposed Government which, like others in Latin America, was keen to reduce its dependence on the United States for trade and aid and looked increasingly towards Europe for this purpose.

12

Peru and the Falklands: London

An article on one of the inside pages of the *Sunday Telegraph* on 7 October 1984 carried the headline: 'Will the *Belgrano* buck stop here?' It recorded an interview with Sir Anthony Kershaw, M.C., Chairman of the House of Commons Foreign Affairs Committee, following the decision by the committee to conduct an inquiry into the circumstances surrounding the sinking of the *Belgrano* on 2 May 1982, against the background of the Peruvian Government's intervention on the weekend of 1–2 May 1982.

At the time I had already been in Uruguay for about a year, having left Lima in September 1983 after almost exactly four years in Peru. I had taken my leave with mixed feelings. Privately, I was satisfied with the manner in which my embassy had acquitted itself in Lima in unusual and professionally challenging circumstances. There had been a long, worrying, and anxious period throughout the Falklands crisis during which President Belaúnde had rejected public demands for my expulsion from Peru; anonymous bomb threats had caused the evacuation of our offices, attempts had been made to interfere with our essential communications with London, and, in separate incidents, real bombs had damaged the British Council premises and injured the Peruvian policeman on duty at my house. But these were only some aspects of the situation which had affected me personally. I shall not dwell here on the many friendships and affinities I was sad to leave behind; suffice it to say that I left with regrets, and not only of a personal nature. Professionally, I had cause also to lament 'all the things that might have been' but for General Galtieri's folly. The tide from the South Atlantic had washed away recent achievements and many current plans and proposals, as well as

217

eroded the foundations on which some of our interests and objectives were based, not only in Peru but in other Latin American countries as well.

In other ways, the aftermath of the Falklands crisis provided me also with an unusually rewarding experience, not least because of the courtesies and facilities I received from Peruvians at all levels in sometimes difficult circumstances. With the approval of the Peruvian authorities we had taken a number of initiatives calculated to promote locally the fence-mending and bridge-building on which all our embassies in Latin America had begun as soon as hostilities in the South Atlantic had ceased. In Peru the United Kingdom contributed an imaginative hovercraft medical service which was established to serve isolated communities in the river valleys of Peruvian Amazonia, supported by medical posts along the riverside villages (some now, alas, threatened by the Sendero Luminoso). The project was jointly funded by the the Amazon Foundation of the United Kingdom and the Overseas Development Administration, and many and varied were the enthusiastic individuals, both British and Peruvian, who worked tirelessly, to bring the project to fruition. At the time, it was described by the BBC as 'the most positive action for restoration of good relations during a difficult year in South America', and was also the subject of an entertaining book* (with a foreword by the Rt. Hon. Edward Heath M.B.E., MP) published shortly after by members of the Joint Services team primarily involved in the project. An eminent Peruvian political personality (and international jurist of note) was appointed Ambassador to the Court of St James's after a long hiatus which might have encouraged some to regard this as a mark of official disapproval. Missions from the British Overseas Trade Board and Canning House, headed respectively by the Earl of Limerick and Viscount Montgomery, were made welcome in Lima and contributed materially to the bridges and fences. Appropriately, we provided emergency help for the Peruvian Government in the form of much needed Bailey bridges following a winter of disastrous floods and avalanches which played havoc with vital road communications in the north. Much favourable publicity was generated, also by

*Peter Dixon (with Dick Bell), *Amazon Task Force* Hodder & Stoughton, 1984.

Peruvian sources, for these developments and other similar initiatives.

One less publicized failure was not altogether unexpected. When I tried to get Peru included in the itinerary of that year's 'course' at the Royal College of Defence Studies (usually made up of middle-ranking officers of the three services of NATO and Commonwealth countries) no reply was forthcoming in time to include Peru in their field study tour. My Defence Attaché, a Captain in the Royal Navy, told me afterwards with a curl in his lip that when the proposal, as was inevitable, had been referred to their potential hosts in the Peruvian armed forces, it had been rejected out of hand by the Minister of War and Chief of Staff of the Armed Forces, still General Galtieri's ertswhile classmate in the Argentine military academy. In July 1983 the local celebrations of the bicentenary of the birth of Simon Bolivar had enabled us to obtain widespread publicity for the British contribution to independence movements in South America in general and, in particular, build on the role of notable British soldiers and sailors in Peru's own historic struggle.

All these things helped slowly to overcome the feelings and attitudes generated by many public demonstrations of support for the futile Argentine military adventure. The banners proclaiming *'Las Malvinas son Argentinas'* had disappeared from the street of Lima, and I like to think that some sort of a turning point was reached when, three weeks before I left, a beaming Defence Attaché told me that the Peruvian naval authorities had approved our request for permission for a Royal Navy frigate, on her way home through the Panama Canal from the South Atlantic, to put in to Callao to refuel and provision ship. When she arrived, Peruvian journalists boarded HMS *Falmouth* and questioned her captain about his experiences in Falklands waters without causing any waves either in the local press or on the part of the transport and labour unions which had been active in 'blacking' British ships and aircraft during the crisis. The usual football games and children's parties were well attended, and I was happy to see the local authorities and the Peruvian Navy fully represented at the farewell cocktail party in the wardroom.

More than anything we could do, it was perhaps the decision of the provisional Argentine authorities in Buenos Aires to prosecute and bring to trial those principally responsible for the conduct of the Falklands war that brought about a change in the attitudes of the press and public opinion in Lima. In any case, with the one exception noted above, our initiatives received the full support of all those Peruvian authorities and officials I approached. The seventeen months I stayed in Peru after the end of the Falklands conflict provided me with reiterated opportunities to appreciate the facilities and assistance made available to us in our efforts to overcome some of the difficulties generated locally by the ill-starred Argentine adventure, at a time when the Peruvian Government was having to deal with serious new problems of its own.

During this period in Peru I was an interested observer of the continuing controversy in Britain's Parliament, press, and television about the timing and purpose of the sinking of the *Belgrano*. The accusations made by Mr Tam Dalyell and others in Parliament and the press centred on the suggestion that the *Belgrano* had been torpedoed deliberately in order to put an end to the prospect of a negotiated (and peaceful) settlement with Argentina. I do not propose here to embark on an account of the controversy as it developed in the United Kingdom, and will assume that any reader who has got this far may recall the circumstances in which the charges were made. Some of the Government's early statements were inconsistent and served to fuel the parliamentary controversy. Declarations made by other personalities in Britain also raised questions which were pursued and developed by the press and television with persistence. Suggestions that the Government had witheld the truth or misinformed Parliament added to the sound and the fury. At one stage it seemed that nothing the Government could say would help to clear the air. An admirable account of the whole episode with a clear chronology of events was published in *The Economist* of 12 November 1983 by Sir Nicholas Henderson, British Ambassador in Washington during the Falklands crisis. His comprehensive 'Case Study in the Behaviour of an Ally', as his article was titled, could hardly be faulted and should have dispelled any lingering doubts about the relative timings of the Peruvian initiative, the conversations in Washington and New York, and the sinking of the *Belgrano*. But this was not to be, and the questions and doubts persisted, both in Parliament and in the media in the

United Kingdom. Most of the time, the press in Lima had in the main confined itself to the publication of agency reports on the goings on in Britain. One Peruvian weekly news magazine carried a report of the BBC programme 'The Sinking of a Peace Plan,' but needlessly embellished it with imaginative extrapolations and sensationalistic comparisons with the crisis provoked many years earlier by the Profumo resignation. But nobody in the Peruvian Government ever thought it necessary to approach me about the British Government's alleged inconsistencies as claimed in Parliament and the press in the United Kingdom.

Then, in March 1984, Mr Desmond Rice and Mr Arthur Gavshon published a book entitled *The Sinking of the Belgrano** which refuelled the controversy. It summarized the origins of the Anglo-Argentine dispute, outlined the political background in Argentina and in the United Kingdom, and argued that until the *Belgrano* sank a negotiated peace 'still seemed possible' and that 'a peace plan acceptable to both sides was only hours away'. Mr Tam Dalyell published a review of this book in the *London Review of Books*, 5–18 April 1984, in which he referred to his own visit to Lima and conversations with President Belaúnde, dismissed out of hand the possibility that I might have failed to keep the Foreign Office informed (in time to stop the sinking), and argued powerfully for a full investigation on the lines advocated by Messrs. Gavshon and Rice. When I obtained a copy of the book I was interested to see that it included transcriptions of some of the telephone conversations between Lima and Buenos Aires on the eventful weekend of 1–2 May 1982. I recognized these as translations of the tape-recorded conversations produced in evidence (and published in full in several Buenos Aires weeklies) to the Commission, headed by retired Lt. General Benjamin Rattenbach, which had been appointed by the provisional authorities in Buenos Aires to judge the actions of those responsible for the conduct of the Falklands war. These and other recorded conversations had also been reproduced in a remarkable and absorbing book published in Buenos Aires in September 1983 and reprinted half a dozen times even before the end of that

*Desmond Rice and Arthur Gavshon, *The Sinking of the Belgrano*, Secker and Warburg, 1984.

year. It was researched and written by three Argentine journalists, Oscar Raul Cardoso, Ricardo Kirschbaum, and Eduardo van der Kooy of the Buenos Aires daily *El Clarin*. The book was called *Malvinas – La Trama Secreta*,* and when I obtained a copy in Montevideo a day or two after publication in Buenos Aires I could not avoid reading the whole book at one compulsive sitting. It was written mainly in factual and objective terms, where not actually critical of the Argentine military.

In the meantime, I was interested to note that since my transfer from Lima to Montevideo certain insinuations about my own role in the episode had been published in the press in the United Kingdom. This was a notable departure from the standards maintained by the Government's principal political critics who had all, without exception, dealt with me courteously and politely in their writings or interviews. When my move from Lima to Montevideo was announced, Mr Gavshon wrote a piece in *The Observer* in which he generously (if inexactly) described my new job as a 'political appointment' and a 'promotion', and me as 'one of the most experienced specialists on Latin America in the Diplomatic Service.' Other journalists were to be less charitable. *The Sunday Telegraph* article of 7 October 1984 on the Foreign Affairs Committee's decision to conduct an enquiry into the sinking of the *Belgrano* also referred, in questionably frivolous terms, to my intervention in the episode. Then the *Times* Diary column on 26 October 1984 carried a piece about the evidence to be given to the Foreign Affairs Committee by the authors of *The Sinking of the Belgrano*, and added that tapes of an exclusive interview with General Alexander Haig in the possession of Mr Gavshon 'revealed that while President Belaúnde Terry and Haig were negotiating the terms of the Peruvian peace proposals in the Presidential palace, the British Ambassador to Peru, Charles Wallace, was in the room'.

Inevitably, this added grist to the mill in the United Kingdom, but caused hardly a ripple in the River Plate. Montevideo is, for some months of the year, almost like a suburb of Buenos Aires. While maintaining its own distinctive character and history, Uruguay is invaded every summer by

*O. Cardoso, R. Kirschbaum, E van der Kooy, *Malvinas – La Trama Secreta*, Editorial Planeta Argentina, Buenos Aires, 1983.

222

hundreds of thousands of Argentines on their way to the splendid beach resort at Punta del Este, some 120 kilometres east of the capital, where holidaymakers of all nationalities singlemindedly devote themselves to the relentless pursuit of fun in the sun. But the Argentine proximity is all-pervasive at any time. The rest of the year an air bridge linking the two capitals enables businessmen on both sides of the river to make daily visits to banks or business firms, returning home in the evening much as a commuter would return to Wimbledon after a day in the City. As a result of the then mounting controversy in the United Kingdom, one or two Argentine journalists visited me in Montevideo with rather academic interest. The press on both sides of the River Plate seemed to be well aware of the timing and details of the Peruvian initiative as revealed in a comprehensive, detailed, and frank interview given some time before by President Belaúnde to an Argentine journalist named Felix Luna. The text was printed in a review called *Todo es Historia* (No. 191) in April 1983; in it Belaúnde answered most of the questions being asked in London and also referred to the (Peruvian) military pressures which had made themselves felt during the Falklands crisis. This interview was widely disseminated by news agencies throughout the area, but possibly because it was in Spanish it appeared to escape the attention of the press in the United Kingdom. In any case, this may explain why those cuttings I have retained from the Argentine and Uruguayan press at the time consist mainly of agency reports retailing the commotion in the United Kingdom with, perhaps, an additional paragraph of rather bemused comment.

For my part I refrained, as I was duty bound, from making any statements to the press while in Montevideo, which seemed to irk some of my visitors from London. Perhaps this was the wrong policy. On one occasion I was specifically authorized by the Foreign Office to speak to Mr Paul Foot, who had himself visited Lima shortly after my departure. In the course of a transatlantic telephone conversation, Mr Foot asked me a number of relevant questions, heard out my detailed answers and, after some final exchanges, courteously agreed with me that in reporting the nature of the Peruvian initiative to London my first and last objective at the time could only have been to get the news and details back to the Foreign Office with the utmost urgency. To the best of my knowledge,

Mr Foot never again put pen to paper about this.

When, therefore, the Foreign Office suggested to me in Montevideo that I might myself give evidence to the Foreign Affairs Committee, I cheerfully acquiesced, confident in my ability to dispel firmly and finally the speculation about my intervention and the insinuation (made only by the press) that I had somehow failed to get the news back to London in time. Accordingly, I flew to London from Montevideo on 10 November 1984 to appear before the Committee, taking with me a copy of *Malvinas – La Trama Secreta* which I proposed to introduce in evidence. I was confident that the findings of the Foreign Affairs Committee and particularly my own evidence before it would dispel any misconception about the timing of the Peruvian initiative and my role in the event. Some other suggestions made in London by various commentators and journalists were that:

(*a*) I had been informed by the Peruvians of their proposals on 1 May, that is, the day before these were communicated to me;

(*b*) a piece of paper in my handwriting existed in the Peruvian Ministry of Foriegn Affairs which proved my cognisance, at its inception, of the Peruvian 'seven-point plan';

(*c*) a red leather bound peace treaty had been prepared in Lima for signature (by implication by me) on the evening of 2 May 1982.

I appeared before the committee on 14 November 1984. To the Committee's questions I replied factually and, I believe, accurately. I made no attempt to prevent or deflect any question or divert any members of the committee from their planned approach by introducing at the outset the decisive evidence of the book *Malvinas – La Trama Secreta* until the chairman had signified that they had completed their questioning. Only then did I draw to the committee's attention the verbatim reproductions of the taped telephone conversations (the Rattenbach tapes) between the principal protagonists in Buenos Aires, Lima, and Washington. Some of these had been reproduced by Mr Rice and Mr Gavshon in their book, but there were others. In particular, I translated in evidence a conversation between the Peruvian Foreign Minister, Dr Javier Arias Stella, and his Argentine counterpart, Dr Nicanor Costa Méndez, on the morning of 3 May 1982. This conversation made it clear that in the preparation of their seven-point plan the Peruvian authorities had had exchanges with the Argentine and United States Governments, but no contact with the British. The evidence was taken by the Committee in public, in one of the main committee rooms of the House of Commons; there were present the Peruvian Ambassador and one or two others, and representatives of the national press and international news agencies. But not, apparently of the *Times* Diary column which returned to the charge with an item published appropriately on 1 April 1985 which among other things again reported that 'our man in Peru, Charles Wallace, was in on every bit of the negotiations' and quoted General Haig as the source of this statement.

As a result of my evidence the committee had pages of *Malvinas–La Trama Secreta* (including my favourite telephone conversation) translated and incorporated in their report,* which did much to clear the air in Parliament and dispel the speculation and innuendo surrounding the events of 2 May 1982. But the committee's report was not published until 24 July 1985, by which time the press (but not Parliament) had clearly lost interest. In a short article about the report, *The Economist* of 27 July 1985 noted that the committee had also produced a minority report and that members of the same committee had reached different conclusions based on the same evidence; it nevertheless came down firmly in favour of the evidence given by Mr (now Lord) Pym and myself.

It may be that few other journalists bothered to read either the committee's report or *The Economist*. In the event, speculation about my role persisted until it was announced that I would retire on my sixtieth birthday in 1986. This resulted in an imaginative report from a London-based Argentine journalist, published first in the Buenos Aires press and subsequently rehashed under the heading 'Wallace Sunk' in the Diary column of *The Times*, to the effect that I was not being employed after my retiring age (Mr Gavshon's 'political'

*Third Report from the Foreign Affairs Committee, Session 1984–5, *Events surrounding the weekend of 1–2 May 1982*, (Report, together with the Proceedings of the Committee, Minutes of Evidence, and Appendices, HMSO, 1985.

appointment may be responsible for this) because I had in some way failed in my task. As though no report had ever been published by the Foreign Affairs Committee, the item in the Diary column stated that I had become 'involved in a global slanging match with the American Secretary of State, Alexander Haig, who had accused him [me] of witholding information about the *American* [my italics] peace initiative until after the sinking of the *Belgrano*'. With less than perfect recall of what its own newspaper had previously printed, the item went on to say that the previous November, 'during a grilling over the affair from the Foreign Affairs Commitee, he *denied knowing anything about the initiative* (my italics), a statement which may also suggest that the *Times* Diary journalists no longer read *The Times*. Ah well, *autres temps, autres moeurs*, if the unintended pun may be forgiven. One or two friends wrote to *The Times* in protest; a deputy editor said he would 'investigate the information with the reporter concerned' and the Foreign Office took the hapless (and blameless) *Times* diplomatic correspondent to task. He agreed that the item was not acceptable and undertook to kick his Diary colleagues on our behalf. But nothing was published, and all this time I was blissfully incommunicado on a slow boat from South America, not arriving in London until it was too late to get anything done effectively.

In any case I was not really surprised. Ministers make policy; the Foreign Office carries it out. Despite being an institution which as an instrument of policy is admired, envied, or imitated by almost every country in the world, the Foreign Office and its servants abroad are conditioned to a bad press in the United Kingdom. Unlike the problems faced by, for instance, the Ministry of Agriculture, Fisheries and Food, which has on occasion been split down the middle while trying simultaneously to defend the opposing interests of domestic producers and consumers, the task of the Foreign Office is relatively simple. The interests of the United Kingdom are not difficult to identify when confronted with foreign proposals or initiatives; and foreign affairs seldom become domestic political issues, (although the reverse can be true, as evinced by the Argentine invasion of the Falklands, which some have attributed to the domestic decision to reduce costs as well as Britain's capacity to deploy force in the South Atlantic). But I learned many years ago that it was fruitless, whether at home or abroad, to try to correct errors in newspapers, since they seldom bother to print a retraction and can always have the last word. Far better to invite the foreign sub-editor to lunch and try to make a friend of him. As a lifelong addict of *The Economist* I have always admired their practice of printing letters from readers pointing out errors in previous editions. But even *The Economist* writers seem to me to have had a tendency to praise the Foreign Secretary and blame the Foreign Office.

Be that as it may, I have an interest to declare in wishing to clear the record, not least in order to pay tribute to the staff of the embassy in Lima at the time. They all made a remarkable contribution, in wholly exceptional and sometimes hazardous circumstances, to the work of the embassy and the unusual burden it was called upon to assume. Their individual diligence, perseverance and initiative enabled us to maintain vital communications between London and Lima, in both directions, without delays, at all hours of the day or night, and sometimes in conditions of physical danger. The communications officers in charge of the constantly chattering teletext machines; the alert press officer retailing news and views to me on my car radio; the Head of Chancery deploying typists and cipherers to receive and despatch messages while dealing simultaneously with a threatened bomb evacuation; the Defence Attaché's vital liaison with the Peruvian military and police; my personal secretary's clairvoyance in always being where needed, her cheerful efficiency unimpaired by the day of the week or time of the night; and all the others, also nameless, who contributed so much to ensure, whether I was there or not, that none of the eggs rolled off my table. No, no mistakes were made, and theirs is the credit.

I appeared before the Foreign Affairs Commitee on the afternoon of 14 November 1984. That afternoon the Committee was made up as follows:

Sir Anthony Kershaw, in the Chair

Mr Robert Harvey	Mr Nigel Spearing
Mr Ivan Lawrence	Mr Peter Thomas
Mr Jim Lester	Mr Bowen Wells
Mr Ian Mikardo	

The questions put to me predictably concentrated on those aspects of my intervention in Lima which had been the subject of speculation in the press. The committee had heard evidence from Mr Gavshon and Mr Rice in their session that morning, when Mr Rice referred to a document in my handwriting in Lima which 'proved' that I had been involved in the negotiations. Mr Gavshon rehearsed his interview with General Haig, suggesting that I was in the room with President Belaúnde on at least two occasions while General Haig was on the telephone from Washington. When it came to my turn in the afternoon I was first asked some general questions designed to establish the circumstances prevailing in Lima during the crisis and the nature and frequency of my contacts with the Peruvian authorities. My replies tried to convey something of the realities of the situation in Peru and the conditions in which we were operating at the time. They may be worth recalling at this stage.

While the Peruvian authorities were unfailingly courteous, friendly, and helpful at all times, in Peru there had been an overwhelming public reaction in support of the Argentine invasion of the Falklands. Some of the reasons for this reaction have the emotional origins to which I have already referred. As a result we had to contend from the beginning of the crisis with obscene and threatening phone calls, bomb threats, one or two attempts by representatives of students' and labour associations to 'occupy' the embassy offices as well as (later) more serious attempts to interfere with our communications.

There was also an effective Argentine disinformation campaign rapidly gathering momentum and force. Argentine television programmes were shown on Peruvian television, and the wildest rumours were being disseminated by the local press. At one stage it was reported that I had left the country (my car had been to the airport) and, after the sinking of the *Belgrano*, the Argentines put it about that we were planning pre-emptive strikes against Argentine air bases on the mainland as well as a blockade of the River Plate estuary, among other things.* For these reasons, one of my principal tasks

*(A comprehensive account of the Argentine military junta's misinformation campaign is included in Chapter 6 of *The Land that lost its Heroes* by Jimmy Burns, the *Financial Times* correspondent in Buenos Aires from 1981 to 1986 (Bloomsbury Publishing, 1987).

throughout the crisis was to keep the Peruvian authorities informed of the realities of the situation, both after and sometimes before the event. I spoke regularly to the Peruvian Foreign Minister and supplied him with the texts of statements in Parliament, speeches, and all the relevant background details. Sometimes he asked me for the latest BBC news. Several times I was instructed to convey details of Falklands exclusion zones and other initiatives to the Peruvian authorities. In the general nature of things, Dr Arias and I also met on official or public occasions. All this meant that we frequently compared notes and exchanged information, either on the 'phone or in person. It was therefore perfectly true to say that the Peruvian authorities were in close touch with the British Ambassador (and vice versa) throughout this period.

We were not, however, in touch about the details of the Peruvian proposals first announced in the Presidential broadcast at 1800 hours on 2 May. During the previous day (and night) these had been discussed on the telephone with General Haig on the one hand and, inconclusively, with the Argentines on the other; they were not worked out with me nor was I consulted at any stage about their formulation or their chances of success. I made this clear when Mr Lester took up the questioning at the Chairman's behest.

Mr J. Lester

Could I then come to the question of the critical weekend? Could you confirm the Foreign and Commonwealth Office's evidence that you went to see Dr Arias Stella on the morning of Saturday 1 May 1982 and that this meeting was in pursuance of an instruction to a number of overseas posts?

Wallace

That is right. I had in fact asked for an appointment with the Deputy Foreign Secretary on 1 May, on instructions from London, to discuss certain aspects, the extension of our exclusion zone, the bombing of the runway in the Falkland Islands, but when I arrived at the Foreign Ministry I saw first the Deputy Foreign Minister, and then the Foreign Minister himself invited me to see him. The ensuing conversation was reported to the Foreign Office at the same time in the normal way. I was given no indication that any new initiative was being considered. In fact Dr Arias gave me a copy of Mr Haig's message to the Peruvian Government, what is known as the "tilt" message, that Haig handed in when he decided to end his arbitration and the United States Government decision to support the United Kingdom as a result of the ending of the Haig mediation. In my conversation with Dr Arias he also asked me if there were any ways in which the Peruvians could help to break the diplomatic deadlock.

Sir Anthony Kershaw
I did not quite hear what you said – did you ask him or did he ask you?

Wallace
He asked me. Dr Arias asked me if I thought there were any ways in which the Peruvians could help to break the diplomatic deadlock which had been established as a result of the ending of the Haig mediation. I said I had no instructions to convey any specific suggestions to him but I reiterated, I took the opportunity to reiterate, our insistence on the implementation of Security Council Resolution 502. I also spoke about the difficulties caused to Mr Haig by the different lines taken by some of his interlocutors in Argentina. I also reminded Dr Arias that it was clear that Argentina attached great importance to the attitudes and opinions in Peru, and I thought Peru could usefully exert its influence on Argentina in convincing Argentina to implement Resolution 502 without any preconditions as soon as possible. After some further conversation of a general nature in which references were also made to the imminent visit of the Secretary of State to Washington, I left the Peruvian Foreign Ministry.

Sir Anthony Kershaw
So that there was no indication from that of a Peruvian peace initiative? It was not your perception

that that was so? Was there a telegram? Did you send a telegram after that meeting in which the Peruvian peace proposals could have been mentioned?

Wallace

I sent a telegram reporting my conversation in the terms that I have described to the Committee without any reference to any new proposals because no such proposals had been mentioned to me.

Sir Antony Kershaw

When did you next see or speak to Dr Arias Stella or any other representative or official of the Peruvian Government?

Wallace

There must have been a telephone call on the Sunday morning summoning me to appear before the Foreign Minister at 1830 that evening. It may have been a telephone call made by the Foreign Minister himself or it may have been, as was more usually the case, a telephone call from his private secretary. I do not remember which of the two but in any case what I do remember is that it was a totally unremarkable telephone call which summoned me to appear at 1830 that evening.

Sir Anthony Kershaw

That was on the 2nd?

Wallace

That was on the morning of the 2nd. I then went to the Ministry of Foreign Affairs at 1830 local time on the evening of the 2nd. As I was driving down to the Ministry of Foreign Affairs I heard on my car radio part, only part, of the Presidential broadcast which had begun at 1800 hours local time, in which the President announced that a series of proposals had been elaborated and that if these were acceptable to both parties the signing of an interim document would take place in Lima. A report of this broadcast was, incidentally, also sent by the Embassy in Lima to London at about the same time but I only heard

231

part of this broadcast on the radio because I was, in fact, travelling in my car to the Ministry of Foreign Affairs. The Minister received me at 1830 when he first conveyed to me the details of the Peruvian proposals. This was half an hour after the Presidential broadcast. My report was received in London shortly after 0100 hours GMT on 3 May, which is, in fact only one and a half hours after my conversation with the Minister had begun, and, given the constraints of transport and communications and the fact that the Ministry is about 25–30 minutes away from my office, I think it would have been difficult to improve on that timing. At 1830 Dr Arias began our conversation by saying that he hoped that we would have very good news very soon. I would like to emphasise the next sentence, if I may. He then said to me that after our conversation the previous day the President had decided to make a further attempt to break the deadlock and bring about an immediate ceasefire and various proposals had been considered with the hope of finding a formula which might bring about a withdrawal of the Argentine troops. Procedural difficulties had arisen during the course of various telephone conversations with Mr Haig but a seven-point formula had eventually been worked out. Dr Arias then gave me details of the seven-point formula. In reply to my specific question Dr Arias said that this formula had the approval of the Argentine Foreign Minister, that General Galtieri was 'well disposed towards it' but that he had his military Junta to consult and convince. The Peruvian authorities were, however, anxious not to lose any momentum and it had been suggested to Washington that if the formula was acceptable the signature of some sort of interim document would take place in Lima.

Sir Anthony Kershaw
Your reaction to that, in the sense that somebody from Britain would have been needing to sign it, must have been one of puzzlement because pre-

sumably if it was as close as that in terms of a negotiated settlement we, as a party to it, must have been very much involved in the negotiations?

Wallace

There were certainly no negotiations which had taken place in which I was involved. I was not at any stage involved in the formulation or the production of these proposals. We know from two sources, the Presidential broadcast, which was relayed in the international wire services by API and various other people, that the signature of an interim document was due to take place if both parties accepted these proposals, and the Foreign Minister also had said to me the same sort of thing, as I mentioned in my earlier evidence. I was aware of the fact that by this time it was about a quarter past seven local time, about 45 minutes after my conversation had first begun, therefore I could not help feeling that the Peruvian assessment was rather optimistic and if they hoped that the signature of a document was to take place imminently it was going to be jolly difficult to do it that evening because while it is true that in Lima we had four and a half hours left of today, it was already tomorrow morning in London.

Then came the question I had been waiting for:

Sir Anthony Kershaw

Ambassador, it has been suggested to us and in the press, I think, that you were very close to the negotiations and that General Haig was under the impression that sometimes when he telephoned to President Belaúnde you were actually sitting in the President's room. Is that a correct impression?

Wallace

No, Mr Chairman. I would not relish being put in the position of having publicly to contradict Mr Haig. We all owe him a tremendous debt of gratitude for everything he did during those critical weeks and, indeed, what he has done subsequently, but I do not

233

think I am, in fact, being put in the position of having to contradict him. I have seen a transcript of the words actually used in this interview and while he said that the British Ambassador "was in on every bit of the negotiations in Peru, he was right in with the President", this could be a reflection of the close working relationship which I had established with all members of the Peruvian Government and it was a great privilege for me to work in those conditions. But be that as it may, I can categorically deny that I was in any room at any time when anyone was speaking to General Haig on the telephone.

I thought I could hardly put it any clearer, and I hoped that this particular canard would be firmly put to rest. After some further talk about what General Haig had really meant when he said that the British Ambassador was 'right in on' the talks, negotiations or whatever, we came to the piece of paper in my handwriting which allegedly existed in the Peruvian Foreign Ministry. By this time Mr Mikardo had taken up the questioning.

Mr I. Mikardo
I believe you were present when we had our session this morning and if so you will have heard references to a document to which Mr Arias Stella was said to have referred, of which it was said that it evidenced your being *au fait* throughout with the proposals. What do you have to say about that?

Wallace
Yes, thank you very much. I am glad to have the opportunity of clearing that up. I think it must refer to the fact that when Dr Arias showed me the seven points there were two versions, one was an English version and the other a Spanish version, but he only had one copy of each. So therefore we scribbled down together the Spanish and the English so that I could have a copy of each in order to ensure there could be no possible risk of subsequent misinterpretation.

234

Mr I. Mikardo

Don't they have a photocopier at the Foreign Office?

Wallace

Not that evening. In order to ensure there could be no possible risk of misinterpretation or ambiguity in the terms used. Therefore I think he has a copy of a piece of paper with my writing on which the English words were put, so that I could be sure that those were the English words that he had in fact agreed with me and vice versa. I wanted to have copies of the Spanish text. I do not think there is anything sinister about this. I think it was perfectly correct and illustrates the manner in which I was privileged to work with Dr Arias, whom I also hold in very high regard.

Mr P. Thomas

When you were shown that document was it on the evening of 2 May?

Wallace

On the evening of 2 May.

Mr P. Thomas

And was it a seven-point plan, as we heard this morning – seven headings in other words?

Wallace

Yes.

Mr P. Thomas

It consisted solely of that?

Wallace

Yes, it consisted of seven headings, seven items.

Mr P. Thomas

And is it right that when you saw the Minister that night on 2 May, which I think was about 6.30 – is that right?

Wallace

Yes.

Mr P. Thomas

Did it come as a surprise to you that this initiative on the part of the Peruvian Government had been made?

Wallace

Yes, it did come as a surprise. I was presented, as I have indicated previously, with a *fait accompli*. It was something of which I had no prior knowledge. But I did not stop to argue about it. Clearly my primary interest was in getting the report back to London as soon as possible, and this is what I did.

Mr P. Thomas

And then of course you reported back to HMG here?

Wallace

I reported back to London, copying I think to Washington and New York in the light of the Foreign Secretary's. . .

Mr P. Thomas

What is the difference between Lima time and London time? Is it about five and a half hours?

Wallace

London is Lima plus 5 G.M.T.

Mr P. Thomas

We were told for instance the difference between Argentine time and London time is four hours. The difference between Lima and Argentina time is I think one and a half hours. So I thought it might be a combination of those two. In any event, when you met the Minister on 2 May in the evening, the time then being 6.30, it would be roughly 10 o'clock at night London time?

Wallace

11.30.

Mr P. Thomas

And the *Belgrano* had been sunk at 8 o'clock London time?

Wallace
That is so.

Mr P. Thomas
Were you told at the meeting that the *Belgrano* had been sunk?

Wallace
No.

There then followed some questions designed to establish beyond any doubt that nothing had gone from London to Lima that might have had a bearing on the decision to sink the *Belgrano*. This was followed by a question about the connection between the Belaúnde/Haig formula and the sinking of the *Belgrano* to which I was able to reply with truth and conviction that during the seventeen months I remained in Lima after the Falklands war no one had suggested to me that the *Belgrano* had been deliberately sunk in order to prevent the Peruvian proposals from prospering.

A further point of interest was raised by Mr Lawrence when he asked me if Dr Arias had known the *Belgrano* had been sunk when he saw me at 18.30 hours. I replied that I was certain Dr Arias did not know and that therefore he did not tell me. There was no question but that he would have told me had he known at the time. This was followed by a question about the significance of the word 'aspirations' in the Peruvian seven-point plan with the obvious purpose of determining if I had contributed in any way to the wording of the seven items.

I explained that the word 'aspirations' was simply an example of the sort of thing to which the British Government would not agree. I said that from previous experience (probably everybody in the Diplomatic Service has dealt with the Falkland Islands dispute at one stage or another of his career) I knew that we had always maintained that the 'wishes' of the islanders were paramount.

Mr I. Lawrence
Can I ask you a bit more detail about the proposals as you understand them at that time. We know that there is a dispute as to how you test or how you react to the wishes of the Falkland Islanders or

the interests of the Falkland Islanders or the aspirations of the Falkland Islanders. That is an issue which has been perpetual. Did he indicate to you what the Peruvian proposal thinking was on that issue of whether they were going to have regard to the wishes, the interests or the aspirations of the Falkland Islanders?

Wallace

The question of the wishes, aspirations and so on is a matter which clearly had occupied the Peruvian mind because I remember discussing this aspect of the situation in the bits of paper that we scribbled in order to get the wording right, and my report giving the terms of the seven-point proposals includes the word 'aspirations'.

Mr I. Lawrence

So did Dr Arias Stella give you any indication that there were differences amongst the contact group of nations as to whether there should be 'aspirations' or 'interests' or 'wishes'?

Wallace

No.

Mr I. Lawrence

You have got the conclusion that everybody had agreed that 'aspirations' would be the factor in the plan?

Wallace

I do not think that aspect was covered in the terms in which you have put it. I got the conclusion and I got the wording which I wrote down, which was that the Peruvian proposals would include the word 'aspirations'.

Mr I. Lawrence

Did he tell you of any other differences that had arisen in the course of negotiating the detail of the plan, and if so, what?

Wallace

He said that a number of procedural difficulties

238

had arisen which had been the subject of many telephone conversations with Mr Haig, on the one hand, and with the—

Mr I. Lawrence
Can you give us some indication? Did he elaborate?

Wallace
No.

Mr I. Lawrence
He just said procedural—

Wallace
Procedural difficulties had arisen with Mr Haig, on the one hand, and with the Argentines, on the other. This is something which he emphasised also and in the subsequent telegram which I sent adding a certain amount of comment on the question of our previous conversation with Dr Arias he confirmed on two separate occasions that the Peruvians now regarded the ball as being in the Argentine court at this moment in time.

Mr I. Lawrence
That there had been other differences than procedural ones or not?

Wallace
That I do not know.

Sir Anthony Kershaw
Ambassador, did you regard the proposals at that meeting at half past six as a completed plan which had been worked out and was presented to you or did you regard it rather as a basis for further negotiation?

Wallace
Yes, I regarded it, frankly, as a basis for further negotiation because there were one or two aspects of the proposals which it was clearly agreed should be developed and continued further. We have mentioned one of them, the question of 'aspirations'. Hitherto we had always thought of the wishes of the

Islanders as being paramount. There were one or two differences of that nature which clearly would have to be developed and considered further.

Sir Anthony Kershaw
    So he indicated there and then that there was further work to be done?

Wallace
    Dr Arias did not indicate that, Mr Chairman. He merely said this is the basis on which the Peruvian plan is being launched and we hope that if its provisions or its outlines are acceptable to both parties there would be the signing of some agreement in Lima. But as I have mentioned earlier, I thought at the time, I remember clearly thinking, this was rather optimistic.

Mr I. Lawrence
    And also that General Galtieri had to convince his *Junta* first?

Wallace
    That is one of the points which was made – by subsequent conversation with Dr Arias in which he stressed, on two separate occasions, that they regarded the ball as being in the Argentine court. If I may add a word of explanation of my own, it was clear to me that there was one major objection to this proposal and that is that if required the Argentine withdrawal of troops from the islands. We knew jolly well they were not going to do that. Resolution 502 provided for two aspects of the situation. One was Argentine withdrawal and the other one was negotiations, and had they been disposed to withdraw their troops, I venture to think we might not be here this evening.

Then came my first opportunity to refer to *Malvinas – La Trama Secreta* when the chairman asked me if Dr Arias thought that the Peruvians had overcome Argentine objections to the withdrawal of their troops, particularly as the Peruvians had included this condition in their seven-point plan. Had he conveyed a feeling of triumph at having overcome this problem?

In my reply I said that Dr Arias had not conveyed that feeling at all. I then referred to the committee's session that morning when they had questioned Mr Rice and Mr Gavshon. Each member of the committee had been given a copy of *The Sinking of the Belgrano*, which I had seen in front of them. I said that there was another book which had been written earlier by three Argentine journalists. This gave a detailed and comprehensive account of events before, during, and after the Falklands invasion. It quoted the transcriptions of the telephone conversations beween Lima and Buenos Aires, including one or two which clearly revealed General Galtieri's state of mind when he refused to commit himself when speaking to President Balaúnde. The Argentine book also produced some of the conversations not included in their book by Mr Gavshon and Mr Rice. In any event, the conclusions reached by the Argentine authors of the book were that General Galtieri was not disposed to give a reply to the Peruvian proposals, either one way or the other, even though his foreign minister, Dr Costa Mendez, appeared to have been hopeful that some solution might be based on the Peruvian initiative.

As the Argentine book was in Spanish the committee did not immediately take an interest in it, but I had prepared a translation of the crucial telephone conversation about me between the Peruvian and Argentine foreign ministers early in the morning of 3 May 1982. I proposed to hand this over, with a copy of the Argentine book, to the clerk to the committee at the end of the session, but first came further questions about my meeting with Dr Arias at 18.30 hours on the evening of 2 May, 1982. These attempted to establish how much detail of the Peruvian initiatives had been passed on by General Haig to Mr Pym in Washington, Mr. Mikardo had again taken up the questioning.

Mr I. Mikardo

I want to get absolutely clear the answers you gave to some questions of Mr Lawrence – and the lack of clarity is probably due more to deficiency of my perception than of your explanation. You say that Dr

241

Arias Stella in that conversation you had with him from 1830 onwards on the 2nd indicated that he had been in touch with General Haig, and he indicated, I thought you said, that he was under the impression that all he was saying to General Haig was being passed on to and discussed with Mr Pym. Is that right?

Wallace
That is correct.

Mr I. Mikardo
That being so, though you say that the information you were then given was the first of your cognisance, it was not the first of Her Majesty's Government's cognisance of the peace proposals, if in fact they had been passed on by General Haig to Mr Pym. Do you have any information which can give any guidance as to whether they were or were not, apart from Dr Stella's impression?

Wallace
I believe that Mr Pym gave evidence before this Committee on the subject, in which he referred to this very aspect of the situation. I think I could probably find the text of the evidence.

Mr I. Mikardo
I have that in mind. What I am trying to get is, what you got out of what Dr Stella said about it.

Wallace
The only thing I got out of my conversation with Dr Stella was the implication he believed – Dr Arias said that he believed that these conversations with General Haig had been relayed or had been communicated to Mr Pym.

Mr I. Mikardo
Indeed, Mr Wallace, would there have been any point at all in Dr Stella's representations to Mr Haig if they were not going to be or had not been discussed with Her Majesty's Government? Wasn't he talking to Mr Haig as an intermediary? Thus the chain of

intermediaries was: the Argentines to the Peruvians to the United States to Great Britain; so that just as President Belaúnde was the first link in the chain of intermediaries of communication, General Haig was the second, and there would have been no point in communicating with him unless he was passing on to the next link. Is that not so?

Wallace

That is what Dr Arias said and obviously thought.

Mr B. Wells

At this meeting at 6.30 with Dr Arias Stella, what did he ask you to do? Did he want you to find out the British Government's reaction to these proposals? Was he asking you to get the British Government to negotiate directly with Lima? What was he wanting you to do, if anything?

Wallace

I think that your question has a bearing on the answers I have just given. We must remember that he had also summoned the Argentine Ambassador at 1800 hours that same evening to communicate to him the same piece of paper, the same seven-point plan. This was regardless of the fact that, as we all know, conversations had been taking place on the telephone both with General Galtieri and Costa Mendez on the one hand and with Mr Haig on the other. He asked me only to report back to my Government as soon as possible, which I did, and to let him have an answer as soon as possible.

Mr B. Wells

From that conversation then you concluded, I imagine, as I would from what you have just said, that no British agreement had been obtained to adhere to those seven points?

Wallace

Certainly.

Mr B. Wells

Or to a cease-fire?

Wallace
Absolutely not. In fact the instructions I received in the middle of the night from New York were that while reiterating our profound gratitude to the Peruvian authorities for their continuing efforts to find a peaceful solution, we needed more time to consider the proposals, we needed more time to analyse them. I was explicitly told to try to forestall any suggestion, as had indeed been suggested in one of the phrases used in the press annoucement made the previous evening, to forestall any suggestion that these had in fact been accepted, and my instructions were to say that we neither accepted nor rejected them but that we wanted more time, and we were very grateful.

Mr B. Wells
And indeed negotiations continued did they not?

Wallace
Indeed they did.

Mr B. Wells
Through your office.

Wallace
I was involved in some negotiations until 24–25 May – subsequent attempts by President Belaúnde.

Mr B. Wells
So that would indicate the sinking of the *Belgrano* by no means dampened the enthusiasm of the President in Peru in pursuing his proposal?

Wallace
That is my impression. That is my conviction.

Mr Mikardo
It was not his ship, was it after all?

Then Mr Spearing asked me for my opinion of Argentine reactions to the sinking of the *Belgrano*. This gave me a further opportunity to quote from *Malvinas – La Trama Secreta*.

Mr N. Spearing

Following that last point, it may indeed have stimulated President Belaúnde, but surely there was a change of attitude – and perhaps you can tell us of it if you knew of it – on behalf of the Argentine Government?

Wallace

I would again refer to this book, which I think purports to give a very comprehensive account.

Mr N. Spearing

Can we know the name and title?

Wallace

Malvinas – La Trama Secreta, which means *The Secret Web*. It is written by three Argentine journalists called Cardoso, Kirschbaum and van der Kooy. They belong to a newspaper called *El Clarin*. They have written an extremely interesting and to me truly fascinating account. They claim to have access to all the tapes of the conversations which took place between Buenos Aires and Lima. Indeed, I have reason to believe that these tapes are true because they are the same tapes which were subsequently quoted by the military authorities in Argentina in the famous Rattenbach Report, which was a judgment on the conduct of the war and on the conduct of those personalities, those military officers principally concerned. The conclusion that these journalists reached is that it did not really make very much difference at all because President Galtieri would find it politically and domestically impossible to withdraw the troops from the Falklands anyway.

Mr N. Spearing

If I may ask a few questions arising out of what has been said and adding to that, can I ask you, Ambassador: the United States' tilt or the dual declaration by the Senate and Secretary of State Haig came, I think, on the Thursday morning—

Wallace

Friday.

Mr N. Spearing

The Friday morning. From your Latin American experience what impact was that likely to have or did it have in Lima and was likely to have had in Montevideo?

Wallace

I was not in Montevideo at the time but in Lima I also reported on the—

Mr N. Spearing

It need not be extensive, just brief.

Wallace

The Peruvian authorities took a fairly poor view, there is no question about it, and I was given a copy of the Peruvian views. The Peruvian reply to the Haig tilt was as follows: 'The Peruvian Government had been actively trying to avoid confrontation and had expressed their position clearly in a communique which they issued on 3 April at the United Nations. They had also produced a truce proposal on 11 April and in a declaration which they had made at the most recent, which was the first, OAS meeting. They consider the possibility of an armed conflict on Latin American continent as anachronistic and inadmissable, with incalculable consequences. The Peruvian Government deplored the measures adopted by the US Government which clearly favoured one of the parties and which had put an end to the good offices mission. The US offer to provide military and material assistance to the UK contravened Security Resolution 502 by adding to the conflict and by prejudicing the peaceful objectives of the OAS Resolution, and the Peruvian Government was ready to continue the search for a peaceful settlement and would adopt any initiatives necessary to achieve that end within the limits of international law.'

Mr N. Spearing

In other words, they almost, using colloquial terms, took the baton from Secretary of State Haig and particularly President Belaúnde, so in the last sentence there was in a sense an obligation for him to carry on. Is that broadly right?

Wallace

I would not myself use the word 'obligation' but it is clear to me that since Mr Haig had been conducting his shuttle, his mediation, for several weeks previously, when Mr Haig decided to end his mediation attempt the Peruvians as a starting-point obviously thought that he was the best person to get in touch with and, indeed, references were made this morning to a telephone call which was made by Dr Arias Stella to the American Ambassador in Lima at the time. Curiously enough, this book refers in a number of places to the intervention of the American – and I repeat American – not the British Ambassador in the events leading up to the presentation of the seven-point plan.

After some questions in which individual members of the committee re-established some of the points previously made I was given an opportunity to deal with the red leather bound treaty when Mr Spearing asked me if the 'seven points' were on a single sheet of paper, or in a file, or perhaps in a bound volume:

Wallace

The seven points were on a single sheet of paper given to me by Dr Arias. I had heard of references to the red leather bound treaty which was prepared or said to have been. I myself would not be prepared to seek to disprove the existence of this treaty. I never saw the treaty, I was not told about the treaty. I was never consulted about any terms or told what it might contain. But I know that a number of people claim to have seen it. All I would say is that we know from two different sources, that is from the presidential announcement at 6 pm and from my conversation with Dr Arias Stella, that the Peruvians were hoping that if their proposals were acceptable

247

an interim document would be signed in Lima. The Peruvian diplomatic service is a highly professional, very skilled and dedicated organisation, and I have no doubt that if they thought a treaty was likely to be signed they would have made all necessary contingency arrangements.

Mr N. Spearing
So this rumour or story is compatible at least with optimism in Lima that night?

Wallace
Certainly.

Mr N. Spearing
Can I ask you about the press wire? You mentioned the presidential statement at 6 pm. Was that the one which later on in the evidence we heard this morning was transferred to New York and the witness said to London by the AP and the UPI? In other words, what I am really asking you is was there widespread knowledge in Lima at that time, presumably after the broadcast was heard on the radio, that big news might be happening shortly?

Wallace
Certainly.

Mr N. Spearing
And although you no doubt exercised diplomatic caution, did you entirely rule that out as being over-optimistic or entirely unlikely?

Wallace
I think it is a question of timing. My references to over-optimism were made to the prospect of signing an interim agreement in Lima within the foreseeable, the immediate future. I thought that was slightly over-optimistic, but I did not stop to argue. My interest was clearly to get my report back to London as soon as possible, and this is what I did.

Mr Mikardo later returned to the red leather bound treaty:

Mr I. Mikardo

I want to ask about this mysterious little red book about which I have heard for the first time. I want to know something about it. You have told us you cannot prove or disprove its existence and therefore I am asking questions about something for which you are not responsible. I am just picking out the information that you must have. From what you know about it or have heard about it, does it purport to be the text of an agreement between Britain and the Argentine to bring the conflict to an end?

Wallace

I do not know. I have never seen it. I have never been shown it. I have never been told what was in it. I simply do not know.

Mr I. Mikardo

Who told you of its existence?

Wallace

For one, Mr Paul Foot. That was not meant to be a humorous remark. There are a number of people who have claimed to have seen it. I would not myself seek to disprove this in spite of the fact that I have never seen it myself and do not know what it contains.

Mr R. Harvey

So far as the Peruvians themselves were concerned, do you think the seven-point proposal was in fact a complete draft agreement or were they expecting further negotiation on it?

Wallace

The reference made in the presidential broadcast was to an interim document being signed and this is what was reported in fact by the international wire services.

Mr R. Harvey

So far as you were concerned this was the interim document?

Wallace

I did not see any interim document. I did not see any treaty. I had a piece of paper given to me containing seven points which the Peruvians had advanced and worked out with Mr Haig. But the treaty which was to have been signed, I have never seen.

Mr R. Harvey

And the treaty was to have been much longer than seven points was it not?

Wallace

I can only speculate.

At the end of the session the chairman courteously asked me if there was anything I wanted to add. I took this opportunity to introduce the transcription of the telephone conversation between Dr Arias Stella in Lima and Dr Costa Mendez in Buenos Aires on the morning of 3 May 1982. This particular conversation was not included among those reproduced in the book *The Sinking of the Belgrano* by Mr Rice and Mr Gavshon.

Sir Anthony Kershaw

Have we failed to ask you any question which you would like to explain?

Wallace

I am very grateful, Mr Chairman. There is one particular point. I am very conscious of my own role in the events and I would like, with your permission, to refer again to this very good book which is very comprehensive.

Sir Anthony Kershaw

Is it in Spanish?

Wallace

It is in Spanish, but I would like to translate, if I may, one of the telephone conversations which is not quoted in the book by Mr Desmond Rice and Mr Gavshon. This is one of the appendices which is on page 344–Appendix 10. It purports to be a conversation which took place between Dr Arias Stella and Dr Costa Mendez on the morning of the 3 May 1982. Leaving aside the usual greetings and so forth – Dr Arias Stella went on to inform Costa Mendez as follows: 'I want to tell you, in addition to reiterating my solidarity and my compliments, Minister, the news that this morning very early the Ambassador of England in Peru has transmitted to me. We, as you know, have been – the President – in contact with the Secretariat of the American Department of State, but not directly with England. Therefore, this message which has been transmitted to us may be interesting for any subsequent evaluation you may make. He has told me as follows. First he is very grateful for the intervention, the intention of Peru, and he believes that Peru can continue helping – that is what he said. In the second place, that is the official message of the Government to our Ministry of Foreign Affairs. The local Ambassador has told me – now this is my own affair, but it is not in the message that I have to transmit, which is only the first part – 'I wish to tell you that in my view what England needs is more time in order to analyse this proposal at the corresponding levels'. And the last thing that they (sic) told me 'the door is not totally closed within the framework of what has been proposed'. Now the fact that Dr Arias put these words into my mouth could be again Peruvian diplomacy at work, for which I have the highest regard. Nonetheless I think it is fairly conclusive, if not absolutely, in its references to the fact that this is the first direct contact which had taken place with the British.

Sir Anthony Kershaw
Ambassador, we are very grateful to you. You have taken a great deal of trouble to come and help us with this matter and we are very grateful to you. Thank you very much.

Because of its particular relevance to my story the following is the complete text of the telephone conversation as translated and reproduced from the book *Malvinas – La Trama Secreta* and printed as an Annex on page 174 of the Foreign Affairs Committee's Report:

Costa Méndez – Arias Stella Conversation (3 May 1982)

Costa Méndez How are you?

Arias Stella Minister: How do you feel this morning?

Costa Méndez Full of pre-occupations and with a great disappointment yesterday, because we were all in the meeting of the Junta studying the paper – it was not easy that all should be convinced, but I think there was a great probability that this might be the case, as I had anticipated something on these lines to the President – it was really a discussion only of words, and in the middle of the meeting of the Military Junta there arrived news of the torpedoing, and this created a great deal of indignation in the Navy, in my judgement very justly so, because they say that this could not have been determined other than by the satellite. They therefore see behind this the hand of the United States.

In any case, even if this were not so, it is evident that Great Britain cannot be negotiating at the same time, compromising a gentleman and a President like Architect Belaúnde and initiating actions. Correct?

Arias Stella The President has fully made the point, in relation to the Argentine reaction, there was no other way.

Costa Méndez Above all, what disappoints me most is that we have spent the whole day talking and in reality speaking of very few words of difference, as you are aware.

Arias Stella I want to tell you, in addition to reiterating my solidarity and my compliments, Minister, the news that this morning very early the

Ambassador of England in Peru has transmitted to me.

We, as you know, have been – the President – in contact with the Secretariat of the American Department of State, but not directly with England. Therefore, this message which has been transmitted to us may be interesting for any subsequent evaluation you may make. He has told me as follows. First, he is very grateful for the intervention, the intention of Peru, and he believes that Peru can continue helping – that is what he said—.

In the second place, that is the official message of the Government to our Ministry of Foreign Affairs. The local Ambassador has told me – now this is my own affair, but it is not in the message that I have to transmit, which is only the first part – 'I wish to tell you that in my view what England needs is more time in order to analyse this proposal at the corresponding levels.' And the last thing that they (*sic*) told me 'the door is not totally closed within the framework of what has been proposed.'

Costa Méndez You know, Minister, this is the first time we received anything direct from Great Britain.

Arias Stella For us it is also the first time.

Costa Méndez We had not received anything direct through any channel, the Haig thing was a special action of his.

Arias Stella This is what has been transmitted to me, and they have not said transmit it to Argentina, but I am doing so, because it is my duty to let you know so that you may have the framework for the corresponding judgment.

Costa Méndez Yes, this is important for us, I am very grateful, Minister.

Arias Stella For anything at the opportune moment . . . I understand that now the feelings . . .

Costa Méndez What I would like is that you should transmit to the President that what he spoke about

253

with the President last night, that this morning President Galtieri told me about and what I had been speaking about with you, what we wished to emphasise are two things. First, we really are moved by the interest and dedication that the President and you all have put into this initiative and that we have been enormously mortified that this initiative, which could have been successful, has had to be interrupted by this news which the Admiral brought at the moment when the Junta was meeting in order to consider the subject.

Minister, many thanks, etc. . . .

Arias Stella Unless you judge necessary an effort on our part when the conditions are suitable. You may take it for granted that we shall not spare any effort to offer help in obtaining peace and justice for Argentina.

Costa Méndez I am very grateful to you, I know it and I feel the fraternal spirit of Peru by my side.

Thank you very much, Minister. Thank you very much for your call.

* * *

The following morning the London dailies factually reported the main points made in my evidence, namely, that I was not in the room with President Belaúnde, and that I had first been informed by the Peruvian Foreign Minister of the Peruvian initiative at 1830 hours local time on the evening of 2 May 1982, that is, about three and a half hours after the *Belgrano* was sunk, although this was not known to the Peruvians at the time. The next day I flew back to Uruguay to find the press in the River Plate even less interested in the developments. I only saw one report, in the Buenos Aires daily *La Prensa* of 16 November 1984, which mentioned my 'intervention' in the 'debate' about the sinking of the *Belgrano*. It reported that I had learned of the Peruvian peace plan – which 'failed because of the sinking' – about three hours after the *Belgrano* had gone down. The report added that this 'detail' supported the posture of the British Government, which had been 'accused' by the Opposition of

254

having ordered the sinking in order 'deliberately to frustrate the Peruvian peace efforts'.

The Foreign Affairs Committee subsequently took evidence from Admiral of the Fleet Lord Lewin and Sir John Nott (Defence Minister during the Falklands war) on 15 December 1984, and the committee's report was published seven months later, on 24 July 1985. The committee divided on party lines and published also a minority report which gave me personally a clean bill of health, even though it did say that the Foreign Office should have been alerted by the tenor and content of my first conversation with Dr Arias on 1 May 1982 and 'could well have concluded that something might originate in Lima'. It also added that even if I was not (as had been alleged) 'right in on it' I was very close – 'exactly where one would expect a British Ambassador to be' which, in the circumstances, I took as an unusual compliment.

But the committee's report was conclusive on a number of points relating to my own intervention. I make no apology for having selected the most relevant extracts from the report and conclusions. Understandably, the timing of the initiation of the Peruvian proposals came under very close scrutiny, and I was pleased to note that the committee had seen fit to have parts of the Argentine book I had introduced in evidence translated for this purpose:

5. THE PERUVIAN PEACE PROPOSALS
The initiation of talks between President Belaunde and Mr Haig

5.1 According to the account of President Belaunde Terry reported by Mr Gavshon and Mr Rice, the so-called Peruvian peace initiative got under way on the evening of Saturday 1 May 1982, when President Belaunde telephoned his ambassador in Washington to tell him of his worries about the situation developing in the South Atlantic. President Belaunde said:

'Half an hour later Haig himself rang me. He told me: "President Reagan's not in Washington right now. He's in Knoxville, opening an exhibition. But I know that you are very concerned, and so are we. What can we do?

255

How can you help us?" I told him plainly that I was on very good terms with Argentina and that I understood that his negotiations with her had not succeeded. "That's right," Haig agreed, "there was intransigence on both sides." I said then that some acceptable formula had to be found. We talked by phone for three-quarters of an hour and I finally asked him please to dictate to me the essential points from Britain's viewpoint. Haig read them over to me, and I for my part told him what word was unsatisfactory and what condition unacceptable for Argentina. We finally agreed on a plan which covered seven points, and I left it that I should call President Galtieri at once to put that formula to him.'

Although there is some discrepancy as to dates and times in this account, General Haig's memoirs confirm that the initiative for this new round of negotiations came from Peru.

5.2 Some other accounts, however, place the beginning of the Peruvian initiative rather earlier. The authors of *La Trama Secreta*, for instance, suggest, first, that President Belaunde was 'encouraged' from Washington to act as mediator in the dispute, quoting the then United States Ambassador to the United Nations, Mrs Jeane Kirkpatrick, as affirming that the Peruvian peace initiative was 'a new Haig mission in disguise'. Second, they claim that the peace initiative effectively got under way 'very early on the 1st [May]', when President Belaunde got in touch by telephone with Mr Haig, 'who immediately perceived the possibility of establishing through Lima a new bridge between Argentina and Great Britain'. Both men then began work on the formulation of proposals based on those previously rejected by Argentina, 'but with some finesse Belaunde was suggesting improvements which would make the proposal palatable to the military junta'.

Then a comparison was made between the relative timings of the Peruvian initiative as given respectively by the authors of the Argentine book on one hand and Messrs Gavshon and Rice on the other. This calls for an additional gloss on the wording of the next two paragraphs of the Committee's Report which some may have regarded as a little ambiguous:

5.3 Mr Gavshon and Mr Rice tend to confirm the Argentine authors' account, placing the actual start of the process a little earlier. Mr Gavshon told us that 'the actual action to launch this late initiative began on Friday 30 April shortly after lunch when Foreign Minister Arias Stella made contact with US Ambassador in Lima, Frank Ortiz. . .the American Task Force, looking after the Falklands problem at that time in the State Department, was immediately alerted. And although the first conversation between Belaunde and Haig only took place on Saturday night, 1 May, in fact there were a good deal of exchanges taking place on an official level between Lima and Washington.'

5.4 In view of other evidence of diplomatic activity in Lima during Saturday 1 May, it seems probable that Mr Gavshon's version of events is substantially correct namely that the first direct talks between Mr Haig and President Belaunde were preceeded by contacts at official level in Washington and Lima which may have begun soon after the United States Administration's public announcement of support for the United Kingdom on Friday 30 April.

My only comment is that the reference to contacts 'at official level in Washington and Lima' which may have preceded the first direct talks between President Belaúnde and General Haig applies exclusively to contacts with United States officials including, of course, my American colleague in Lima, Frank Ortiz. Although I was not asked questions about this during my sessions with the Foreign Affairs Committee, I believe the point may be worth making here. There were certainly no contacts with British officials in Lima, nor did the American Ambassador tell me (until much later) about his intervention when the Peruvians began their initiative. But, with the benefit of hindsight, this was the obvious thing to do. General Haig's mediation ended on 30 April. It is logical that in their attempt to pick up the pieces the following day, the Peruvians should have turned to General Haig in Washington in the first instance, and to the American Ambassador in Lima for assistance in getting in touch with him. As a result of the Haig mediation the Peruvians obviously regarded the Americans as their immediate interlocutors, if only to take full advantage of General Haig's earlier hard work.

At all events, the Committee's conclusions were quite clear. First on the timing of the Peruvian exchanges with me:

'We have concluded:
(i)   that although there is no doubt that the Peruvian Government and the Argentine junta believed that Mr Haig was in close contact with Mr Pym on the details of the Peruvian proposals on the morning of 2 May, nothing from British sources suggests that that was in fact the case (*paragraphs 5.14 and 5.17*);
(ii) that there is no evidence that the British Ambassador in Lima was informed of the detailed Peruvian proposals until some time after the attack on the *Belgrano* (*paragraph 5.24*); and
(iii) that we have no reason to disbelieve the evidence of the participants that the War Cabinet was not aware of the Peruvian peace proposals at the time of the decision to authorise an attack on the *Belgrano* (*paragraph 5.8*).'

The point was made even more clearly in a later section of the report which also referred in unequivocal terms to the telephone conversation between Dr Arias in Lima and Dr Costa Méndez in Buenos Aires on the morning of 3 May 1982, as transcribed in the book *Malvinas – La Trama Secreta*:

5.24 We have no reason to disbelieve Mr Wallace's account of his relations with the Peruvian President and Foreign Ministry during the weekend of 1 and 2 May 1982. There is, in particular, no evidence to support the hypothesis that Mr Wallace was advised of the detailed Peruvian proposals until his meeting with Dr Arias Stella on the evening of Sunday 2 May, some time after the

Belgrano had been attacked. This view is supported by the telephone conversation between Dr Arias and Dr Costa Mendez on the morning of Monday 3 May 1982, in which Dr Arias specifically stated that the Peruvian authorities had not been in direct touch with 'England' during the weekend. It is, perhaps, not without significance that of the many telephone conversations reported by them between Lima and Buenos Aires, this particular conversation was not reproduced by Mr Gavshon and Mr Rice.

5.25 How much did the War Cabinet know? Assuming as we do, that the accounts given to us by Mr Pym, Ambassador Henderson and Ambassador Wallace are correct, the first account of the outline Peruvian peace proposals was not despatched from Washington until after 5.00 p.m. local time (10.00 p.m. London time). Mr Wallace's account of his conversations with Dr Arias Stella, and of the Peruvian President's press conference, was not received in London until shortly after 1.00 a.m. (London time) on Monday 3 May 1982. If these accounts are correct, the first news of the Peruvian peace initiative cannot have reached the War Cabinet earlier than about 10 hours after they had authorised the change in the Rules of Engagement which permitted the sinking of the *General Belgrano*, or more than two hours after the cruiser was torpedoed.

The Committee reported on their own exchanges with General Haig about the evidence given by Mr Pym (and others) and myself:

5.29 Because of the apparent conflict of evidence between the statements of British participants and other participants and observers on the diplomatic events of 1 and 2 May 1982, we sought information from Mr Haig about, in particular, the nature of his discussions with Mr Pym in Washington on 2 May and his assessment of Ambassador Charles Wallace's involvement in negotiations in Lima on that date, both of which could have a direct bearing on our assessment of the information available to the War Cabinet on that date. Although Mr

259

Haig did not feel that it would be 'appropriate' to comment in detail on these points, he nevertheless told us that

> 'At no time during that weekend, or during preceding or subsequent events, did I have reason to question the motives of the officals of Her Majesty's Government with respect to the *Belgrano* nor do I have any basis for challenging the statements made by responsible representatives of the government at that time.'

Mr Haig appears to be telling us that the evidence given to us by Mr Pym and Mr Wallace, which was quoted to him, was correct.

I was interested to see that, in another section of their report, the committee had drawn again on *Malvinas – La Trama Secreta* when considering the acceptibility or otherwise of the Peruvian 'seven-point plan'. They had translated the conversation in which General Galtieri had refused to commit himself (on the telephone) in spite of President Belaúnde's insistence. The Argentine authors do not appear to have been sanguine about the chances of success of the Peruvian proposals, even though their existence (but not the details) was revealed to the world for self-evident reasons by President Belaunde in his news conference at 1800 hours (local time) in Lima:

5.34 Significantly, the Argentine journalists' account of the communications between Lima and Buenos Aires, from which Mr Gavshon and Mr Rice evidently drew much of their material, comes to quite other conclusions. Although, with even greater confidence than Mr Gavshon and Mr Rice, they base their account on the assumption the UK Government was directly involved in the negotiations, they do not give the impression that the junta's agreement to the terms of the agreement could be confidently expected. First, they stress the Argentine foreign Minister's insistence that 'the word "wishes" is unacceptable', and the difficulty of finding an acceptable compromise on this point. Second, they stress General Galtieri's 'annoyance' with President Belaunde during that afternoon, Galtieri insisting that, although 'what you discussed with Costa Mendez is all right', 'it does not oblige me to give you a reply, because I can't. You understand, I also have my Senate and I must consult it'. Finally they suggest that, by the time of President Belaunde's press conference on the evening of 2 May (before news of the attack on the *Belgrano* had reached the Argentine junta), 'it was certain that Belaunde's proposal seemed destined to fail'. 'The impression that the agreement promoted by Belaunde was failing also increased in Buenos Aires, in spite of *the untimely announcement of the Peruvian President* (our italics). There was an enormous gap between expression of optimism and the depression noticed above all among Argentine diplomatic staff.' Moreover, their account conveys no sense of any pressure from the Argentine military to sue for peace at that time.

But in his reply to the committee's written questions, General Haig was even more categorical on this aspect of the situation:

5.39 *Was an agreement in sight?* Despite the fact that he has been widely quoted in more optimistic terms elsewhere, General Haig's evidence to us about the chances of a settlement being reached during the weekend of 1 and 2 May is categorical:

> 'At no time during that difficult weekend of 1–2 May 1982 did I believe we were on the verge of a settlement. This subjective attitude on my part was the result of weeks of tedious negotiations with the then Government of Argentina involving a comparable political framework for settlement. It did not, however, dampen my enthusiasm for exploring any possible political solution which would not condone rule of force.'

I have little more to add. The committee's report was summarized by the Central Office of Information in the following terms:

The committee believes that the claim that the

Argentine Junta was on the brink of agreeing to the Peruvian proposals on the evening of 2 May is a highly speculative and selective interpretation of the information available.

The report goes on: 'Although there is no doubt that the Peruvian Government and the Argentine Junta believed that Mr Haig (the US Secretary of State at the time) was in close contact with Mr Pym (British Foreign Secretary at the time) on the details of the Peruvian proposals on the morning of 2 May, nothing from British sources suggests that that was in fact the case. There is no evidence that the British Ambassador in Lima was informed of the detailed Peruvian proposals until some time after the attack on the *Belgrano*.

'We have no reason to disbelieve the evidence of the participants that the war cabinet was not aware of the Peruvian peace proposals at the time of the decision to authorise an attack on the *Belgrano*.'

The House of Commons committee is not convinced that the avoidance of military action would have been justified even if the War Cabinet had known of the proposals at the time, unless the Argentine Junta had directly informed the British Government that it intended to suspend hostilities. The Committee also concludes that adequate notice had been served on the Argentines of a change in the British rules of engagement in a warning of 23 April 1982. However, the committee adds that the purpose of the exclusion zones around the Falklands was unclear and ultimately misleading and that the establishment of the zones did not contribute to Argentine understanding of the actions which British forces might take against their forces outside the zones.

Since the British War Cabinet was not aware of the Peruvian peace proposals when it authorised the attack on the *Belgrano* it could not have been motivated by a desire to frustrate a negotiated settlement. The report goes on: "Evidence of Argentine intentions to attack the British Task Force before 2 May casts doubt on the idea that Argentine military activity after 2 May was merely a response to the sinking of the *Belgrano* and other British military actions.

'The continued willingness to negotiate of both the Argentine and British Governments does not support the belief either that the United Kingdom Government had decided to abandon the search for a peaceful solution on or by 2 May 1982 or that the Argentine Government was compelled to reject a peaceful solution as a result of the attack on the *Belgrano*.'

Few journals bothered, by this time, to use much of this material. The report undoubtedly did much to clear the air in Parliament, and the allegations of a Government cover-up subsided. But it was the height of the holiday season in the United Kingdom and my impression was that the impact of the report on the awareness of the general public (if the Diary column of *The Times* is anything to go by) was minimal. *The Economist* gave it a brief paragraph in their edition of 27 July–2 August 1985. I shall refrain from reproducing it here in the whole since the second half of the paragraph consisted of *The Economist*'s own judgement on the allegedly partisan attitudes of the members of the committee, which I have no interest in rehearsing here. The first part read as follows:

'It was always wishful thinking that the house of commons select committee on foreign affairs would 'solve' the matter of the sinking of the Argentine cruiser *General Belgrano* during the Falklands war. But the reports of the committee – two of them, the Conservative and Labour members having come to different conclusions from the same evidence – have revealed the basis of disagreement between the Belgranauts.

'This disagreement has little or nothing to do with whether sinking the old ship was a deliberate attempt to scupper the Peruvian peace initiative – the original claim by Mr Tam Dalyell, MP. Even the Labour report can only conclude that linkage between the sinking and events in Peru and New York is 'an open question'. But to keep the question open it is necessary either to believe that both Mr Francis Pym, then foreign secretary, and Mr C. W. Wallace, then ambassador to Peru, lied to the committee – or that Mr Pym lied and Mr Wallace was kept in the dark about negotiations with the Peruvians. Neither hypothesis is plausible.'

PART

5

Look thou again Sir Francis!
  I see the flags a-flapping!
Hearken once more, Sir Francis!
  I hear the sticks a-tapping!
'Tis a sight that calls me hither!
  'Tis a sound that bids me come'!
'Tis the old Trafalgar signal!
  'Tis the beating of my drum!'

Dudley Clark, *Called up*

13

The Birth of a Legend

I have elsewhere recorded that when I arrived in Paraguay in 1947, I shared a house with Winton Irvine. A close friend of his (and neighbour, with whom I also became friendly) was the director of the British Council Institute in Asunción, officially *El Centro Cultural Anglo Paraguayo* but known throughout the land simply as *el Anglo*. Like most of these establishments in Latin America it enjoyed a high reputation and a privileged position as a purveyor of British culture, education, history, traditions and, above all, the English language, for the teaching of which there then was (as even now) a seemingly ever-increasing demand. The Director of *el Anglo*, Duncan Targett-Adams, was a large, extrovert, jovial figure with a plump, smiling face and a small moustache, above medium height, with thinning hair, and always attired in suits and shirts which seemed to be one or two sizes too small. He was married to an equally engaging Colombian lady called Magola (a Colombian pet name for Magdalena) whom he had married on his earlier British Council assignment in Bogotá. When we first met, the Targett-Adams were then expecting their second child. They already had a small boy, then aged about two. His name was Eugen; it was explained to me with some pride that his godfather was Sir Eugen Millington-Drake.

This was virtually the first time I had heard of this remarkable man whom I was not to meet until many years later. But in 1947, in Asunción, anecdotes about his personality and stories of his many and varied achievements were legion. Of these, perhaps the most notable was the decisive role he had played, while Minister in Uruguay, in the circumstances which led to the sinking off Montevideo of the German pocket

267

battleship *Graf Spee* after the Battle of the River Plate in December 1939. This was the first naval engagement between British and German naval forces in the Second World War, and a notable naval occasion in a number of other ways. When I arrived in Asunción in February 1947 I moved, so to speak, into Sir Eugen's sphere of influence. The fact that he was shortly retiring made him the subject of general comment and public expressions of genuine regret.

In 1941 Sir Eugen Millington-Drake was seconded from the Foreign Service to be Director General of the British Council in South America after completing an unusually lengthy tour of duty as Envoy Extraordinary and Minister Plenipotentiary in Uruguay, to which post he was appointed in 1933. Before that, he had spent five years across the River Plate, as deputy head of mission at the Embassy in Buenos Aires. In this subsequent British Council role he had done much to put Britain on the map, even in Paraguay, in then new and original ways. He had endowed scholarships in the United Kingdom for suitably qualified Paraguayan students, he had invited Paraguayan musicians to perform in London, he had organized international sporting events, and provided facilities (and funds) for meetings between British athletes and sportsmen from the southern cone. Sir Eugen's retirement was lamented by all in the countries of the River Plate and so far as I know he never again visited Asunción.

It was not until I arrived in Montevideo in 1964 that I fully realized the extent to which in Uruguay Sir Eugen had been a sort of one-man, individual precursor of the Overseas Development Administration and the British Council in single-handedly creating and promoting Anglo-Uruguayan friendship and trust based on the sort of bilateral cooperation and technical aid which, together with the English language, comprise today perhaps the most effective tools of the trade available to Britain's representatives abroad when invited to give substance to the traditional expressions of goodwill and close links. There were in existence Millington-Drake challenge trophies, cups, medals, scholarships, and bursaries. Boxing and rowing were among his many interests. He was tireless in his promotion of British-whatever sporting and cultural exchanges. His efforts and initiatives were exceptionally matched by a seemingly limitless personal generosity which enabled him to disburse considerable funds from his and his wife's ample private means to endow scholarships, pay for journeys and expenses, or indeed build the tennis courts or gymnasium or whatever other proposal had been the subject of his interest and philanthropy. I learned that his wife, Lady Effie, was a member of the wealthy Inchcape family, and that she supported her husband's official activities with equal enthusiasm and unflagging generosity. As a result, his initiatives and achievements in the pursuit of British interests and objectives had become almost legendary; there were few areas of public life where his activities had not left their mark, to the greater and deserving glory of Britain in general and Sir Eugen in particular, supported as these were by a rare freedom from the monetary constraints which today severely limit the extent of our technical cooperation and bilateral aid, even where these exist.

Her Majesty's Government realized many years ago that something more than words might be necessary to win friends and influence people abroad, and ambassadors today have sources of funds available for approved initiatives which will, it is hoped, redound in favour of British interests or even further the shorter-term efforts of a particular head of mission. Other (smaller) funds are available even for more altruistic objectives, but in Sir Eugen's day these instruments of policy were conspicuously absent, hence the notable and almost disproportionate impact, still felt today in Uruguay, of Sir Eugen's personally funded pioneering efforts. These were rendered even more effective by the fact that Uruguay had for long been a country with a special affinity towards Britain; an appreciative people and successive governments readily recalled the historical role played in Uruguay's struggle for independence by British statesmen, encouraged by a convergence of interests and objectives, both in Europe and South America. Even so, there can be few countries where a British envoy privately provided the financial backing for the establishment of the first national airline, where a street was named after him in his lifetime, or where the municipal authorities chose to erect, on a suitably prestigious site on one of Montevideo's principal arteries, a dignified bust tastefully reproducing in bronze the chiselled features of their benefactor. In addition to streets and parks, his or his wife's name was perpetuated in tennis clubs, hospitals, schools, and theatres, not only in Montevideo but also in many of the more remote provincial capitals and towns throughout the country.

When I arrived in Montevideo in 1964 the Ambassador's social secretary was a remarkable and almost equally legendary lady called Esther Shaw, who had been Millington-Drake's private secretary. As I got to know her better in the months that followed I sometimes joined her in the bar across the street from our offices where she took her frugal lunch. Some time previously she had been seriously ill. As a result she was on a strict diet and never accepted invitations to meals out. Whenever I joined her she always had a small piece of cold boiled ham and a leaf of lettuce which was apparently enough to sustain her petite figure and her unfailing good spirits.

I was fascinated by Esther's unending fund of stories and anecdotes about the great man, his effortless charm and winning ways, his studied and engaging eccentricities, his incessant and wide-ranging activities, and his remarkable and unquestioned popularity. I was shown photographs taken at the time of his first arrival in Montevideo, when he was a youthful 44 years of age. They showed an erect figure with an unusually handsome face with even, well-proportioned features that can only be described as patrician, a broad brow and well spaced eyes, a full head of hair, a straight nose, and a firm mouth. Eton and Magdalen and an appointment in the old Diplomatic Service before the First World War were followed by a first appointment to St Petersburg, service in Buenos Aires during the First World War, and then Paris, Bucharest, Brussels and Copenhagen, until he returned to Buenos Aires as counsellor in 1929, being promoted to the rank of Minister Plenipotentiary in Uruguay in 1933. His personal appearance, education, background, marriage, and wealth all combined in the admiring eyes of his Uruguayan hosts and Latin American colleagues to render him into the very model of the (then) popular image of the aristocratic English diplomat, an image which he secretly enjoyed and contrived in various ways to perpetuate and enhance.

As a result of his strong personality, his generosity, and his unusually long sojourn in Uruguay, Montevideo became one of the posts where all British envoys were forever after bound to be judged by the impossible benchmarks established by a famous and privileged, long-departed predecessor. When I arrived there I found that, with almost no exception, virtually all the other titular incumbents of the embassy, both before and since, had disappeared without trace from the public memory. In 1964, my chief in Montevideo was Sir Norman Brain, a gifted linguist, musician and Japanese scholar who had been Minister in Tokyo and assistant Under-Secretary of State in the Foreign Office before being appointed Ambassador to Uruguay, where he and his wife were popular and well liked and where they stayed until he retired in 1967. But the memory of Sir Eugene Millington-Drake was still afresh in the collective Uruguayan mind, even though I was told that he had not revisited Uruguay for many years since his retirement. But even this omission was shortly to be repaired.

During the long years after his final departure, a stream of Uruguayan friends and other admirers or beneficiaries of Sir Eugen's generosity had visited the great man in both London and Rome, where he lived part of the time in his retirement. He had arranged suitably to celebrate the tenth, fifteenth, and twentieth anniversaries of the battle of the River Plate in various ways which always involved individuals and personalities of the three countries primarily involved. For the tenth anniversary, the ship's bell of HMS *Ajax* was formally presented to the Uruguayan Chargé d'Affaires in London at a formal luncheon offered at the Dorchester by the Friends of Uruguay Society, of which the president was Sir Eugen. The dedication on the luncheon programme reads:

For presentation to the Uruguayan Government and People in appreciation of their friendly attitude at the time of the Battle of the River Plate.

The formal presentation was made by Admiral Sir Henry Harwood in conjunction with Sir Eugen; the first 'on behalf of the Captains, Officers and Ship's Companies of the South American Division 1939–40', and by Sir Eugen 'on behalf of the Members of the British Legation and Consulate, Montevideo, 1939–41'. In 1939 Commodore Harwood had been in command of the Royal Navy's South American station, wearing his flag on HMS *Ajax* at the time of the battle. The *Ajax* bell was later ceremonially installed and unveiled on the

271

harbour of Montevideo in the presence of the President of the Republic, assembled ministers and officials as well as the British ambassador of the day.

For the fifteenth anniversary, special occasions were arranged following the Royal Command Performance of the Rank film *The Battle of the River Plate* at the Empire Theatre, Leicester Square, in the production of which film Sir Eugen was characteristically and heavily involved. This was followed by the formal presentation of a bust of the Uruguayan Foreign Minister at the time of the battle, Dr Alberto Guani, to the then Chairman of Canning House, Viscount Davidson, which again brought about the reunion of a large gathering of former combatants and personalities. I need hardly add that the presentation was made by the President of the Friends of Uruguay Society in London, again Sir Eugen.

In the meantime, Sir Eugen had been compiling a book which, whatever the original intention, had by this time developed into a major anthology* on the Battle of the River Plate and its participants. It drew on the historical connections between the pocket battleship *Graf Spee* in 1939 and the naval battles at Coronel and the Falklands in 1914 in which the eponymous Admiral Maximilian Reichgraf von Spee was victorious in the first but suffered defeat in the second, the admiral and his two sons, both naval officers serving on other vessels in the German naval formation, all losing their lives on 8 December 1914.

By the time the twentieth anniversary came round Sir Eugen had his book well under way and, having conveyed to the appropriate German naval authorities and survivors of the *Graf Spee* his wish to include German texts and documents giving German versions of the event, was sufficiently encouraged to invite former *Graf Spee* officers to meet some of their British counterparts and survivors in London. He also caused special ceremonies including memorial services to be arranged at Plymouth and at the German Naval War Memorial near Kiel, which were attended by veterans of the battle on both sides who also laid wreaths.

When I arrived in Montevideo I found that in his spare time Sir Norman Brain was also heavily engaged in correspondence

* Sir Eugen Millington-Drake, *The Drama of 'Graf Spee' and the Battle of the Plate: A Documentary Anthology 1914–1964*, Peter Davies, 1964.

with Sir Eugen over the book. Every diplomatic bag from London brought an increasing volume of letters asking for dates and numbers to be checked, names and spellings to be corrected, and quotations and sources to be identified. Esther Shaw was the irreplaceable intermediary in this process, not only as the former private secretary of Sir Eugen but because she had actually been in the job when the battle took place and the *Graf Spee* was scuttled. Her own capacious memory contributed to most of the replies to Sir Eugen's queries; those few answers she did not know she could find out instantly from her unlimited circle of relatives, friends, and contacts throughout the country. I know that her contribution was substantial; curiously, her own labours are not mentioned in Sir Eugen's lengthy list of acknowledgments in the book finally produced in which, to add insult to injury, she is referred to several times in the text by Sir Eugen but confused by the compilers of the index with another Miss Shaw (the Hon. Jean, daughter of the then Chairman of the P. & O.) who was also in Montevideo staying with the Millington-Drakes at the time of the battle and who subsequently wrote an eyewitness account of the scuttling at Sir Eugen's behest.

By his own account, Sir Eugen's interest had been stimulated by the fact that he arrived in Buenos Aires on his first Diplomatic Service posting to the River Plate area in December 1914, immediately after the two naval battles of Coronel and the Falklands, and read a confidential report of the battles which happened to be in the absent ambassador's safe. Years later, when appointed to Montevideo, Sir Eugen found that Commander Lloyd Hirst, a retired naval officer who subsequently served during the Second World War as Assistant Naval Attaché in Buenos Aires and Montevideo, was himself a survivor of those two famous battles. When eventually he decided to compile his anthology, Sir Eugen's researches engaged him in correspondence with naval sources in Germany and in the United Kingdom, his principal theme being to draw together some of the strands of history which had curiously linked names, naval actions, individuals, battleships, and nations after a gap of twenty-five years in two separate wars. He was punctilious in making his anthology an account of individual courage and naval distinction without regard to uniform or country. In particular, the tone of the narrative was

273

set by the tragic decision taken by the commander of the *Graf Spee*, Captain Hans Langsdorff of the German Navy, to shoot himself in Buenos Aires in December 1939 after seeing his crew safely evacuated and scuttling his battleship outside the port of Montevideo. His choice of a pre-Nazi German naval battle ensign for his body to rest on, in preference to the new-style red flag with the odious central swastika, added a further thought- provoking dimension to the unusual story. Sir Eugen's treatment of the episode with the emphasis on naval tradition, duty, and honour also formed the background for his account, often based on official documents, of the hunt for the *Graf Spee* in the South Atlantic and Indian Ocean, after the German raider had sunk nine British merchant ships without the loss of a single life.

The exciting chase by the cruisers HMS *Ajax* and *Exeter* and the *Achilles* of the Royal New Zealand Navy culminated in the closing engagement on 13 December 1939, with many instances of individual gallantry in action, devotion to duty in hazardous conditions, and bravery under fire, in the waters of the River Plate estuary off the splendid Uruguayan coastal resort of Punta del Este. When the stricken *Graf Spee* headed into the River Plate the British cruisers held their fire in order to avoid shelling the Uruguayan shores; after urgent representations by the German Minister in Montevideo and Sir Eugen's more effective intervention, the Uruguayan Government (whose sympathies were wholly democratic and less 'neutral' than those of other Governments in the area) gave their permission for the damaged *Graf Spee* to enter the harbour, transfer her prisoners, and bury her fallen in a ceremony also attended by British merchant officers who were prisoners in the *Graf Spee* during the battle. After a technical inspection of the damage, the Uruguayan authorities, in accordance with certain terms of the Hague Convention of 1907, gave the Germans a period of seventy-two hours to carry out repairs and leave Uruguayan jurisdiction, while urgent efforts were made to refuel and reinforce the British cruisers (which had also suffered heavy casualties) waiting to pounce outside Uruguayan territorial waters. The *Exeter*, with all her turrets out of action and her forward bulkheads flooded, had been ordered to withdraw and make for the Falklands for repairs. She was replaced outside Montevideo by HMS *Cumberland*. The rest is history.

Although Captain Langsdorff was initially attacked by the pro-German press in Argentina for not having gone down with his ship, it may be worth recording again that his principal concern had been the fate of his crew of nearly one thousand officers and men, not to speak of the numerous British prisoners on board. Only when he had seen them safely across the River Plate within the less 'neutral' boundaries of Argentine territory, having previously obtained assurances about their fate, did he put into practice his decision to take his own life. That his body was found lying in his Buenos Aires hotel room on an old-fashioned German naval ensign did not pass unnoticed among the large and powerful German communities in the River Plate countries. His funeral in the German cemetary of Buenos Aires was attended the next day by, among many others, the master of one of the British merchantmen sunk by the *Graf Spee*, in representation of the British sailors who had been held prisoner on board, whose many individual tributes to Captain Langsdorff are reproduced in Sir Eugen's book.

In December 1939 the thrilling chase in the South Atlantic, concluding with the British naval victory after three months of 'phoney war', made a notable impression throughout the world, providing a timely illustration of Britain's reiterated mastery of the seas. This was also probably the last recorded instance of a naval commander taking his life following the loss of his ship, and this, together with the generous and humane manner in which Captain Langsdorff and his men had treated the British crews he had made prisoner, all lent a romantic aura of naval tradition, chivalry, and courage to the Battle of the River Plate and all its participants, in this first major engagement of the Second World War, at a time when the full horrors that were to follow could not be envisaged. The preface of the book, written by Admiral of the Fleet Sir Philip Vian, refers to 'a page of history whose unfolding was watched by a spellbound world', and in his own foreword to Sir Eugen's anthology, Lord Mountbatten of Burma was to write that this was 'the last old-type naval battle between cruisers and pocket battleship – without aircraft-carriers, submarines, destroyers or effective radar'. Even though explosive charges were used to scuttle the *Graf Spee*, parts of her superstructure were clearly visible above the muddy waters of the River Plate when I arrived in Montevideo in 1964. The remains of the *Graf Spee* were always pointed out to passengers arriving at Montevideo or leaving the harbour on the many regular sailings which then existed between the United Kingdom and River Plate ports; they remained visible and identifiable for many years after as a result of the shallow waters and sandy bottom.

In the Montevideo embassy in 1964, the arrival of every diplomatic bag with Sir Eugen's letters continued to maintain among those who had to deal with his ceaseless correspondence a lively interest in the compilation of the anthology, an interest that was shared and indeed stimulated by the many Uruguayan personalities and officials who had been involved in some way in the drama played out during the days Montevideo held the attention of the whole world. Dates and names, anecdotes and contributions flowed into our offices in a steady stream, to be relayed to the compiler in London, whose declared aim was to have the anthology published for the twenty-fifth anniversary of the battle, on 13 December 1964. Characteristically, the proceeds from the publication of the book had already been assigned to King George's Fund for Sailors.

One morning I arrived in the office to find a rare atmosphere of excitement. A beaming Esther Shaw told me that the latest bag from London had brought a personal letter to the Ambassador from Sir Eugen. In it he announced that, in response to reiterated and insistent requests from numerous Uruguayan and other personalities, veterans' associations on both sides of the River Plate, and individuals in the area he had decided to visit Montevideo, for the first time since his retirement, for the twenty-fifth anniversary of the battle, when his personal intervention and supervision would be available for the proper and most suitable commemoration of the event. He would be staying for several weeks, also visiting towns in the interior of the country, and proposed to bring, as his personal guests, a number of personalities closely connected with the battle, including officers who had served on the vessels involved, as well as members of Captain Langdorff's family. His intention was to organize a number of ceremonies and commemorative events (in which no doubt the Uruguayan authorities would wish to be involved), including memorial services and other religious occasions, with the laying of

276

wreaths on the graves in the German and British cemeteries in Montevideo. At the other extreme, there would be reunion dinners and other social occasions for the former combatants and their Uruguayan hosts. All the events were to have a strong ecumenical Anglo-German flavour, set against the exceptional Uruguayan background, as befitted a very special reunion of former wartime enemies, comrades-in-arms and 'neutral' Uruguayan participants.

At our staff meeting that morning the Ambassador said that it was clearly in our interest to ensure that all arrangements were made properly and that nothing marred the success of the visit. Apart from the intrinsic importance of the event, Sir Eugen's visit would pay handsome dividends in fomenting and renewing bilateral goodwill and historical links. Sir Eugen had no representatives in Montevideo; we would obviously have to see to all the local details. The preparation and planning for the visit would impose an additional burden on our resources, but it was well worth it. At that point the Head of Chancery and Consul, then Keith Hamylton Jones, looked at the ceiling thoughtfully and said (in tones of sincere regret) what a pity it was that he would be away on mid-tour leave in the United Kingdom at the time; whereupon the Ambassador turned to me and lifted his eyebrow.

Thus was it decided. From that moment, Sir Eugen's increasingly urgent correspondence, with proposals, after-thoughts, additions and alterations, was all deposited on my desk by a merry Esther Shaw, who had usually provided most of the answers in her marginal scribbles. My knowledge of the great man, his preoccupation with minutiae, his constant changes of mind, and his many other foibles all became increasingly familiar through the months that followed. The local announcement of the forthcoming visit became immediate front-page news and caused great excitement and public interest. It also generated its own additional momentum, not a day passing without a request or suggestion from the local authorities or, at the very least, a call from somebody who had once met Sir Eugen and wished, if no more, to have the opportunity of shaking the great man by the hand once again.

All this gave me a rare insight into the remarkable extent to which Sir Eugen had involved himself in almost every aspect of Uruguayan life during his long years in Montevideo, having had the aptitude, the means, and the ability to get through to all those parts of the fabric of Uruguayan society that other ambassadors could not always reach, perhaps lacking the will, the money or, more usually, the time to do so. From the highest in the land in the Swiss-model, yearly rotating, collegiate presidency (a system modified later by the 1966 Constitution) through the Supreme Court and the Senate, ministries and departments of state; all the way to remote provincial chambers of commerce and municipalities; stockbreeders' associations; schools and universities, meat-canning plants; hospitals; rowing, tennis, football and every other sporting association in existence; down to individual retired soldiers and sailors and more humble tinkers and tailors – each and every one in Uruguay wished to pay homage to their legendary benefactor.

14

A Great Naval Occasion

In 1964 General de Gaulle visited Montevideo in the course of a historic goodwill tour of Latin America. When the General arrived large, cheerful crowds turned out to greet him at the airport and lined the coastal road to the centre of the capital, enthusiastically applauding when they saw the official entourage of vehicles approaching with the unmistakable figure of the General, his head, shoulders and both arms perilously leaning out of his car window waving and smiling at his well-wishers.

The local press gave much prominence to the general's programme, activities, and sayings, choosing in a good-humoured way to make much of the fact that the Uruguayan Government had felt obliged to commission and install a special bed in the official (but then seldom-used) presidential residence in the suburb of El Prado in order to accommodate their lofty visitor, who was invariably photographed with the then Uruguayan Foreign Minister smiling at his side. The minister himself, Alejandro Zorrilla de San Martín, a genial and gifted member of a gifted family which had for generations enriched the theatre, literature, and the arts on both sides of the River Plate as well as the political scene in Uruguay, usually and gleefully contrived to create this juxtaposition for the benefit of the press photographers, having for many years been affectionately known throughout the land as *el Chiquitúa* because of his exceptionally short stature which obliged him, when both were standing, to address himself to the fourth or fifth button on the General's military tunic.

General de Gaulle's brief sojourn in Montevideo during his whirlwind tour of South America pleased his Uruguayan hosts and undoubtedly did much to reinvigorate France's relations with a part of the world which French governments had relegated in recent years, no doubt as a result of other, more pressing commitments. I recall drafting a report for the Ambassador's signature in which I tried to analyse the significance and value of the visit, concluding that high-level visits had an important part to play even in countries with which there were no pressing bilateral problems.

But in the busy weeks leading to the anniversary of the battle, the local press increasingly devoted more and more time and space to our own imminent visit. When our great day dawned and Sir Eugen's ship docked in the harbour of Montevideo, the newspapers estimated the following day that more than one hundred thousand people had gathered in the port area to greet the visitor. This may have been a fulsome exaggeration, but even if the multitudes amounted to only fifteen or twenty thousand people, the milling throngs, the banners of welcome, the delegations from the interior, the unscheduled orators, the proud and happy British community (among whom Sir Eugen was affectionately known as 'Fluffington-Duck'), all combined to render the good-natured chaos in the harbour total and absolute. TV teams with their cumbersome cameras, lights, and endless cables cluttered the approaches to the vessel. Police in large numbers were trying to control the enthusiastic crowds, if only to permit the other passengers to disembark. Ambulances, police cars, official vehicles and, for some reason, even the fire brigade all contributed to the confusion. Sir Eugen had been declared an honoured guest of the city for the first few days of his stay. Representatives of the Government, the mayor and city council, countless officials, retired and serving officers, members of the dozen or so British community organizations, old friends and well-wishers, all wanted to make their presence known to the great man. A group of bewildered Argentine tourists on their way to Punta del Este dis-embarked from the night ferry which had brought them from Buenos Aires and fruitlessly tried to drive their cars through the crowds. When, in response to their enquiries, they were told that Uruguay had turned out to greet a former British envoy who had left the country twenty-odd years previously, they flatly refused to believe it.* A colleague at the French Embassy subsequently told me with more than a trace of acerbity that only a visit by Millington-Drake or, in his default, Sir Winston Churchill could so rapidly have eclipsed the effect of the French presidential visit. Why had we done this to them?

Sir Eugen was then a sprightly seventy-four years old, his age betrayed only by his stooping shoulders, his face still handsome with intense blue eyes and thick white hair. He had shaken every hand within reach for several hours, spoken with hundreds of individuals in his voluble but accented Spanish, recalled names, events and personalities at will, and given several TV and dozens of press interviews. I remember musing that the Uruguayan popular concept of the archetypal 'aristocratic English diplomat' was somewhat at variance with what I had seen of his behaviour with the welcoming crowds. He had an engaging but rather un-British penchant for public displays of emotion, tears and embraces, energetic gesticulation and theatrical exaggeration, all of which, together with his admirable and facile turn of flowery phrase, were to be put to good use in the weeks that followed. When he was eventually extracted from the ship after long hours of emotional reunions, extemporaneous speeches, and improvised departures from the prepared arrangements, he was whisked away in a car, his hair dishevelled from the many embraces, his face bearing traces of tears, but otherwise trim and elegant in his smart beige tropical Palm Beach suit, brown suede shoes, and Old Etonian tie.

Sir Eugen had invited a number of retired British and German ex-combatants to join him for the commemoration in Montevideo. The British contingent consisted of Captain D.M.L. Neame, D.S.O., who had been Executive Officer on HMS *Ajax* at the time of the battle, Commander H.W. Head, D.S.C., of HMNZS *Achilles*, and Surgeon Commander R.W.G. Lancashire, D.S.C., of HMS *Exeter*. With Commander F.W.

* In 1941 Millington-Drake was appointed Director General of the British Council in South America, in which guise he doubtless revisited Uruguay. He retired from the Foreign Service in 1947, although he may have held his British Council appointment for some time after. When he returned to Montevideo in 1964 he said in his speeches that he had not been back for 'nearly fifteen years', but his appointment as Minister to Uruguay had ended twenty-three years previously.

Rasenack, who had been a technical gunnery officer of the *Graf Spee*, they were to be the principal naval guests at the commemorative events in Montevideo. After the scuttling of the *Graf Spee* Commander Rasenack had been evacuated with the rest of the crew from Montevideo and interned in Argentina, subsequently escaping and making his way back to Europe to rejoin the German Navy. He returned after the war to establish himself in business in Buenos Aires where he wrote a book on the battle and his wartime experiences. A brother of Captain Langsdorff, Dr Reinhardt Langsdorff (formerly a high court judge in Dusseldorf), together with a sister, Fräulein Annelise Langsdorff, had also been invited by the *Graf Spee* Association of Argentina to visit the River Plate for the twenty-fifth anniversary, and were to be in Montevideo for some of the events.

The German Defence (naval) Attaché in Buenos Aires, together with his British counterpart, were both in attendance in Montevideo, specially delegated to emphasize the bipartisan, ecumenical flavour of the commemoration. The social part of the programme included dinners by the Minister of Foreign Affairs and by the President of the Foreign Affairs committee of the Senate, receptions by the British Ambassador and formal sessions by the municipality of the capital as well as by other municipal councils of towns in the interior who wished to be associated with the visit.

There were also other occasions organized by institutions and organizations which Sir Eugen had either founded or even endowed. These included formal sessions and lunches with various chambers of commerce, the Club de Lunch Uruguayo-Britanico (CLUB), the Rotary Club, a number of personal friends, the Association for the Promotion of Anglo-Uruguayan Exchanges and, last but by no means least, the Committee of the Chauffeurs' Protection Centre (an association of Montevideo taxi-drivers) which had no doubt long ago benefitted in some way from Sir Eugen's generosity. All this against a background of daily TV and radio interviews, round-table discussions by the participants, and, of course, Sir Eugen's *pièce de résistance*, his personal lecture on the battle of the River Plate, delivered many times in different venues, in evocative language with dramatic effect and the corresponding histrionics to appreciative and enthusiastic audiences.

Sir Eugen's memory and delivery could not be faulted. A contemporary German account tells of a similar occasion when 'the old gentleman' stood without desk or notes before his audience and held them spellbound for an hour and a half: 'It was fascinating to see how he lived this piece of history, how he had in his head dates, hours, minutes, and every detail of the various events.' After the first week or two some of the more irreverent members of the embassy who were in attendance during the daily lecture began to feel that they, also, had lived through those eventful days twenty-five years previously. And in the days that followed, once or twice I sensed the patches of thin ice which still existed on the boards of the stage the old *maestro* had chosen for his grand performance. Although hardly discernible even as the merest bat squeak of a discordant note, there were one or two events on the programme which seemed to me to reveal the wholly understandable underlying emotions which the commemorative events could hardly fail to engender.

Visitors to South America in the past used to find that some of the long-established British communities resident in the various capitals were not always, perhaps, among the most radical and forward-looking bodies of public opinion. Some families had lived there for many years, and most of the elders were very conservative and viewed the prospect of change with caution. Others were the second and third generation born in their adopted countries. Many had volunteered and gone to the war in 1939. Some had failed to return, while others had been prisoners of war, or suffered greater hardship. In Montevideo in 1964, the battle of the River Plate was still regarded, both by the British community and their Uruguayan hosts, as 'their' battle and, having had a rare grandstand view of the sinking of the *Graf Spee*, 'their' victory. At the time, the Second World War was still fresh in the global memory, Uruguay was a bastion of democracy which had sided with the Allies from the first moment, and Uruguayans had experienced at first hand the dramatic conclusion of the Royal Navy's victory in their very own battle of Punta del Este, which is how the Battle of the River Plate is known in Uruguay.

One of the more solemn events on the official programme took place the morning after Sir Eugen's arrival. This was the ceremonial laying of wreaths on the corresponding graves in the British and German cemeteries. Both ceremonies were attended by representatives of the Uruguayan armed forces, civic dignitaries, and members of the local German and British communities, including a colour party provided by the Montevideo branch of the British Legion, complete with medals, banners, and ensigns. While the long-retired former British and German naval combatants all wore, naturally, civilian suits, the appearance of the German Defence Attaché in Buenos Aires resplendent in his then new-style khaki summer uniform contrasted strangely with the rather old-fashioned Iron Cross displayed on his tunic.

On this occasion, by the time the Uruguayan bugler had finished playing the Last Post, the small group laying the wreaths was surrounded by a visibly moved, nervous and divided audience as well as some rather boot-faced members of the British Legion colour party. In the ensuing and unexpected coolness the departure of the German and British participants in the ceremony took place separately in a chilly silence broken only by Sir Eugen's agitated efforts to break the threatened ice. The event generated no more than a faint wisp of cloud much smaller than a man's hand on the otherwise serene horizons which surrounded us, and was soon overtaken by the Millington-Drake lecture of the day, with its strong ecumenical flavour.

The formal dinner offered by the Minister of Foreign Affairs, the diminutive Alejandro Zorrilla de San Martín, proved to be the most memorable event of the celebrations. This took place one evening at the unoccupied suburban presidential residence in El Prado, then used as a government hospitality venue. The residence was unoccupied mainly because of the yearly rotating, Swiss-style, collegiate presidency system then in force, sensible and practical Uruguayan political wives flatly refusing to move into the large and imposing house, with its extensive grounds, for only twelve months. On this occasion however, the gates to the handsome driveway were thrown open and the imposing rooms with their high ceilings splendidly lit and decorated. The stately waiters circulated refreshments to the large gathering of distinguished guests, which included many former ministers, generals and admirals who had been in office at the time of the battle of the River Plate (but who had since seldom been seen socially) as well as the visiting British and German contingents and some prominent members of the British community. Evening dresses and uniforms lent additional colour to the scene. Every arrival added to the excited, cheerful, noisy group within as they were greeted with effusive handshakes and warm embraces by the elegantly black-tied and dinner-jacketed Minister for Foreign Affairs.

Alejandro Zorrilla de San Martín was small of stature but eminent in many other ways. He combined great personal charm, a ready smile, and a mischievous wit with rare perception and clarity of vision, and a prodigious memory for names and faces. He was also a firm and loyal friend, popular and respected by all, including his political opponents. Above all his many attributes, he was renowned for his impressive oratory. With effortless excellence and without text or notes he could speak on his chosen subject with eloquence and emotion, coherently, without repetition or digression, deftly gauging the sentiments of his audience and matching their changing mood with responsive words and phrases. His introductions were models of clarity and detail, his evocations exemplary displays of erudition and research, his sonorous words logical and consequential, his exhortations compelling and inspiring, and his concluding toast an intoxicating combination of animation and invitation which invariably brought his audiences to their feet, rapturously and spontaneously, as one man. With their customary irreverent humour his compatriots had dubbed him *el pico de oro*, a notable tribute to an acknowledged grand master in a country which boasted a multitude of accomplished public speakers. All ambassadors found him a hard act to follow.

His speech that evening was no exception. Although some of the German visitors had also been invited, the dinner was unequivocally in honour of Sir Eugen and the British naval officers who had accompanied him. Smart in their white dinner-jackets, Commanders Lancashire and Head were, together with Captain Neame, the centre of much attention and interest, as were of course the members of the Langsdorff family, Commander Rasenack, and the other German guests. The British Ambassador, Sir Norman Brain, was also somewhere in the throng. He had wisely and with good humour insisted on his relegation to an unaccustomed place below the salt on all those numerous public and private occasions to

285

which he was, inevitably, also invited during the Millington-Drake commemorative visit.

By this time, Sir Eugen had identified me as being involved in the arrangements and had therefore requisitioned me as his 'personal ADC'. Characteristically, he was not content merely to be the centre of attention of a chattering and enquiring group and was excitedly moving from one part of the throng to the other end of the room, with a word, a greeting, or an embrace for all those who crossed his path. 'Ah, there you are, dear boy,' his voice exclaimed behind me after I had lost him the second time. 'Please see if General Campos has arrived.' A few minutes later: 'My dear Wallace, a dreadful problem – I have mislaid my spectacles!' Later still: 'Dear boy, someone just told me Señora de Morelli is here. I must see her before we sit down!' When eventually we sat down to dine, the animated conversation continued through the several courses and excellent wines even though, as was his wont, Sir Eugen nodded off for fifteen or twenty minutes between the third course and the dessert. He was gently wakened by the persistent musical chimes of the Foreign Minister's fork on his wine glass while an expectant hush gradually descended on the gathering.

It is difficult to convey the range, content, or sentiments of the speech that followed. Speaking in his customary, well-modulated tones to a predisposed and appreciative audience, Zorrilla de San Martín referred to the battle, to the participants, to their valour and individual gallantry and to the course of history, before and since the battle. Without hyperbole or exaggeration, but in an atmosphere which his extensive vocabulary and superlative eloquence rendered increasingly emotional even for those of his foreign guests who imperfectly understood his words, his fluency and the manner of his delivery brought a lump to many throats round the tables. Sir Eugen's was not the only face with traces of ill-suppressed emotion, and there were moist handkerchiefs and unexpectedly misty spectacles by the time our host turned towards Sir Eugen to begin his eagerly anticipated evocation of the character and personality of the guest of honour.

The Minister's panegyric was a stylish and polished eulogy of the career, activities, background, and birth of this 'typically English' guest, this paragon among ambassadors who embodied all the traditions, virtues and attributes of the distant island race with which Uruguay had shared so many pages of history. At the end of his magnificent peroration Zorrilla de San Martín raised his glass and, with shining eyes and a catch in his voice, invited his guests to join him in a toast to this paradigm of the English man* whose achievements would never again be equalled and who, in his lifetime, had become, far from his island home, a legend which Uruguay would honour through the ages. The ensuing pandemonium was quite spectacular.

Against a deafening background of thunderous applause, cheers and banging of tables, Sir Eugen leapt up and rushed across to embrace his host. Other close friends clambered over chairs to congratulate both the speaker and his principal guest, by this time closely embraced and thumping each other on the back. Many of the guests were wiping their eyes. All raised their glasses to a beaming Zorrilla de San Martín. Some were trying to catch the agile Sir Eugen on his way back round the room. Waiters were hurrying to recharge glasses. Someone collided with a tray of champagne. The cheers and continuing applause drowned any attempt at conversation. Only the German contingent (whose turn it seemed to be to look a bit wooden-faced) remained seated, applauding politely, without enthusiasm. Much of what had been said had no doubt escaped them and, to be fair, they had hardly been mentioned. When, eventually, order was restored Sir Eugen retrieved his glasses from me and said in an aside, 'Well, well, goodness me, what on earth can I say after all that?'

Needless to say, he rose to the occasion without difficulty. Handsome and courtly in his dinner-jacket, he spoke in his accented but fluent Spanish, with his customary loquacity and felicity of phrase. He clutched a few sheets of paper in his left hand, which he forgot to consult throughout his speech, merely

* In his speech, Zorrilla de San Martín made an elegant literary reference to 'the English Man', quoting the poem *Canto al Hombre Ingles*, an ode to 'the English' (as all the inhabitants of the British Isles were generically known throughout Latin America) by the Uruguayan poet Fernan Silva Valdéz. The poem was inspired by the Battle of Britain in 1940 and dedicated to Sir Winston Churchill. It was later gracefully translated into English and entitled *Song to the English* by the Scottish poet Walter Owen, who spent his childhood in Montevideo and later lived in Buenos Aires. A more literal translation of the sense of the Spanish title would have been 'Song to the Man from England'.

waving them above his white head when he wished to emphasize a point. He began by disclaiming any credit or responsibility for the outcome of the event which was being commemorated, and then went on to introduce to his audience, separately and individually, the former British naval officers present, giving in each case a brief biographical sketch of their careers or achievements before they joined the ships in which they had served during the battle. Thus we learnt that Captain Neame had been an Olympic hurdler and that Commanders Lancashire and Head had also achieved distinction in other ways. Sir Eugen then went on to describe, in precise detail, three incidents in which each had been separately involved during the battle, giving rise to exceptional acts of gallantry and bravery under fire. Each narrative was accompanied by excited gestures and vivid descriptions of their actions and duties: the battle positions of the ships, the damage caused by the shelling, the changes of course and the individual officers' skill and resourcefulness, all graphically illustrated with the aid of various plates, finger-bowls, candelabra, and assorted wineglasses on the snowy linen before him. Having thus skilfully captured both the imagination and the attention of his enthralled audience, with a gesture towards the embarrassed former naval officers, he addressed the Minister in ringing tones: 'It is fitting that you, Sir, should know what manner of men have sat at your table this evening!' Waving aloft his unread sheaf of notes he cut short the ovation which followed his words and again addressed himself to the Minister. 'As for me . . .' and with impeccable timing after a long pause in which the suspense mounted, finally added, 'If I am indeed a legend, it is a legend which only you, my dear friends, could have created!' his voice sounding like a fanfare of trumpets and his widespread arms figuratively embracing the whole of Uruguay. The explosion which followed shook the massive beams of the lofty room. A standing audience applauded and stamped and shouted. Once again the cheers were mixed with tears. The noise, according to some of the drivers on duty by their cars, was heard four city blocks away. Even though he could hardly match the Minister in fluency and style as a speaker (in Spanish), such was the dramatic atmosphere he had contrived to create that 'e'en the ranks of Tuscany' (in the shape of the now visibly less formal German guests) 'could

288

scarce forbear to cheer', as Sir Eugen himself noted in a later letter to the Ambassador.

Although the Minister's dinner was unquestionably a high point in the visit, Sir Eugen's triumphant progress continued unmarred, each day with a TV interview, another Battle of the River Plate lecture, another press conference, a formal session of the municipal council, a lunch or dinner, the dedication of a plaque or whatever; for the first fortnight in Montevideo and subsequently in the principal provincial capitals of the interior, all were anxious to pay homage to their old friend and benefactor. The growing volume of unanswered correspondence on my desk obliged me to decline Sir Eugen's pressing invitation to accompany him on his tour of the interior, which happily coincided with the arrival of the English-language edition of his anthology, which sold like the proverbial hot cakes to the greater benefit of King George's Fund for Sailors, especially as the compiler liberally autographed all copies submitted to him. The Spanish version was even then being prepared and was to benefit from a quantity of additional photographs and articles which had appeared in the Uruguayan press during the twenty-fifth anniversary commemorative visit.

On his return from the interior, a day or two before he was due to leave the country, Sir Eugen (Lady Effie had already gone) gave a private dinner at the Victoria Plaza Hotel in Montevideo, to which he invited those friends and other persons who had been involved in the arrangements for his visit. All the other visitors had already left. For some reason he chose my wife to act as his hostess and asked her to see to the *placement* and other details. We arranged to meet in the bar of the Victoria Plaza where I had a drink while my wife went to check the table, flowers, and so forth in the private dining-room. A few minutes after she rejoined me, a dapper Sir Eugen came through the door, again in his Palm Beach suit and Old Etonian tie. We had not seen him since his return from his provincial tour. He looked well and fit, his white hair and intense blue eyes accentuated by his tanned face. 'Come along, come along, dear lady,' he boomed across the room. 'Don't forget to have me awakened during the dinner!'

Some weeks later, when Keith Hamylton Jones returned to Montevideo, we ourselves left for Britain on mid-tour leave.

Miss Jill Quaife, Sir Eugen's secretary, had sent me numerous bread-and-butter letters which I had dutifully forwarded to their destinations. In those days home leave journeys were undertaken by sea, either on the Blue Star Line's comfortable and less crowded mixed passenger and cargo vessels or on the beautiful Royal Mail liners, both of which had regular services from the United Kingdom to the River Plate ports. Perhaps unwisely, I had undertaken to carry with me to London several tardy gifts and souvenirs of Sir Eugen's visit which had been delivered to the embassy after his departure, one or two quite bulky. On arrival in London, I telephoned Miss Quaife in order to deliver the goods. This resulted in an immediate invitation from Sir Eugen to the theatre and supper. The invitation was repeated after a few days. We were told that we would be joining a group of Argentine and Paraguayan visitors he was entertaining, but, unfortunately, we had to decline, and we did not see him again before we returned to Uruguay at the end of our leave.

When I was transferred to the Foreign Office in 1967, I found myself dealing with Latin American affairs. It was not long before correspondence about Sir Eugen again crossed my desk. From his home in Rome, Sir Eugen's persistent efforts to interest the rest of the world in his Battle of the River Plate lecture were not always appreciated in countries which had neither been involved in the event nor known the great man in the plenitude of his generosity and success. By this time he had outlived many of his friends and contemporaries, and current developments and frequent crises were yearly superimposing layer after layer of more recent events on overburdened official and personal memories. Some time later I heard that he was again in London. The invitation to 'join a small party for the theatre and supper' was not long in coming, but this time I was saddened to find that his health no longer permitted him to accompany his guests. I was even more shaken just before we left for Italy in December 1969 to have a member of my department walk into my office one day and ask, 'Who's this fellow Millington-Drake they keep on writing about?'

The last time I saw him was at the Queen's Birthday party at the British Embassy in Rome in June 1971. This was still at a time when all and sundry were invited to the embassy on this annual occasion. The splendid lawns on the Villa Wolkonsky were graced by the presence of many of the ancient Britons locally resident. The Ambassador, at the time Sir Patrick Hancock, greeted his numerous British and Italian guests in the garden under one of the large trees facing the house. In this task he was aided, as is usual in most large capitals, by a long-serving member of the staff. In Rome this was Gus Nash, an indispensible member of the commercial section who was by this time the only person who could identify almost all the many guests generously invited. The tall, portly figure of the silver-haired Gus was flanked by the equally impressive figure of the Ambassador to whom all arrivals were presented as they queued up beneath the the spreading branches of the tree. Before Sir Patrick Hancock's appointment, those of his pre-decessors whose appearance failed to match the handsome, morning-coated Gus Nash in dignity and grace, had found that many of the less-frequently invited guests mistook the one for the other. On this occasion, about an hour later, when most of the guests had arrived and the staff could circulate, Gus wandered over to me at the other end of the garden where I had joined some friends listening to the Italian police band playing on the lawn. 'I was looking for you,' he said. 'You'll never guess who's actually turned up this year,' he said in wonder. 'Old Fluffington-Duck no less. There he is, under the second tree beyond the rose bushes.'

When I walked across to great Sir Eugen where he was standing. I was shocked by his appearance. He was escorted by the loyal Miss Quaife who had accompanied him to Monte-video in 1964. Sir Eugen had aged noticeably, but most cruelly the passing years had accentuated his stoop until his back was so bent that he was obliged to turn his head to look up at the face of any person who addressed him. He was leaning against the tree, and I assumed he had been brought there in a wheelchair. I remembered the old photographs shown to me by Esther Shaw of the youthful, upright, handsome minister in Montevideo. I exchanged a few words with him, but I do not think he really remembered me. It was only when I mentioned Uruguay and the Battle of the River Plate that his expression changed. 'Ah, yes,' he said. 'That was a great naval occasion.'

15

Uruguay, 1983–1986

When I moved from Lima to Montevideo in October 1983, I was looking forward for a second time to a post where I had enjoyed an earlier spell of duty, years before, in a junior capacity. I was happy to return to a country where I had made many enduring friendships among a people who, on my previous tour of duty from 1964 to 1967, made no secret of their belief that there existed a rather special historical relationship between their country and the United Kingdom. This was in part the result of the intervention of two British foreign secretaries, Lord Castlereagh and, later, George Canning, in the process which ultimately led to the emergence of an independent buffer state between the two giant rivals, Argentina and Brazil, after the overthrow of Spanish rule in South America. Subsequent British investments in stock breeding, meat-packing plants, railways, dry docks, gas companies, tramways, telephones, and other public utilities recreated as in Argentina the same sort of pervasive British involvement in many aspects of Uruguayan economic and social development, with the concommitant educational and cultural influences on the character of a nation which for long rejoiced in its well-merited reputation as 'the Switzerland of South America'.

For many years, shared historical experiences, the British presence and influence, and a democratic political trajectory unusual in Latin America combined to maintain in Uruguay the special relationship with Britain. This had been made manifest in a number of ways: the development of a cattle-breeding and sheep-rearing economy originally based on Hereford, Aberdeen Angus, Romney Marsh, and other British breeds, as well as the requirements and preferences of the

United Kingdom housewife; the existence of a small but profitable and reliable market where British goods were synonymous with quality and value; the absence of any bilateral problems; and, last but by no means least, informal but traditional assistance in providing the Falkland Islands with a lifeline to the outside world. These arrangements included frequent and welcome calls by the Royal Navy to Uruguayan ports and regular passenger and freight sailings from Montevideo to and from Port Stanley in the Falklands, sometimes even in the face of Argentine objections.

When I arrived in October 1983, the days of the Uruguayan military dictatorship were already numbered. Increasing domestic and international pressures, the overthrow of a distasteful military regime in neighbouring Argentina and, perhaps above all, the harsh economic realities of the Latin American debt renegotiations, led the military rulers of Uruguay to the conclusion that solutions to all these problems were to be found only by an elected civilian regime. As in my previous post in Lima I was destined again to be a privileged witness to the peaceful replacement of a military dictatorship by a democratically elected Government, which was to restore to Uruguay its traditional political character and democratic trajectory.

By the end of 1983 the military were considering their withdrawal to the barracks while difficult and complex negotiations took place with the political parties for the holding of national elections and an orderly transition to an elected civilian government. During this period I gradually became aware of some changes and more subtle differences. The street where the British Embassy was situated was still called 'Calle Jorge Canning', and the American Ambassador in his imposing residence facing us across the park had to put up with living on a street still called 'Lord Ponsonby'. The fashionable suburb of Carrasco boasted a Commodore Harwood avenue and a Millington-Drake street. The great man's bust, unsullied on its plinth, still graced the wide promenade by the sea close to the (formerly British) gasworks and the (formerly British) dry dock. My Uruguayan friends were no less friendly and their welcome equally warm and genuine, but during my long absence a serious outbreak of foot-and-mouth disease in the United Kingdom had been traced by the experts in the

293

Ministry of Agriculture, Fisheries and Food to imports from Uruguayan canning plants. This resulted in a total British ban on imported beef from Uruguay, a Uruguayan search for alternative export markets, and the consequent diminution in Anglo-Uruguayan exchanges. More significantly, the former Switzerland of South America had given painful birth to one of the first underground urban guerrilla movements, and the increasing political and economic instability brought about the replacement in 1973 of the democratic government of the day by a repressive and authoritarian regime formed by the armed forces which, in marked contrast with the normal practice in neighbouring countries, had seldom before intervened in politics.

The circumstances which led to military rule for twelve years had also brought about changes in the nature and character of Uruguayan society. There had been abductions, murders, and torture. A British ambassador had been kidnapped and (perhaps because he was British) providentially released unharmed after suffering eight months of virtual solitary confinement in an underground prison in conditions which could have deprived a lesser man of his sanity. As a result of these and other equally regrettable developments I found that in formerly peaceful, law-abiding Montevideo, ministers, bankers, businessmen (and ambassadors) were escorted by armed bodyguards. The walls of the British Embassy were sometimes defaced by anti-government and 'anti-imperialist' slogans of the sort more usually found on the walls of US embassies in Latin America. My initial calls on the military government's civilian and military ministers and officials revealed attitudes which suggested that the whole fabric of Uruguayan society had collectively discarded its romantic historical nostalgia under the unrelenting daily pressures of a harsh and oppressive economic and political reality. There was also, of course, a new generation of younger men, including many of those bearing traditional political surnames, who had lived through their formative years at a time when Uruguay's tragic internal problems had obliged Uruguayans in all walks of life to relegate to the lumber in the attic of their national consciousness some of the anachronistic heirlooms which had been a notable feature of our bilateral relations during my first appointment to the Montevideo embassy in the middle sixties.

These had since been eroded by the passage of time, by the repressive military dictatorship and the ensuing international ostracism, and by Latin American reactions to the European Community's agricultural policies which removed cheap South American beef from British and other traditional European markets.

Even so, there can be few foreign countries which have as their legal tender banknotes bearing the Union Jack as a reminder of the role ascribed by Uruguay to the United Kingdom in the birth of their nation. The flag is included in the notable painting by the Uruguayan artist Blanes Viale recording the promulgation of the first Uruguayan constitution on 18 July 1830, following the Uruguayan declaration of independence in 1825. This was the final culmination of the arduous and lengthy process begun in 1811 by José Gervasio Artigas,* the man regarded as the principal leader of the initial military struggle, first against the Spaniards and then against the Portuguese. The Uruguayan artist portrays a crowd gathering before the 'Cabildo' building in Montevideo (the headquarters of the municipal government during the colonial period) to cheer the new constitution drafted by the founding fathers of the nation. The joyous group in the foreground are waving Brazilian and Argentine flags in homage to the 'guarantors' of their independence. Others are bearing the blue and white Uruguayan flag. The fourth flag being waved aloft in the painting is the Union Jack, representing the might and main of a Great Britain which, to quote George Canning in a speech made on 12 December 1826 'claimed the initiative in recognizing the independence of the revolted Spanish colonies in South America in 1823'. In a clear reference to the situation then prevailing in Europe and to his own role at the time, Canning went on to say, 'I resolved that, if France had Spain, it should not be Spain with the Indies. I called the New World into existence to redress the balance of the Old.' His famous phrase is often quoted without the qualifying first sentence which, according to modern Uruguayan historians, puts the sentiments into their proper context.

Curiously, the Union flag depicted in the painting is a red ensign of the sort normally flown by British merchant vessels.

*In 1817 Artigas signed with Britain Uruguay's first Commercial Treaty, in which he was recognized as head of an independent state.

There is a probably apocryphal story that the unexpectedly rapid course of events in July 1830 found the then British Consul in Montevideo, a former naval officer called Thomas Samuel Hood away from his post. His British consular Union flag thus being unavailable, the excited groups of Uruguayans promptly made for the port, secure in the knowledge that this was certain to harbour at least half a dozen of the ubiquitous British merchantmen which promoted British commerce, exports, and investment across the southern oceans to the newly liberated former Spanish colonies of the New World, perhaps not for wholly altruistic reasons. An obliging master is said to have lent the Uruguayan patriots the 'red duster' immortalized in the Blanes Viale painting, reproduced in more modern times by Uruguay's Central Bank on the back of a series of Uruguayan currency notes of high denomination.

The Falklands war and its aftermath provided many opportunites for demonstrations of characteristically Uruguayan humanitarian and practical assistance, at a time when the realities of geopolitical life and the all-pervasive Argentine presence across the river imposed constraints on Uruguayan freedom of action both before and after the election of a democratic regime in Argentina. I was given many opportunities to appreciate Uruguayan generosity and friendship, even before the restoration of a civilian regime. Many Uruguayans made no secret of their distaste for the Argentine military Government's Falklands initiative, and I found that officials of the Uruguayan Ministry of Foreign Affairs, all career diplomats in an effective and highly professional service, were ready and willing to help us remedy some of the consequences.

These attitudes were later enhanced and emphasized by the new democratic government installed on 1 March 1985. A gifted and talented but untried team of ministers had been wisely drawn by President Sanguinetti from the ranks of both the principal traditional political parties. Even before the cabinet appointments were announced it was generally known that the foreign minister-designate was to be Enrique Iglesias, a renowed economist of great charm and solid international repute, who had been a youthful director of the Economic Planning Board and later President of the Central Bank during my first appointment in the sixties. When Baroness Young arrived in Montevideo as Her Majesty's special representative to the presidential inauguration. I suggested that he should have a few minutes' private conversation with her before they met officially at the crowded ceremonial occasions. The minister-designate insisted on calling at my house early on the morning of the inauguration because his appointment 'would not be formalized until the President had assumed office later in the day', in a rare but typical gesture which I think was appreciated by my visitor, and for which I was very grateful.

I found many old friends both in the new Government and outside it. Informal meals and gatherings in Punta del Este were attended by holidaying Argentine friends. Press interviews with some of Montevideo's prestigious dailies still resulted in the inevitable questions about Millington-Drake and the Battle of the River Plate – one of the journalists, as a young man, had been the beneficiary of a Millington-Drake bursary. Shortly after, I attended a farewell lunch for Alejandro Zorrilla de San Martín, still as mischievous and witty as ever, before his departure for Italy where he was to be the new Government's first ambassador to the Vatican. His son, a career diplomat with whom I had coincided some years previously in Paraguay, was installed as the new foreign minister's private secretary.

For our part, we were again doing what we could to rebuild bridges and mend fences damaged by the war in the South Atlantic. Britain was able to offer assistance to newly democratic Uruguay in a number of welcome ways, and I think a turning point may have been reached when, once again, circumstances happily contrived to create a situation which in 1985 saw, for the first time since the Falklands war, the Royal Navy's white ensign again flying in the port of Montevideo.

In the comfortable embassy house, I frequently thought of the many former incumbents who had previously sat at the head of the table in the gracious dining room. Still the most famous of them all, Sir Eugen Millington-Drake had, in the long years since his departure, become a sort of cross which all British Ambassadors in Uruguay were bound to bear throughout the period of their appointment. Formal occasions frequently took place in the Millington-Drake Theatre and the best Uruguayans surgeons operated in the Lady Effie Ward of

297

the British Hospital. 'El Drake'* was an inescapable con-
versation-opener with new arrivals. This was deliberately
ambiguous play on the name of the bogeyman invoked in the
Spanish-American colonies by exasperated sixteenth-century
mothers with recalcitrant children. Amiable Uruguayan
interlocutors invariably asked visitors if they had ever met Sir
Eugen and, without prompting, relayed hoary and much-
embellished anecdotes about his generosity. Admiringly and
without guile, they averred that there would never again be
another ambassador like 'el Drake'.

This was true, of course. Of my more distinguished predecessors, none had 'sunk a battleship without firing a single
shot', although others had achieved a measure of notoriety, not
always for the best of reasons. Remarkably, his kidnapping and
long personal calvary had left Sir Geoffrey Jackson admirably
equitable and objective; he showed neither bitterness nor pain
when talking after his retirement of his memories of Uruguay.

Many of the former occupants had left their mark in some
way on the house, if only in the ghastly colours chosen when the
drawing-room curtains were last renewed. But there were more
lasting achievements. One had persuaded the Ministry of
Works to install central heating. Another had planted ornamental rose bushes by the disused (no money for maintenance)
grass tennis court at the back of the house. Somebody had
managed to get the ancient, coal-burning boiler modernized

---

* Part of the Millington-Drake mythology in Uruguay, fostered enthusiastically
during his time by Sir Eugen, was that he was a descendant of Sir Francis Drake,
widely regarded by historians of Hispanic inspiration as a 'pirate' or 'corsair' for
his successful raids on Spanish colonies and captures of Spanish vessels,
enterprisingly undertaken even before formal hostilities had broken out between
Britain and Spain. Here, Uruguayan historians face a conflict of loyalties
between the Spanish motherland's founding rights in the Americas on the one
side and, on the other, the later struggle for independence which the initiatives of
Sir Francis Drake and his successors did much to further, and which led
ultimately to the convergence of interests identified by Castlereagh and
Canning. Uruguayans are therefore more balanced than some other Hispanic
writers in their attitudes to the British 'pirates' or Admirals of the Blue who
plagued Spanish shipping and interests in the Americas. According to their
records, Sir Francis Drake visited Uruguay on at least one occasion. He called at
Punta del Este on 14 April 1578 and stayed there for a week, becoming the first of
the famous tourists who have visited what has since developed into a splendid
international playground resort, as well as the setting for the Battle of the River
Plate in December 1939.

and converted. During the Jacksons' tenancy a long-sought-after swimming pool was added to the staff amenities (they left before it was built). The Millington-Drakes' annual Christmas trees had been planted in the garden, where they had grown and prospered. Their impressive size by the time I arrived made it imperative that they should be drastically pruned, if only to allow adjacent trees and bushes to survive. I told myself that this was not a Freudian reaction to the long shadows cast both by their branches and by the man who had planted them.

But there was nothing in the house which recalled its most famous tenant. It was as though subsequent incumbents had found that the plethora of Millington-Drake memorabilia in Montevideo and the country as a whole more than made up for his conspicuous absence from his former home. One idle day, in a seldom-visited storage room with bits of old carpeting, broken floodlights, dilapidated garden chairs and other lumber, I found in a corner two formal, official portraits of King George V and Queen Mary which had long since given pride of place in the main entrance hall to more recent members of the Royal Family. There was also a framed portrait of Sir Eugen, together with an ornate glass case containing a silken and embroidered reproduction of a full-sized Uruguayan flag given to him by the Uruguayan authorities when he left, and a large brass tray with an engraved map of Uruguay which had been presented to him by the loyal staffs of the British consulates on his final departure. Characteristically, he had in turn dedicated the tray to the staff of the British Legation and had so had it re-engraved on the back.

On an impulse, I retrieved the Millington-Drake photograph, the glass case with the flag, and the tray and put them on one of the tables in the upstairs corridor where they could be seen by visitors from the UK and other house guests. If there were streets and theatres and hospitals and tennis courts bearing his name in Montevideo, the least we in the embassy could do was to display a photograph of the great man on the premises, together with his tray and flag. However, a long-serving member of the domestic staff told me with a smile that one or two previous incumbents had retrieved the exhibits from the store only to have them again consigned to the lumber room by their successors, some of whom may have found the still-intrusive presence of the long-departed excellency more than they could bear.

When I left Uruguay in 1986 I felt strongly that some sort of wheel had turned a full circle. As I was retiring from the service on reaching the statutory age of three score years I decided to put the clock back twenty years or more and travel to the United Kingdom by sea, on one of the small but comfortable Uruguayan mixed passenger and cargo ships, by this time the only vessels plying between Montevideo and the Thames estuary. I felt I could at last again take my time to travel in comfort, with all my luggage, secure in the knowledge that on this final occasion my departure would not be preceeded by an urgent message from London saying that plans had changed and . . .

One calm evening we steamed out of the harbour of Montevideo heading for the navigable channel away from the dangerous shallows of the 'English bank'. The captain invited us up to the bridge, the better to see the receding harbour and the skyline of the city. As we set an easterly course for the lights of Punta del Este on the way to our first Brazilian port of call and our leisurely journey to Europe, I searched the darkening waters of the estuary for my last glimpse of the masts and residual superstructure of the *Graf Spee*, which had for so many years been such a notable navigational hazard on the approaches to Montevideo. In the gathering dusk I borrowed a pair of binoculars, still to no avail. When I eventually turned to the captain he confirmed that, during a violent storm some years before, the last vestiges of the *Graf Spee* had quietly and finally disappeared beneath the muddy waters of the River Plate.

SELECT BIBLIOGRAPHY

Burns, J., *The Land that Lost its Heroes*, Bloomsbury, 1987.

Cardoso, Oscar, Ricardo Kirshbaum, and Eduardo van der Kooy, *Malvinas – La Trama Secreta*, Editorial Planeta Argentina, Buenos Aires, 1983.

Dixon, P., *Amazon Task Force*, Hodder & Stoughton, 1984.

Harriman, Brenda, *The British in Peru*, Editorial Grafica Pácific, Lima, 1984.

Innes, N., *Minister In Oman*, Oleander Press, 1987.

Jackson, Sir Geoffrey, *People's Prison*, Faber & Faber, 1973.

Jackson, Sir Geoffrey, *Concorde Diplomacy*, Hamish Hamilton, 1981.

Johnston, Sir C., *The View from Steamer Point*, Hutchinson, 1964.

Millington-Drake, Sir E., *The Drama of the Graf Spee and the Battle of the Plate*, Peter Davies, 1964.

Pendle, George, *The Lands and Peoples of Paraguay and Uruguay*, A. & C. Black, 1959.

Phelps, Gilbert, *The Tragedy of Paraguay*, Charles Knight, 1975.

Philip, George E., *The Rise and Fall of the Peruvian Military Radicals*, Athlone Press, 1978.

Plá, Josefina, *The British in Paraguay*, Richmond Publishing Company in association with St Antony's College, Oxford, 1976.

Rice, D. and A. Gavshon, *The Sinking of the Belgrano*, Secker & Warburg, 1984.

Stark, Dame Freya, *Dust in the Lion's Paw*, John Murray, 1961.

Trevelyan, Lord, *The Middle East in Revolution*, Macmillan, 1970.

Trevelyan, Lord, *Worlds Apart*, Macmillan, 1971.

Trevelyan, Lord, *Diplomatic Channels*, Macmillan, 1973.

INDEX

A

Acción Popular (AP) 201, 214
Achilles, HMNZS, 274, 281
Aird, Major J.R. 207
Ajax, HMS, 271, 274, 281
Alexandra, HRH Princess, 207
Al-Khalifah, His Highness Shaikh Sir
  Sulman bin Hamed, 97
Allen, Sir Roger, 49, 59
Amazon Foundation of the United
  Kingdom, 218
Amin, Sayed, 101
Anderson, Lt. Col. Frederick (Derek) 99
Alianza Popular Revolucionaria
  Americana (APRA) 201, 214
AP (Accion Popular) 201, 214
APRA, (Alianza Popular Revolucionaria
  Americana) 201, 204
Aranguren, Fernando, 147, 150, 151, 154,
  161, 163, 165
Arias Stella, Dr Javier, 199, 225, 229, 230,
  231, 232, 234, 235, 237, 238, 239, 240,
  241, 242, 243, 347, 250, 251, 252, 253,
  254, 255, 257, 258, 259
Artigas, Jose Gervasio, 295
Assyrians, 24
Audland, Christopher J. 112

B

Babylonians, 24
Baird, Brig. 'Robert', 87, 88
Ba'quba, 50
Barzani, Mullah Mustapha, 40
Beagle Channel, 209

Belaunde Terry, President Fernando, 199,
  200, 201, 202, 203, 204, 206, 207, 211,
  212, 213, 217, 221, 222, 228, 233, 241,
  243, 244, 245, 247, 252, 254, 255, 256,
  257, 260, 261
Belaunde Terry, Juan, 200
Belgrave, Sir Charles Dalrymple, 98
Belgrave, James Hamed, 107
Binnie, Deacon & Gourlay, 24
Blakemore, John, 159, 160, 161, 162
Blanes Viale, Pedro, 295, 296
Bligh, Tim J. 128
Bolivar, Gen. Simon, 208, 210, 211, 219
Bowden, Col. Guy, 29, 30, 31, 32
Brain, Sir (H) Norman, 271, 272, 285
Braithwaite, Ron A. 61
British Council, 177, 267, 268
British Overseas Trade Board, 218
Brown, David C. 107
Brown, Mervyn, 112, 113
Brown, Patricia, 107
Burrows, Sir Bernard A.B. 98, 107
Burton, Sir Richard, 168
Butler, Major H.W. 207

C

'Camilo' 165
Campos, Gen. Alfredo, 286
Campo Grande, Cavalry Regiment, 176
Canning, George, 292, 293, 295
Canning House, 218
Cardenas, President Lazaro, 144
Cardoso, Oscar Raul, 222, 245
Castlereagh, Lord, 292
Chippendale, William H.J. 171, 172, 173,
  174, 175, 191

Chopra, Ambassador Inder Sen, 42
Churchill, The Right Hon. Sir W. 281
Cochrane, Lord, 210
Comfort, Anthony F. 115
Concepción, 177, 178, 179, 188
Condor Mountains, 208
Costa Mendez, Dr Nicanor, 225, 241, 243, 250, 251, 252, 253, 254, 258, 259, 261
Cousteau, Cdr. Jacques-Yves, 90
Cowdray, Lord, 139
Craig, A. (James) McQ, 129, 130, 131
Cumberland, HMS, 274

D

Dalyell, Tam, 220, 221, 264
Danson, Ian, 58, 59, 60
Davidson, Viscount, 272
Dennison, Brig. Malcolm G. 107
Derbendi Khan, 25, 39, 43, 45
Diaz, Gen. Porfirio, 145
Doherty, Dr Peter F. 106
Dokhan, 25, 37, 45
Dombrowski, Baroness von, 167
Downing, Henry J. 115
Drake, Sir Francis, 298

E

Ednam, Viscount, 207
Erbil, 39, 41
Exeter, HMS, 274, 281
Estigarribia, Marshal Jose Felix, 169

F

Falmouth, HMS, 219
'Florentino', 152, 159
Foot, Paul, 223, 224, 249
Franco, Col. Rafael, 178

G

Galtieri, Gen. Fortunato, 207, 211, 217, 219, 232, 240, 241, 243, 245, 254, 256, 260, 261

Gaulle, Gen. Charles de, 279
Gavshon, Arthur, 221, 222, 224, 228, 241, 250, 255, 257, 259, 260
Giddens, Richard (Dick) G. 104, 105, 107
Gloucester, TRH the Duke and Duchess of, 143, 145
Grace, W.R. & Co. 150, 204
Graf Spee (Pocket Battleship) 272, 273, 274, 275, 276, 282, 283, 300
Greenwich Bay, USS, 87
'Gaudalupe', 159, 160
Guani, Dr Alberto, 272

H

Haas, Dr Hans and Lotte, 90
Habbaniyah, 54
Haig, Gen. Alexander, 213, 222, 225, 226, 228, 229, 230, 232, 233, 234, 239, 241, 242, 243, 245, 246, 247, 250, 253, 255, 256, 257, 258, 259, 260, 261, 262
Hall, George E. 136
Hall, Maureen, 143
Hall, Norman, 143
Hamilton, Wing Cdr. W.E. 54, 56
Hancock, Sir Patrick, 291
Hardinge, Douglas, 146, 147, 148
Harriman, Brenda, 205
Harvey, Robert, 227, 249, 250
Harwood, Adml. Sir H. 271, 293
Haskell, D. Keith, 60
Hassan, Prince Moulay, 116, 117
Hay, Mary, 83, 87
Hay, Lt. Col. Sir Rupert, 41, 42, 47, 81, 82, 83, 84, 86, 87, 88, 99
Hay, Lady (Sybil), 83, 86, 87
Haya de la Torre, Victor Raul, 201, 214
Hayman, Peter T. 21, 49
Head, Cdr. H.W. 281, 285, 288
Heath, The Rt. Hon. Edward, 218
Henderson, Sir Nicholas, 220, 259
Herdon, Christopher de L. 25, 26, 34, 36, 40, 47
Herdon, Virginia, 25
Hillary, Sir Edmund, 106
Hood, Thomas Samuel, 296
Horsley, Wing Cdr. Robert (Bob) 28
Hunt, Sir John, 106

303

Huntingdon, Capt. Robin, 89, 91, 107
Hurlingham Club, Buenos Aires, 183
Hyde, Chief Supt. James, 95, 101

I

Iglesias, Enrique, 296
Iguazu Falls, 193
Irvine, Winton, 173, 179, 180, 267
Itaipu Dam, 193

J

Jackson, Sir Geoffrey, 298
Jalisco, Governor of, 147, 149, 150, 151, 152, 153, 154, 155, 156, 157, 158, 159, 160, 161, 162, 163, 164
Jockey Club, Buenos Aires, 182
Jones, Keith Hamylton, 277, 289
'Jose', 159, 160
Joy, Michael G. 115
Juarez, Benito, 140, 145
Jufair, HMS, 74

K

Kent, HRH the Duke of, 207
Kershaw, Sir Anthony, 217, 227, 230, 231, 232, 233, 239, 240, 250, 251
Khadhamain, 101, 102
King Feisal (of Iraq), 50
Kirkpatrick, Ambassador Jeane, 256
Kirkuk, 35
Kirschbaum, Ricardo, 222, 245
Kurdistan, 42

L

Lancashire, Surg. Cdr. R.W.G. 281, 285, 288
Langsdorff, Annelise, 282, 285
Langsdorff, Capt. Hans, 274, 275, 276, 285
Langsdorff, Dr Reinhardt, 282, 285
Lawrence, Ivan, 227, 237, 238, 239, 240, 241

'Leila', 66, 68, 69, 70, 72
Le Quesne, Charles Martin, 98
Leonhardy, Terrance, 144, 165
Lester, Jim, 227, 229
Lewin, Adml. of the Fleet Lord, 255
Lezcano, Mario, 171
Liebig's Extract of Beef Co. 176
Limerick, Earl of, 218
Lloyd, The Right Hon. J. Selwyn, 117, 118
Lloyd Hirst, Cdr. 273
Lloyd Thomas, Hugh, 207
Lopez, Carlos Antonio, 167
Lopez, Francisco Solano, 167, 169
Lucas, The Hon. I.T.M. 94
Luna, Felix, 223
Lynch, Eliza Alicia, 167

M

MacDermot, Brian C. 168, 169
MacGinnis, Francis R. 113
Macmillan, The Right Hon. Harold, 128
Mais, Lord, 141
Makepeace, Roy, 187
Marshall, Peter H.R. 115
Maude Square, (Gen. Sir Frederick Stanley Maude), 52, 53, 56, 60
Maudsley, William P. 77, 78, 79, 80, 94, 95
Maximilian, Emperor of Mexico, 140, 144, 145
'Miguel', 151, 152, 154, 155, 157, 158, 159, 160, 161, 162
Mikardo, Ian, 227, 234, 235, 241, 242, 244, 248, 249
Millington-Drake, Sir (John Henry) Eugen, 267, 268, 269, 270, 271, 272, 273, 274, 275, 276, 277, 280, 281, 283, 284, 285, 286, 287, 288, 289, 290, 291, 293, 297, 299
Millington-Drake, Lady Effie, 269, 289, 297
Mitchell, David G. 127
Montgomery of El Alamein, Field Marshal, 192
Montgomery, The Hon. David, 192
Montgomery, Viscount, 218

Morales Bermudez, Gen. Francisco, 197, 200, 201, 202
Morelli, Mrs 'Tina' 286
Moriñigo, Gen. Higinio, 169, 176, 178, 187, 188
Mosul, 34, 39, 43
Mountbatten of Burma, Earl, 275
Munro, Robert (Rab) W. 49, 53, 56, 60

N

Nairn Transport, 66, 68
Napoleon III, 145
Nash, A.A. (Gus) C. 291
Neame, Capt. D.M.L. 281, 285, 288
Nineveh, 39
Norkay, Sherpa Tensing, 106
Nott, The Right Hon. Sir John, 255

O

ODA (Overseas Development Administration) 218, 268
Odria, Gen. Manuel, 214
Ogilvie, The Hon. Sir Angus, 207
O'Higgins, Gen. Bernardo, 210
Orozco, Jose Clemente, 149, 153
Orozco Guzman, Pedro, 165
Ortiz, Ambassador Frank, 257
Overseas Development Administration (ODA) 218, 268
Owen, Walter, (footnote) 287

P

Paraguari, Artillery Division, 179, 193
Parker, Plewes, 89
Pearson, Sir Weetman, 139
Peron, Gen. Juan Domingo, 173, 182, 187
Phelps, Gilbert, 168
Pla, Josefina, 168, 169
Ponsonby, Lord, 293
Prado, President Manuel, 126, 128
Pritchard, Sir Montague, 143, 146, 148
Profumo, John D. 221
Punta del Este, 274, 280, 283, 298

Pym, The Rt. Hon. Lord (Francis), 225, 241, 242, 258, 259, 260, 262, 264

Q

Qasim, Brigadier Abdul Karim, 19, 22, 23, 40, 46, 49, 50, 51, 56, 61
Quaife, Jill, 290, 291

R

Rasenack, Cdr. F.W. 282, 285
Rattenbach, Lt. Gen. Benjamin, 221, 245
Reagan, President Ronald, 255
Regente (of Mexico City), 138, 141
Rice, Desmond, 221, 224, 228, 241, 250, 255, 257, 259, 260
Rich, Charles, 51
Rich, Mary, (Baghdad Embassy launch named after), 51
Richards, Francis Brooks, 98
Richter Prada, Gen. Pedro, 202
Robey, D. John B. 49
Rodriguez de Francia, Dr Jose Luis Gaspar, 167
Rodriguez, Gen. Andres, 169
Rowanduz, 39, 41
Royal College of Defence Studies, 219
Russell, Sir John, 10

S

San Martin, Gen. Jose de, 210, 211, 215
Sanchez Juarez, Delfin, 140, 141, 143, 145
Sanguinetti, President Julio M. 296
Shaw, Esther, 270, 273, 276, 277
Shaw, The Hon. Jean, 273
Silva Valdez, Fernan (footnote) 287
Sindall, Adrian J. 20
Smith, Howard F.T. 120, 121, 123, 124, 125
Snellgrove, John A. 115
Snelson, Kenneth, 25, 26, 34, 35, 36, 37, 39, 43, 44, 45, 46
Snelson, Moyna, 26
Spearing, Nigel, 227, 244, 245, 246, 247, 248

Spee, Adml. Maximilian Reichgraf von, 272
Stark, Dame Freya, 58
Stewart, The Rt. Hon. Michael, 206
Stimson, Robert, 139
Stirling, Alexander J.D. 26
Street, John E.D. 115
Stroessner, Gen. Alfredo, 169, 191, 193
Sucre, Gen. Antonio Jose de, 211
Suleimaniyah, 39, 41

T

Targett-Adams, Duncan W. 177, 267
Targett-Adams, Magdalena, 267
Taylor, Leslie J. 107, 108
Thomas, Richard (Dick) J.E. 59
Thomas, Peter, 227, 235, 236, 237
Tolsa, Manuel, 156
Trefgarne, Lord, 215
Trevelyan, Susan (Mrs Harald Busse), 62
Trevelyan, Lord, 14, 19, 20, 22, 49
Trevelyan, Lady, (Peggy) 19
Trew, Frank S.E. 107

V

Van der Kooy, Eduardo, 222, 245
Van Ollenbach, Aubrey, 90

Van Ollenbach, Norah, 90
Velasco Alvarado, Gen. Juan, 200, 201
'Velasquez', 159, 162, 164
Vian, Adml. of the Fleet Sir P. 275

W

Wales, HRH the Prince of, 207
Wall, John W. 103, 104, 105, 106
War of the Pacific (Chilean/Peruvian War, 1879–82), 208
Warren, Ambassador Fletcher, 186, 187
Wells, Bowen, 227, 243, 244
White, Ambassador Robert, 192, 193
Wilkins, Dennis H. 107
Williams, Dr Anthony, 146, 147, 148, 150, 151, 161, 162, 163, 164, 165
Wren, P.C., 68

Y

Young, Baroness (Janet), 296, 297

Z

Zahara, Princess Fatima, 116
Zeballos-Cué, 176
Zorrilla de San Martin, Alejandro, 279, 284, 285, 286, 287, 297

306